KATHY BARTON
939 HAMILTON CT
PALM HARBOR FL 34683

D1314838

The
Self-Defeating
Organization

The Self-Defeating Organization

How Smart Companies Can Stop Outsmarting Themselves

Robert E. Hardy and Randy Schwartz

ADDISON-WESLEY PUBLISHING COMPANY
*Reading, Massachusetts   Menlo Park, California   New York
Don Mills, Ontario   Wokingham, England   Amsterdam   Bonn
Sydney   Singapore   Tokyo   Madrid   San Juan
Paris   Seoul   Milan   Mexico City   Taipei*

Many of the designations used by manufacturers and sellers to distinguish their products are claimed as trademarks. Where those designations appear in this book and Addison-Wesley was aware of a trademark claim, the designations have been printed in initial capital letters (e.g., Kodak).

Library of Congress Cataloging-in-Publication Data

Hardy, Robert Earl.
   The self-defeating organization : how smart companies can stop outsmarting themselves / Robert E. Hardy, Randy Schwartz.
      p.   cm.
   Includes index.
   ISBN 0-201-48313-0
   1. Organizational behavior.   2. Organizational change.   3. Self
-defeating behavior.   I. Schwartz, Randy.   II. Title.
   HD58.7.H36917   1995
   658—dc20   95-45050
                                                                          CIP

Copyright © 1996 by Robert E. Hardy and Randy Schwartz

All rights reserved. No part of this publication may be reproduced, stored in a retrieval system, or transmitted, in any form or by any means, electronic, mechanical, photocopying, recording, or otherwise, without the prior written permission of the publisher. Printed in the United States of America. Published simultaneously in Canada.

Jacket design by Andrew Newman
Text design by Karen Savary
Set in 12-point Bodoni by Weimer Graphics, Inc.

2 3 4 5 6 7 8-MA-0099989796
Second printing, January 1996

Addison-Wesley books are available at special discounts for bulk purchases. For more information about how to make such purchases in the U.S., please contact the Corporate, Government, and Special Sales Department at Addison-Wesley Publishing Company, 1 Jacob Way, Reading, MA 01867, or call (800) 238-9682.

To the memory of Milton R. Cudney,
my teacher, mentor, and friend.
RH

For my mother.
RS

Contents

Acknowledgments

IN DEVELOPING the ideas for this book, we talked to dozens of people in business, government, education, and sports. Among them were executives, managers, administrators, and no few rank-and-file workers. Their insights and recollections were invaluable. We learned something of value from all of them— from those who succeeded as well as those who failed. And we learned the most from the courageous few who toiled to no apparent avail day after day, but who finally prevailed despite daunting odds. They showed us that floundering organizations *can* change for the better, if only they're lucky enough to number among their members people who refuse to flee, hide, or quit.

We also owe a debt of gratitude to the Lazear Agency, where Dennis Cass saw merit in our approach and encouraged us to develop it into a full-length treatment. He helped the completed manuscript find a good home, where John Bell, our editor at Addison-Wesley Publishing, took over. John brought a keen eye and a keener mind to bear on our initial efforts, proposing elegant solutions to tough problems. He applied his editorial and artistic acumen to crude drawings and schematics. The diagrams and charts on the pages that follow are largely the fruits of his imagination.

On a personal level, Bob Hardy would like to acknowledge the love and loyal support of Diane, Tasha, Heather, and Pearl Hardy, and of his friends Loren Brink, Jerry Lutz, and Pat Ogden. He would also like to express his appreciation to his brothers Bruce and Jim, and his father, Melvin Hardy.

Randy Schwartz would like to thank Kerry Cork for proofreading the manuscript and for her unfaltering loyalty and encouragement over the years. He would also like to express his gratitude to Dr. Jeffrey Wallace, who contributed, as ever, his singular combination of inspiration and amusing distraction. And finally, he would like to say that this book would never have been written without the kinship and faith of Jon Schwartz, Trent Schwartz, and Marcia Laase, his brothers—and sister—in arms.

Robert E. Hardy
Randy Schwartz

Introduction

ORGANIZATIONS are a lot like the people who belong to them. Once born, they experience the wonders of growth and development. During early maturity, successful organizations gradually negotiate compromises with the realities of the world, and eventually settle into the patterns of behavior that will come to characterize the organizational culture. Like an individual, a business or agency moves through crises, successes, and failures, consolidating the sum of its experiences into beliefs that serve as a basis for future action.

And just like individual people, organizations develop predictable ways of responding to challenge and change. Any organization—a business, team, division, department, or committee—is prone to acquire, practice, and cultivate standard techniques and strategies for dealing with problems. If these techniques and strategies are healthy, flexible, and appropriate, the organization will continue to flourish. But if not—and here again, there's a parallel with individual behavior—the organization may begin to function at less than peak efficiency. An organization that persists in responding inappropriately to new challenges eventually falls into the systematic practice of what we've come to recognize as *self-defeating organizational behaviors*.

What is a self-defeating organization? Like the individual who practices one or more self-defeating behaviors, the self-defeating

1

organization faces problems with the best of intentions. In its heart, this organization really wants to do the right thing. When crises arise, however, it resorts again and again to expedient courses of action that have helped it weather storms in the past. And for an indefinite period of time, these tried-and-true remedies seem successful: the crisis passes, and organizational life returns more or less to the comfortable pattern that members of the group have become accustomed to. But beneath this glossed-over surface, an ominous change has occurred. The business-as-usual measures the organization has taken in response to the crisis leave in their wake a corrosive residue. This residue gradually eats away at the healthy beliefs at the core of organizational life. If the behaviors that produce it continue to be practiced, the organization will eventually find itself lacking the will and resolve to deal with the demands and challenges the future holds.

Odd as it seems, an organization actually has to work to perpetuate its self-defeating behavior systems. Over a period of years or decades, this sort of organization must consistently fail to anticipate changes in its environment, stubbornly refuse to innovate in the face of challenge, and continually deny the core beliefs that form the basis of its earlier success. While doing this, the organization must simultaneously deal with nagging consequences of prior self-defeating actions; it must put out fires, subdue internal rebellions, and assign blame for its less than optimal performance, all in the interest of denying that changes have occurred or mistakes have been made. Slowly but surely, it comes to focus on damage control and survival, rather than on providing the products or services it was chartered to provide. Organizational performance inevitably suffers, and when this decline is no longer deniable, blame is apportioned among a few unfortunate scapegoats.

Although they are sometimes ingeniously practiced, self-defeating organizational behaviors tend not to be especially complicated or refined. They're so common, in fact, that if you've spent a few years in business, in the military, or as a member of a task force or committee, you can recognize them at a glance. They come disguised in pithy phrases: "We're getting lean and mean,"

"We're going back to basics," or "It's time to separate the boys [or girls] from the men [or women]." The message is clear. Your organization is under siege because you and your colleagues have been lax. Now it's time to tuck in your chins, belly up, and bite the bullet. Only the strong will survive.

No doubt there are scenarios where such draconian measures are justified. But in the course of our work, we've discovered that these situations are relatively rare—much less common, at least, than the ongoing popularity of hard-line remedies would suggest. We'd even go so far as to say that the majority of organizational performance problems are more often the *predictable consequences of heavy-handed remedies that were applied at an earlier time*. In a self-defeating organization, this year's malady is often little other than the by-product of last year's cure.

There's no reason for any organization to rebound constantly between crisis and calm, or between punishment and reward. Like the evolving individual, the functioning organization has the resources required to meet challenges in healthy, pragmatic ways. If allowed to do so, the organization's system of core beliefs will point toward the most appropriate path to follow—the path that will lead to growth on the part of both the larger unit and its individual members. To optimize its performance, the organization need only remain in close and perpetual touch with these core beliefs, while at the same time assiduously avoiding any measures that run roughshod over the very beliefs that have given it life and a sense of higher purpose.

We call this alternative to systematic self-defeating organizational behavior the *high-performance loop*. It draws not only upon an organization's core beliefs, but also on the natural momentum that accrues from repetitive activity. In this sense, the high-performance loop turns the self-defeating organizational behavior pattern on its head. It shows how better and healthier effects can arise from the same initial cause. Most importantly, it shows how an organization accustomed to failure and discord can learn to make a habit of success.

This book grew out of our work with dozens of business and professional organizations, all of them faced with stubborn performance problems. In the interest of confidentiality, we haven't used their real names (none would welcome a public airing of their tales of self-inflicted travail). We've also used pseudonyms for the key individuals we worked with, many of whom have moved on to new challenges and healthier organizational environments. None see themselves as heroes or villains; most simply consider themselves hard-working people who did their best under trying circumstances. For this reason, we've preserved their anonymity.

Although they differed widely in their goals, missions, and ideas about success, these organizations and individuals tended to believe two things: 1) that meaningful change was, for all practical purposes, an impossibility; and 2) that the key to improving group performance lay in addressing the negative attitudes and behaviors of a few problematic individuals. It took us a while to recognize that these two beliefs were somewhat contradictory. Although they saw the value of eliminating personal behaviors like perfectionism, procrastination, and suspicion, the people we talked to told us time and again that in their organizations, these behaviors were subtly encouraged and, in some cases, rewarded. "These change seminars are all the same," one middle manager told us pointedly. "They tell us to be honest, open, sincere, and flexible. But down the road, the promotions and raises still go to the back-stabbers and the office politicians.

"Let's face it," he continued, "in our company, you have to be a little twisted and self-destructive if you want to survive."

Reactions like this one brought quickly to the surface the question of whether it is indeed possible for individuals to function productively in a less than healthy milieu. Our answer remained a qualified *yes*. However, we realized that sooner or later our client organizations were going to have to deal with the dysfunctional patterns that pervaded their internal cultures. If not, the same kinds of problems would continue to plague them, forcing them to look outside their boundaries for quick fixes and temporary solutions.

At this point, we began to talk with organizational leaders about the characteristics of their enterprises and the possibility of changing what seemed to stand in the way of individuals who wanted to improve their effectiveness. To obtain an accurate picture of an organization in crisis, we conducted one-on-one interviews and distributed questionnaires, asking key executives and administrators to describe in detail the counterproductive patterns that persistently plagued their enterprises. We also asked for suggestions on how these problems might be eliminated.

The responses we received were revealing. It suggested that a few dysfunctional behavior patterns were common to all organizations, and that these patterns tended to be replicated at predictable intervals with a variety of enterprises. Perhaps more significantly, the majority of respondents viewed these counterproductive patterns as inextricable components of their larger organizational cultures. When asked how self-defeating processes, procedures, and policies might be changed or eliminated, respondents tended to answer in two curt words: *They can't.*

"So, then," we said, "you want us to help you change the way your organization works, but you don't really believe that change is possible?"

"That pretty much sums it up," more than a few executives and managers told us.

"So you're asking us to do the impossible."

"That's one way of putting it," we were advised. "Let it be your challenge."

It was a formidable task, because many of the organizational leaders we talked to made it clear they weren't interested in solutions that required significant financial investments. They had invested in too many computers, networks, joint ventures, and vertical integration* schemes—and realized too few results—to put much faith in such solutions. What's more, many admitted that

---

*In its most basic form, *vertical integration* is an arrangement where a company owns all the resources required to produce its products. A vertically integrated wholesale bakery, for example, might own a controlling interest in several wheat fields, a flour mill, a sugar refinery, a fleet of delivery trucks, and several retail outlets. The goal of this approach is total control over procurement, production, distribution, and sales. When vertical integration succeeds, it succeeds marvelously. When it fails, the vertically integrated company is often forced to sell off holdings at deeply discounted rates.

they were strapped for capital dollars. They needed to improve organizational performance with the equipment and the people at hand. They challenged us to come up with management techniques and tools that could turn their enterprises around without turning them upside down.

The pages that follow comprise our answer to these leaders, executives, and managers. We've attempted to apply our knowledge of self-defeating systems to problems typically encountered in the worlds of business, government, education, and competitive athletics. We've also tried to demonstrate how entire organizations can fall into self-replicating cycles not unlike those so often found in the lives of unhappy, disappointed, or underachieving individuals. And finally, we've outlined a high-performance loop that can serve as an alternative to entrenched organizational habits, procedures, and attitudes. Not only can this loop help bring about healthy change within a struggling organization—it can also help a business or agency avoid the kinds of jarring, expedient shifts of direction that erode core beliefs and undermine organizational morale.

We realize, of course, that hard, bottom-line business decisions will always have to be made, and that some organizations cannot in fact change unless drastic measures are taken. And we're aware that no organization can keep all its members happy all of the time. But it's a goal worth pursuing—a challenge, we believe, that the leaders of today's struggling, evolving organizations would do well to accept.

PART ONE

Self-Defeating Organizational Patterns

The behavior of an organization can best be predicted by assuming that it is under the control of a cabal of its sworn enemies.

ROBERT CONQUEST

CHAPTER 1

The Self-Defeating Organization in Action

ERHAPS the most memorable portrait of a self-defeating organization in action was drawn more than thirty years ago by Joseph Heller, in his now-classic novel *Catch-22*. Its plot traced the bizarre and increasingly demented antics of an Army Air Corps unit stationed on a Mediterranean island during the height of World War II. Under the auspices of the oppressive General Dreedle and the devious, literal-minded Colonels Cathcart and Korn, the unit becomes progressively less concerned with the objectives of the war (e.g., to end the conflict as soon as possible, with a minimal loss of life) and more and more obsessed with marginally relevant matters such as the number of missions individual members have flown and the "tight bomb patterns" produced by a perfect aerial attack. The cohesiveness of the unit is gradually destroyed, with individual members sensing the futility of the larger effort and focusing exclusively on personal survival and profit. The ultimate beneficiary of all this pointless, wheel-spinning activity is the cold-blooded mess officer Milo Minderbinder, a nightmarish entrepreneur who, at the story's climax, pulls off the coup of contracting with the enemy to drop bombs on his own unit.

Black comedy, you say? Clever, but ultimately hollow, antiestablishment rhetoric having little to do with the realities of the modern organization? We don't think so. For one thing, Heller is on record as saying that his model for the crazed, cyclical milieu of the novel was not in fact the military, but rather the Time-Life Corporation, where he worked as an ad writer. For another thing, the book, if viewed from a nonliterary perspective, provides a virtual diagram of how an organization malfunctions in the absence of clear goals and an intact sense of core beliefs. And finally, the ludicrous systems of thought and action that Heller assigns to a single organizational unit are only slight exaggerations of behaviors that are quite familiar to anyone who has served time in an organization gone awry.

If you're still not convinced, consider the following example. It's drawn from the recent experiences of a large brokerage house, one branch of which came perilously close to self-destruction. The story is instructive and, we assure you, nonfiction.

STRANGER THAN *CATCH-22*

In the midst of the most recent business recession, a large investment firm sought a quick-and-dirty way to improve the sluggish performance of one of its branch offices. After considering a few alternatives in a perfunctory fashion, corporate headquarters decided to do what it had often done in the past: it dispatched a ruthless, much-traveled executive named George to get the laggard branch into shape.

Within the corporation, George was something of a legend. He came to the office each day dressed in the same attire: dark suit, white shirt, and, incongruously, a wildly patterned tie. Regardless of circumstances, he wore on his face an unvarying half-smile, betraying neither approval nor disapproval—nor, for that matter, any other discernible emotion. Although widely traveled in the company, he seemed to have formed few relationships with either his subordinates or superiors. He was the modern-day equivalent of the traveling executioners who roamed the Old West, brought to town to serve a single unsavory purpose.

On arriving at the troubled branch office, George immediately brought to bear what, in retrospect, seemed to be his sole management tool: the weekly Monday morning staff meeting. (Although he never spoke on the subject, he was known to eschew a hands-on involvement in the problems of a recession-plagued brokerage as "touchy-feely," or "micromanaging.") Each Monday, the managers of the six departments within the brokerage were to assemble around a long table in a conference room, with George sitting at the head. In no particular order, he called on managers to spend a maximum of thirty minutes summarizing the past week's sales activities. For the first few weeks, George sat impassively through these recitations. Then, in the middle of one fund manager's belabored explanation of a set of low numbers, George abruptly cleared his throat.

"I'm not happy with this," he said coolly. "You can sit down now."

Over the next few months, George regularly expressed his unhappiness with at least one unfortunate member of his staff. When the person in charge of the waning high-yield bond market made George unhappy on three consecutive Mondays, a memo circulated announcing the manager's resignation "for personal reasons." On the following Monday, George opened the meeting with the following proclamation:

"I want to hear about *results*," he said curtly. "Nothing more, and nothing less."

Such events yielded predictable consequences. Before long, the six department managers were entirely focused on their Monday morning presentations. Paying little attention to long-term goals, staff morale, or the reputation of the firm, they spent their days and nights worrying about the numbers they would have to present at the weekly meeting. The presentations themselves became more and more elaborate, as the department heads strove to disguise less than stellar numbers with four-colored bar and line graphs, computer-generated graphics, and elaborate special effects. No one wanted to make George unhappy; no one dared risk telling him the truth.

The fallout soon spread throughout the branch. The office cold-callers, those shock troops who supplied the firm with new business, were relentlessly badgered to produce "results" that their managers could present to George. Under pressure, they began to take more and more "bad" orders—sales to customers who either changed their minds or lacked the necessary funds. (In this particular brokerage, each bad order tended to bleed the profits from one or more "good" transactions; the paperwork required to undo the transaction was paid for out of branch overhead.) Even worse, when a cold-caller or senior account rep managed to land new business, he or she often found it impossible to get the order booked, *because most of the firm's administrative assistants were busy helping managers prepare for Monday meetings*. The recording of numerous transactions was delayed because the aide responsible was off at a printer, picking up overhead transparencies, or submitting changes to charts and graphs. As an ironic consequence, department heads sometimes faced George with numbers that were *worse* than actual sales performance. But this didn't seem to trouble George, who sat impassively through report after report, taking no notes, calmly oblivious to the chaos outside the conference room walls.

What had happened was apparent to everyone in the office—everyone, perhaps, except George. The branch was no longer in the business of selling stocks, bonds, mutual funds, retirement plans, and annuities. It was in the business of creating colorful, vibrant thirty-minute presentations for the new general manager.

If this strikes you as outlandish, just wait—it gets even more so. It turned out that, among his other endearing qualities, George was an exceedingly impatient man. So after sitting through three-hour meetings for several months, he took to cutting each speaker off once he got the gist of the presentation. "Okay, you can sit down," he'd say brusquely once he was satisfied. Then he'd call on his next victim. The six department managers gradually began to long to hear these dismissive words, and began to compete among themselves to see who could speak for the shortest length of time before being cut off.

At this point, the brokerage had not only shifted its focus and resources to the production of thirty-minute presentations—it was producing presentations *that, if successful, would scarcely see the light of day*. The department managers began joking uneasily among themselves that the best weekly report would be the one that inspired George to cut it short in less than a minute.

Obviously, this situation couldn't go unchecked for an indefinite period of time. After George terminated another department manager—the second of the original six—a third manager entered treatment for alcoholism. Sensing what was afoot, the firm's top account executives and cold-callers resigned and went to work for competitors, taking valuable accounts and contacts with them. Communication among employees was reduced to furtive whispers at the water cooler and coffee urn, or in the rest rooms; absenteeism soared, as employees took more and more sick days for unspecified reasons. Despite a variety of advertising programs and discount offerings, sales at the branch slumped to an unprecedented low. But because George had put a freeze on new hiring, and because so many employees had left the branch, the year-end figures showed the branch to be slightly more profitable than it had been the previous year.

Which, as survivors of the devastation ruefully concluded afterward, was probably what the headquarters office had had in mind all along.

WHAT IS A SELF-DEFEATING ORGANIZATION?

A self-defeating organization systematically inhibits its own performance. The brokerage we just described is but one example of an enterprise at odds with itself. Other examples abound in the worlds of commerce, government, education, and organized sport. Think of the company that constantly laments the low skill level of its employees, but refuses to provide them with appropriate training. Or the legislative committee that deliberates long and hard on a matter of public policy, only to conclude in the end that no action is possible without further deliberation. In the world of education, we see task forces that painstakingly formulate strategic plans, admissions standards, and hiring policies, only to abandon these carefully wrought guidelines at the first expedient opportunity. In the world of competitive sport, we see teams comprising top-performing athletes that consistently fail to measure up to the expectations of fans, the press, and their own organizational leaders.

A division or subgroup of a larger entity may also behave in a self-defeating way, regardless of the practices and policies of its parent enterprise. The purchasing department of a production plant may, for example, buy low-quality materials to save money and shift the cost of extensive testing to the quality assurance department. A government task force charged with highway maintenance may delay its recommendations until they are obsolete the moment they are announced, making an entire agency, legislature, or administration look shortsighted and ineffectual. A humanities department at a generally successful university may become so mired in ideological squabbling that it refuses to grant tenure to its younger members, thereby putting its future in jeopardy. The sales force of a computer company may regularly misrepresent the capabilities of its machines, leading subsequently to the kind of misunderstanding and customer dissatisfaction that makes selling the company's products all the more difficult.

None of these organizations is necessarily lacking in talent, energy, or motivation. All, however, have fallen into group behavior patterns that subtly work against stated goals and expectations, while at the same time reinforcing false beliefs about the nature of the organization and its potential for growth.

It's important to draw a distinction between the self-defeating organization and the organization that is merely ineffective or inefficient. By and large, an ineffective or inefficient organization tends still to be in its formative stages: it lacks a track record of success to draw upon and has not yet formulated a system of core beliefs. Such organizations are often relatively youthful and, like the individual adolescent, are still in search of an identity. If they have not been misbegotten from the start, these organizations will eventually work out their problems, establish their missions, and put themselves in a position to succeed.

In contrast, the self-defeating organization is in most cases a mature enterprise with a history of high performance. It has an image, a market position, and a reputation for success. It has a considerable investment in an entrenched set of products, policies, and internal procedures. Having experienced the ups and downs of growth and expansion, it feels capable of dealing with whatever obstacles arise in its path. But as time passes and crises persist, this confidence is gradually undermined. At this point, the organization's inner confidence begins to deteriorate. Its once-formidable belief in itself atrophies into a sort of brittle lip service to a set of principles that members of the organization have all but ceased to believe in. Feeling at once enervated and threatened, the enterprise collectively hunkers into a defensive, self-protective posture. It becomes increasingly fixated on rituals and formalities, and ever more fearful of ultimate results. Apprehensive of the future, it looks to the past for solutions to current problems. Although unspoken, its overriding goals are survival and maintenance, rather than improvement and growth.

As a result of diminishing confidence and conflicting internal impulses, the organization inevitably falls into patterns of self-defeating organizational behavior. Its internal practices become distorted to the point where they seem to serve no productive purpose, and the energy required to sustain them robs the organization of the vitality it needs to confront new challenges. Accountability either disappears from the organization's daily life, or—as was the case in the brokerage we described earlier—is arbitrarily, crudely, and even brutally enforced. As individual members struggle with the disparity between what the organization claims to believe and the way it operates, productive activity diminishes to a sporadic trickle. When an organization has come to function along these self-defeating lines, organizational life will come to be shrouded by one or more of the following:

- confusion
- deceit
- territorialism
- cynicism
- rationalization

- secrecy
- insecurity
- ritualization
- boosterism
- scapegoating

It's possible, of course, for individual members to take on these characteristics, even in a healthy and productive organization. Certain people will always have trouble adapting to organizational life and may, as a result, fall into unhealthy patterns of thought and action. But in a self-defeating organization, dysfunctional attitudes become tenets of belief for *entire groups* of individuals. When the negative becomes the norm, the organization is well along the path to thwarting itself and performing at a level below its capabilities.

HOW SELF-DEFEATING PATTERNS TAKE ROOT

Behind most self-defeating patterns of organizational behavior lies a single root cause: *fear*. There's nothing particularly groundbreaking about this notion. The renowned management expert W. Edwards Deming long held that the key to quality improvement is the elimination of fear from the workplace. More recently, organizations have focused considerable energy on the "empowerment" of individual members, which, when all is said and done, amounts to little other than ridding individuals of the paralyzing fear that inhibits their performance. Fear is very much on the minds of modern organizational leaders, many of whom have pledged to purge it from the environment.

We wish them the best, but doubt they will ever—or *should* ever—succeed.

Fear is an integral part of individual and organizational life. It is a subtle but marvelously effective mechanism for steering behavior toward healthy and productive ends. It has the complementary effect of helping individuals and groups avoid thoughts and actions that will ultimately prove destructive. In individuals and in organizations, it serves as an early warning system that guards against reckless, expedient, or pointless actions.

Why, then, do so many experts seek to stamp out fear?

As it turns out, these professionals have targeted only one manifestation of a fundamentally healthy response to crisis and discomfort. For just as there are two kinds of stress—the "good" stress that motivates and the "bad" stress that debilitates—there are also two kinds of fear. On the one hand, there's the healthy, realistic fear that inspires the organization. It may be a fear of reduced earnings, of diminishing market share, of falling behind the competition; or, on a more fundamental level, a fear of measures or policies that violate the organization's system of core beliefs. This fear has the salutary effect of guiding the organization when crises arise and key decisions are made. (We call these decision points *strategic moments*; more on them in the next chapter.) If we were to diagram how healthy fear works, it might look like the figure below. As is shown in this figure, a realistic fear of low performance, in combination with a sound set of core beliefs, effectively blocks the kinds of decisions that initiate ongoing cycles of self-defeating organizational behavior. The organization that heeds this fear—rather than denying its existence or attempting to skirt it—takes an important first step along the path toward high-performance behavior.

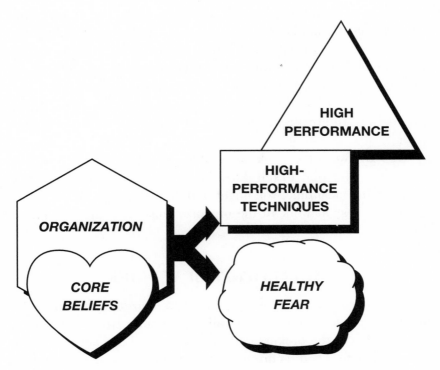

Healthy Fear in a High-Performing Organization

This brings us to the second kind of fear: the bad or limiting fear that management experts and would-be empowerers seek to drive out of organizations. This fear arises when the organization senses that it is out of step with its core beliefs, or when it believes it cannot possibly deal with a looming challenge. Though it may at first seem like a basic fear of failure, it is more often than not an unwarranted dread of change, growth, and the uncertainty of the future. It's an emotion that can cause uncertain individuals and organizations to react frantically in an attempt to establish control in the midst of perceived chaos. It triggers a response intended to freeze the organization at the present point in its development. Sadly enough, the organization usually manages to do just that. But in the process, it allows unhealthy fear to block the path to growth and high performance, and forces itself to resort to cyclical, reactive patterns of behavior that consist of much frenetic motion and little meaningful action. If you were to sketch a diagram of your organization at this crucial juncture, you might come up with something like the figure on page 19. If your organization finds itself in this position, it can hardly help but develop a less than productive approach to solving its problems. Your organization has simply lived too long with corrosive, unhealthy fear. This fear saps the strength inherent in its system of core beliefs, depriving it of the resiliency required to follow a high-performance path.

In Part Two of this book, we'll take a closer look at the role that unhealthy fears play in self-defeating organizational behavior patterns. In the meantime, you might want to think about the kinds of unhealthy fear at work in the organizations you're most familiar with.

UNHEALTHY FEAR AT WORK

Once inappropriate fear takes root in an organization, it eventually branches out to touch virtually all aspects of organizational life. We saw this at the brokerage during George's brief but traumatic tenure. The fear had its origins among the firm's senior managers, who concluded, rightly or wrongly, that a slump in sales and earn-

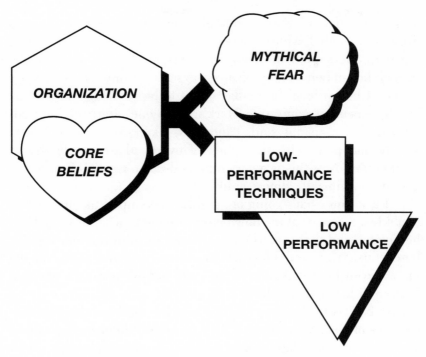

ORGANIZATION

CORE BELIEFS

MYTHICAL FEAR

LOW-PERFORMANCE TECHNIQUES

LOW PERFORMANCE

Unhealthy Fear in a Self-Defeating Organization

ings had put the branch at risk of failing. They did what had worked for them in the past: they dispatched George to "fix" the problem office. George communicated this fear to his department managers by way of the Monday morning performance reviews. Shortly thereafter, the fear had taken hold of every employee in the branch, from top account executives to administrative assistants and other support personnel.

"We were all in panic mode, eight, ten, twelve hours a day," one department manager told us afterward. "Yet time seemed to drag. Every week seemed like a month, every month like a year."

Although George's methods did seem to yield positive, short-term results—a slight increase in profitability, brought about largely by staff reductions—the ultimate consequences for the branch and its corporate parent were ominous. Absenteeism soared, with employees taking their full allotment of sick days and seeking treatment for stress-related ailments. Some took solace in drugs and alcohol, while others—among them, some of the office's top performers—left the company outright. The survivors of the turmoil began behaving in bizarre ways that conformed to George's vision of how a local brokerage ought to be run.

"I remember going into Mark's office one afternoon," an administrative assistant said, "and he's, like, sitting at his desk, sweaty and pale, with this stack of overhead transparencies in front of him. Now this is a very buttoned-down guy, but he's sort of giggling to himself, almost giddy.

"I ask him what's going on, and he looks up at me and sort of chuckles. 'George sat me down after three minutes,' he says. Then he laughs, and that was when I knew we were in trouble. I mean, here's this guy, never shows any emotion unless he's just wrapped up a seven-figure deal, and he's all happy and relieved that George didn't tear into him."

As bad as things were at the time, the most insidious consequences of George's reign did not appear until after he had moved on. Once the dust had settled and the branch had come under more benign management, it became clear that a majority of the employees who remained no longer believed in their company or trusted its motives. Many held the attitude that the corporation, despite its pronouncements on the value of individual workers, in fact cared only about bottom-line numbers—and the employees be damned. Some even believed that any organization that would support the likes of George was at heart hostile to its members and willing to inflict pain upon them to achieve its ends.

More than one survivor of this unfortunate episode would agree with the department manager who told us, "After George, it was never the same. We'd had rough times before, but there was always the sense of being in it together. George changed all that. He drew a line in the sand and said, in so many words, the company's over here, and you're over there."

Statements like this confirmed our suspicions about self-defeating organizational behavior patterns. Though we had long believed that pointless and destructive cycles have the long-term effect of bringing on the very results an organization most fears,

we were not completely aware of their most disastrous consequence. But after working with the brokerage, we became aware
that the definitive characteristic of a self-defeating organizational
behavior pattern was its tendency *to erode and ultimately destroy
the core beliefs from which an organization draws its sense of purpose and strength.* The senior management of the brokerage had,
in turning the branch over to George, accomplished what none of
the firm's competitors—or even its sworn enemies—could hope to
accomplish. They had made the company's own employees believe
they were working for the worst organization in the world.

From this experience, we were able to conclude the following
about self-defeating organizational patterns and how, in the long
term, they tended to play out in group environments:

- Like the self-defeating behaviors of individuals, self-
  defeating organizational behavior patterns arise from
  fear—usually an unrealistic and, hence, unhealthy fear
  of change and uncertainty.
- The fear behind self-defeating organizational patterns
  effectively blocks the path to high performance. In the
  process, these patterns steer the organization inexorably
  toward the low-performance results it wants to avoid.
- The ultimate and most dangerous consequence of self-
  defeating activities within an organization is the gradual
  destruction of the system of core beliefs that give the
  enterprise its strength.

Because these characteristics tended to parallel what we knew
about how self-defeating systems work in individuals, we began
to wonder about other potential correspondences between individual self-defeating behaviors (substance abuse, hostility, procrastination, and so on) and the courses of action organizations
repeatedly pursue in times of change and crisis. We wondered if
general systems theory, which had guided the development of
our self-defeating behavior model, could afford key insights into
why once-successful organizations react in ways that guarantee
failure.

In the next chapter, we'll outline the results of this investigation. We hope to show how problem-plagued organizations systematically react under duress, and how these familiar reactions—restructuring, retrenchment, and the restriction of individual actions, to name a few—serve only to perpetuate ongoing performance problems. You'll see how self-defeating organizations work ingeniously against themselves, and why, in the end, it is futile for an organization to try to carve its niche in tomorrow's world with yesterday's blunt-edged tools.

CHAPTER 2

The Elements of Self-Defeat

T HE MANAGEMENT of Ralph's company saw him as a problem. It was the mid-1980s, and the personal computing revolution had cut deeply into the market for the typewriters, adding machines, and calculators the company manufactured. Stockholders were demanding improvements in the return on their investment, in light of which senior management issued a series of cost-cutting and productivity-improvement directives. When these methods failed to bring about the desired increase in profitability, the firm's business and financial analysts were instructed to isolate the source of the ongoing problem. After three months, they came to the conclusion that the firm's domestic manufacturing plants were dragging down the performance of the company as a whole. Upper management then issued a stern challenge to its plant managers: either increase productivity by 20 percent in the coming year, or shut down.

"No way," said Ralph, the manager of a plant in the Northeast. Even in the best of times, his job was grueling; at various points in a single day, he often had to function as a financial analyst, a technical troubleshooter, a hands-on repairman, and a human resources executive. He knew the plant inside and out, and he strongly believed that management's goals were unattainable. "It's the kind of worker we have to deal with these days," he growled.

"They're inefficient and undependable, and they don't have any of the skills they need to operate new equipment and adapt to new procedures."

There seemed to be two obvious solutions to the problem: the plant had either to remedy the skill deficiency of production workers or to be more selective in its hiring practices. But Ralph adamantly rejected both alternatives. "No point training them," he said with a shrug. "It would cost too much and, besides, by the time we got them up to speed, we'd have to lay most of them off during our slack months." And in response to the suggestion that the plant hire more qualified workers, he shrugged again, saying, "We take who we can get. The kind of people we need can get more money someplace else, where they won't have to put up with layoffs."

The majority of workers at the plant, it turned out, were essentially seasonal employees. Typically hired in March and September to meet mid-year and year-end production quotas, many were regularly laid off in the summer and early winter, in keeping with the "flexible workforce" concept the company had recently adopted. This meant that they had little investment in the fate of the company and little motivation to work harder or smarter, or to pick up new skills. And as Ralph bluntly revealed, they were in effect preselected on the basis of their lack of aptitude: they were chosen from a pool of people whose skill deficiencies forced them to accept the terms and conditions of employment that the plant offered. This put Ralph in the position of having to improve plant productivity with untrained personnel who, he claimed, could not be trained, and who viewed their work merely as a means of earning a paycheck.

The company had a problem, all right. But it certainly wasn't Ralph.

THE SYSTEM TAKES SHAPE

Organizations don't necessarily fall into self-defeating patterns because they are greedy, stupid, or obtuse. These patterns evolve over time, as an organization attempts to meet challenge after challenge in the best way it knows how. Unfortunately, much of what the organization "knows" is often based on expedient* responses at strategic moments in its development. These are often instances where the organization has betrayed or ignored its core beliefs. When a fear-driven organization resorts to such measures, it initiates a self-defeating behavior pattern that continually replicates itself until corrective action is taken.

How does this work? You might want to think of a self-defeating system as a process consisting of the steps shown in the figure on page 26. As this diagram suggests, a self-defeating organizational behavior pattern is more than a single misguided strategy or reaction. Instead, it's a cycle of thought and action that ultimately serves only to validate and perpetuate itself. And our experience leads us to believe that this system of thought and action has taken root in a wide variety of organizational settings, where it plays out time after time in ways that are remarkably similar.

In the system shown in the figure, you can see that once an organization allows unhealthy fear to divert it from the path suggested by its core beliefs, it initiates a series of activities that follows a logical and predictable pattern. Under duress, the organization *reacts* expediently, often by *replicating* one or more of the techniques it has used in the past. Then, when the true *costs* of this decision become apparent, the organization finds it must take measures to *minimize* the consequences and justify its course of action. But despite the organization's attempt at minimization, these costs continue to assert themselves, dragging down both performance and morale. As a result, the organization must ultimately fix the blame for the persistent problem on either an external source or one of its own internal components. This systematic *blaming* completes the cycle. It confirms the organization's worst suspicions about itself and, hence, validates the unhealthy fears on which the behavior pattern was based.

---

*Throughout this book, we use the term *expedient* a lot, and we use it in a specific way. When we refer to a decision or action as expedient, we mean that it looks practical or wise at a particular moment, even though its ultimate results may be disastrous. Expedient reactions aren't necessarily ill intentioned; they are merely convenient or habitual.

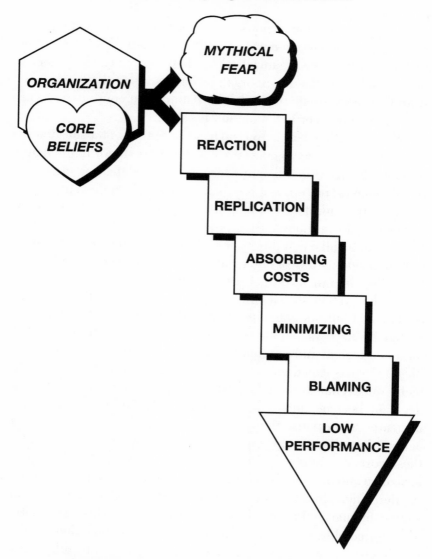

A Self-Defeating Organizational Behavior System

Systems theory tells us that once an organism or functional unit incorporates a response to a particular scenario into its repertoire, that response will continue to be replicated unless it malfunctions of its own accord or an intervention takes place. This is precisely what happens in a dysfunctional organization. Once the organization manages to make a counterproductive behavior pattern part of its repertoire or culture, it acts in accordance with that pattern until it collapses or until the pattern is interrupted midway through the cycle. In the sections that follow, we point out the kinds of insidious consequences self-defeating patterns can introduce into the daily life of an otherwise healthy organizational unit.

Core Beliefs and Fears

Virtually all significant organizational decisions are the result of a delicate interplay between core beliefs and fears. Core beliefs are the healthy principles on which successful organizations are based. They collectively form the organization's conception of itself: why it exists, what it does, and what it needs to do to be successful in the future. Fears, however, warn an organization against certain kinds of activity. Healthy fears block the path to failure, while unhealthy fears steer organizations away from growth and success.

In the course of an organization's life, its core beliefs are continually challenged. If these core beliefs are sound and if the organization continues to honor them, it will continue to meet the majority of its challenges successfully. Nonetheless, the forces of change may weaken even the most staunch set of beliefs. War, natural disaster, or demographic shifts, for example, may force the organization to examine the principles behind its strategies and actions. These periodic internal audits can be a source of revitalization and renewal. But unfortunately, they can also give rise to unhealthy fears. That's what happened at Ralph's company.

For decades, the company had held to a full-employment policy that guaranteed employees their jobs for as long as they wanted them. In the late 1970s and early 1980s, however, the "flexible workforce" concept came into vogue among the nation's industries. Under this concept, plant and secretarial employees were classified as "supplemental" workers who could be laid off and rehired according to the firm's changing needs. (There's nothing inherently wrong with the notion of a flexible workforce; in appropriate situations, it has been creatively and productively applied.) As a result of shifting from a permanent to a transient employee population, Ralph's company realized a temporary surge in profitability, which pleased stockholders and convinced corporate management that the policy could work.

Eventually, though, the unpleasant consequences of this decision began to appear. As Ralph had predicted, the most productive workers began to drift off to new employers who promised greater security. When he needed to hire and call back workers to meet peak demand quotas, he was forced to take on temporary employees with spotty performance records and relatively low skill levels. As a result, plant productivity gradually began to decline, along with overall product quality and employee morale.

The company's abrupt abandonment of its full-employment policy had, in effect, saddled Ralph and his counterparts with workers ill equipped to adapt to change and meet new challenges. Though he didn't put it into so many words, he sensed that the company had put him and its other plant managers in a situation where they apparently couldn't succeed.

If we consider from a long-term perspective the problem that Ralph's company faced, we can see that its leadership had long struggled with the unhealthy fear of losing control of the company. The consensus among senior management was that if the stockholders weren't pleased, they might well entertain leveraged buyout offers from corporate raiders. The company's admirable goal of providing secure employment while expanding into new markets was gradually superseded by the less lofty objective of keeping the board of directors—and, by extension, the shareholders—happy with the rate of return on their investment. Once the latter became paramount, senior management initiated a self-replicating and self-defeating pattern of periodic cost reduction, regardless of what they might have felt about the long-term effectiveness of this measure.

Reaction and Replication

In the grip of an unhealthy fear that threatens core beliefs, an organization like Ralph's invariably shifts its focus from long-term growth to short-term survival. The organization reacts to the imminent threat by taking expedient measures that temporarily stave off danger. The urgent atmosphere in which these measures are taken usually means that they are not carefully evaluated in terms of their ultimate consequences; there simply isn't time. And if there isn't time to pay due heed to potentially disastrous results, there certainly isn't time to formulate a prudent, creative, and ultimately beneficial course of action.

How did Ralph's organization react when faced with a productivity crisis? After only a cursory consideration of the available alternatives, the company replicated the measures it had resorted to in the past. Cost cutting had enabled the organization to survive a previous cash crunch, so it looked immediately to this approach as a solution to its dilemma. By the start of the 1980s, however, the company had cut its operating costs pretty much to the bone. When the next crisis arose, the firm's financial officers reported that any subsequent cuts would have to come out of the cost of labor. This not only sounded the death knell for the company's core belief in full employment, it also dovetailed nicely with the notion of a flexible workforce, at the time highly touted in corporate circles.

"We can make you a hero," company accountants said in so many words to the chief executive officer. "Just relax a little on the full-employment issue and give us a crack at knocking down labor costs."

This temptation proved irresistible, and it was soon announced, via a series of seminars and elaborately staged presentations, that the company had adopted a new approach that would make it more responsive to the marketplace and more competitive within its industry. And so the so-called flexible workforce—conceived, by the way, as a means of limiting the need for large populations of secretarial, clerical, and agricultural employees—became a reality in a firm that manufactured relatively sophisticated electronic equipment.

Though it may have served a purpose in the past, the technique the organization chooses to replicate is rarely the best response to a threatening scenario. No one would argue that cost cutting, staff reductions, and occasional restriction of individual activity are not appropriate measures in certain limited instances; the organization that rejects these remedies out of hand is probably in for trouble. But in our view, they are too often looked upon as cure-all solutions to persistent problems. The very fact that they need to be repeated says something about their ultimate effectiveness.

Absorbing Costs

Self-defeating techniques yield consequences that most organizations would just as soon not deal with. When an organization's core beliefs are undermined, subverted, or blatantly contradicted, individuals within the group become cynical, depressed, opportunistic, and, ultimately, weary. The resiliency of the organization is sapped, and its sense of cohesiveness often destroyed. The once-robust character of the organization disappears, and it gradually manifests symptoms associated with distressed individuals: depression, anxiety, denial, and an increasing preoccupation with the past, the future, and other fanciful scenarios. In behavioral terms, these inevitable results can be thought of as the price—or, in organizational terms, the *costs*—of counterproductive policies and actions.

Now if the organization acknowledges these costs and deals with them head on, it can bring an end to the pattern of self-defeat. In tracing its maladies back to their true root causes, the organization can gain a heightened appreciation of the power of its core values. In other words, it can *learn from experience*—which, educators agree, is the most effective means of incorporating knowledge into behavior.

Unfortunately, one of the hallmarks of a self-defeating organization is its refusal to absorb the costs of its misguided actions. When the costs of errant policies or decisions arise, the dysfunctional organization either ignores them, devalues them, or shrugs them off as part and parcel of life in a complex, demanding environment. But in glossing over the less savory results of its actions, the organization denies itself a rare opportunity. It passes up a chance to learn and grow.

At Ralph's plant, for example, the costs of the ill-starred shift to a flexible employee population emerged within months. He didn't need to read his weekly reports to note the reduction in plant output, the increased amount of downtime on the production line, and a surge in the number of parts and assemblies that required reworking in order to conform to quality specifications. But the reports did reveal some of the less overt symptoms of organizational decline: a rise in absentee rates, sick calls to the plant nurse, and maintenance expenses for repairing abused or misused plant equipment. In all three areas, the numbers showed a steady upward trend.

Ralph duly expressed his concerns about these trends at a quarterly meeting of headquarters and plant personnel. "Don't worry about it," the company's director of plant operations told him. "These things always happen when you have turnover and bring in new people." When Ralph replied that he found the trends ominous, the director said, "Look, keep an eye on this if you want. But try to balance the problems against the drop in your labor costs. You're coming out way ahead in the end."

Minimizing

Minimizing is just what it sounds like—an attempt to ignore or explain away the costs of misguided decisions and actions. The organization may simply deny the existence of these consequences or look on them as the inevitable costs of doing business.

Minimizing is the first technique a self-defeating organization uses to avoid responsibility for the costs of its counterproductive actions. If these costs are addressed—if the organization allows itself to experience the discomfort and temporary dislocation that self-defeating patterns produce—the organization can learn from its mistakes and position itself to make better decisions at future strategic moments. But by minimizing costs and eventually blaming them on uncontrollable forces, an organization denies itself this opportunity for growth and all but guarantees that it will react inappropriately when subsequent challenges arise.

When minimizing measures fail to relieve the discomfort of individual members, the organization may need to take expedient steps to quiet or subdue the resulting waves of discontent. It may, for example, divide short-term spoils among vocal or prominent dissidents, distributing financial bonuses, salary increases, or promotions among the complaining factions. Or it may shift the focus of the organization away from the present circumstances, either by romanticizing its past or encouraging members to fantasize about an idyllic future that will ultimately justify the sacrifices individuals have been called on to endure. And when these measures fail, the organization may engage in a systematic devaluation of the losses it has experienced, saying, in effect, that lost employees, clients, accounts, or opportunities were at best marginally important to overall performance.

Although they consume lots of time, money, and effort, minimizing techniques are seldom effective in the long term. Sooner or later, the resources required to put them into practice are depleted, leaving the organization at a loss to deal with the nagging aftereffects of acting contrary to its core beliefs. When this occurs, the self-defeating organization has little choice other than to assign blame for the low morale, declining productivity, or reduced level of performance it is experiencing. This collective blaming completes the task that minimizing has failed to accomplish. But it does so at a high price, both for the organization and its individual members.

Within Ralph's company, the technique of minimizing played out in textbook fashion. To understand the implications of what occurred, it's important to keep in mind that the company's senior management ordered the shift from a permanent to a flexible workforce largely out of *fear*—in this case, a fear of losing control of the enterprise. When productivity at the firm's manufacturing plants subsequently dropped, the company ignored this ominous signal. Management chose instead to emphasize the labor dollars it was saving and to view outspoken messengers like Ralph as cranks, malcontents, and compulsive worriers.

Still, the company felt a need to address the concerns of its dissident members, at least to the point of obtaining their implied agreement with the counterproductive decision to alter the composition of the employee population. So it divided some of the spoils that resulted from the decision. In an attempt to minimize the difficulties that Ralph and a few of his counterparts regularly reported, it granted plant managers a series of substantial annual bonuses for helping to implement the new policy.

"At first I was relieved," Ralph admitted later, "but after a while I started to feel uneasy and then scared. My numbers were off; I was expecting either a low rating or a pink slip, and instead I open the envelope and find a memo praising my 'commitment' and a check for $5,000.

"But, hey, I'm a company man," he continued. "I took the higher-ups at their word, went back to beating my head against the wall. The next year rolls around, my numbers frankly stink, and, what do you know—another letter of commendation, another bonus. It was like they were trying to pay me off for keeping quiet, to *bribe* me to look the other way. I got scared then, because I knew things couldn't go on."

Blaming

The organization that is looking to assign blame for its self-defeating behavior patterns is seldom at a loss for potential scapegoats. It can cast the onus for its ongoing low performance on one or more of several external agents: customers or constituents, suppliers, competitors, or outside consultants. Simultaneously or concurrently, it can also fragment itself into component parts and blame one or more of these parts—a particular individual, department, division, or internal subculture—for the larger pattern of failure. In situations where a blaming pattern has endured to the point where this list of potential culprits has been all but exhausted, the self-defeating organization may resort to casting blame on its own core beliefs—on the very principles from which it has traditionally drawn its strength. When this happens, the dysfunctional organization typically puts out an urgent call for the sweeping revision of internal culture, an expedient reaction that is often characterized as a "change initiative" or an attempt at "values clarification."

This process of blaming effectively completes a cycle of self-defeating organizational behavior. Though it temporarily alleviates organizational stress and defuses ongoing problems, it ultimately imperils the organization's survival. Why? Because in assigning blame for low performance on uncontrollable agents or forces, it diminishes the organization's ability to act independently of those same agents and forces. The business that blames its difficulties on the ignorance or perfidy of its customers, for example, has ceded the power to shape its own destiny. And once it has forfeited the power to act, the organization becomes both reactive and reactionary. In the face of crisis or turmoil, the best it can do is attempt to accommodate external demands that are themselves often misguided and contradictory.

Think about Ralph's predicament and the role that organizational blaming played in it. When minimizing failed—that is, when Ralph persisted in pointing out the potential consequences of continued low performance—the company, in turn, blamed him for the difficulties. And here, sadly, is where Ralph fell in step with the firm's self-defeating behavior pattern: he passed the blame on to the workers at his plant, arguing that they were unskilled, unreliable, and untrainable. But he then made the strategic mistake of linking the low level of output with the company's earlier decision to rely on temporary workers.

"You can imagine how well that went over," Ralph wryly observed. "All of a sudden, after twenty-six years of service, I wasn't a 'team player' any more. I was out of step with the company's 'new vision.' They said I was too driven by the numbers, and—this really got me—too focused on short-term gains." As you'll see in Part Three, Ralph's story has a happier ending than most. But for now, you should note that at no point did his company appear to question the appropriateness of its earlier decision on plant staffing. Instead, it continued to look for individuals and circumstances to blame for its dilemma, until finally its worst fear—the fear of losing control of the company—became a very real possibility. Its much-heralded flexible workforce had come to hold the company hostage; it couldn't achieve the results that would please shareholders without more skilled and dedicated plant personnel. And in view of this grim prospect, the firm's senior officers began quietly to seek out a "white knight" to buy out the shareholders, oblivious to the irony that any such savior would demand near-total control of the firm's operations.

The combination of minimizing and blaming, in short, makes for an ineffective response to organizational dilemmas. Worse yet, minimizing and blaming cannot help but have a negative effect on a company's healthy core beliefs. We'll talk more about this in Part Two, where you'll see how these two techniques guarantee that an organization will resort to self-defeating action when its next crisis arises.

THE SELF-DEFEATING ORGANIZATION AND THE INDIVIDUAL

So far, we've looked primarily at the consequences of counterproductive patterns for the organization as a whole. We've seen how these consequences all but guarantee low performance, while at the same time validating unhealthy fears and eroding core beliefs. Yet these results seem trivial in comparison to the damage an organization's self-defeating behavior inflicts on its individual members. This damage is difficult to quantify; unlike declining revenue or product quality, it doesn't immediately show up as a bottom-line cost of ongoing counterproductive behavior. Instead, it manifests itself gradually, as healthy individuals struggle to cope with the aimless and confusing activity that swirls around them. It may remain hidden for long periods of time, but sooner or later it emerges.

It's extremely hard for healthy individuals to function productively in an organization at odds with itself. In a self-defeating environment, most people eventually respond in one of four ways. The healthiest and most capable members of a self-defeating organization tend either to fight against counterproductive policies and procedures, or to flee the environment at the earliest opportunity. However, those who are less confident of their own strength and capabilities are more likely to try to hide within the organization or, sadly, to adapt to the situation as best they can. None of these four reactions bodes well for the organization and its members.

Fighting Organizational Behavior Patterns

Strong, healthy individuals have firm convictions and beliefs. Their motivation derives from an inner need to act on these fundamental values and, in times of crisis, to protect them from unhealthy influences. When an organization tells these people to behave in ways that violate their core beliefs, their reaction is to balk, protest, and, eventually, to fight.

We're not talking here about the eternal rebel—the person who reenacts an unresolved inner conflict by defying authority in all its forms and in every circumstance. On the contrary, the person most likely to fight against self-defeating organizational behavior patterns may, in calmer times, seem utterly placid and conventional. But this outward taciturnity masks a core of steel, an inner self that is utterly inflexible when it comes to unhealthy or unproductive activity. In the face of a self-defeating organizational behavior pattern, a person of this sort has little choice other than to fight.

Take, for example, Tom. The sales manager of an auto dealership, Tom was directed by the owners of his franchise to terminate the lowest-performing members of his staff at the end of every fiscal quarter. The goal of this policy was to use fear to drive sales figures steadily upward. A former salesman himself, Tom immediately recognized the unfairness and long-term counterproductivity of this policy. He knew that auto sales fluctuate in accordance with a wide variety of uncontrollable factors, including general economic conditions, the ebb and flow of the seasons, even the weather. So he went to his boss and flatly refused to put the new policy into practice.

"It just won't work," he stubbornly protested. "You'll end up with a crew of panicky people out on the sales floor. They won't represent the company well, and sooner or later they'll start working against each other."

The boss, though taken aback, let it be known that if Tom wouldn't do as he was told, the dealership could find someone who would.

"Yeah, you could do that," Tom calmly replied. "But you'd be cutting yourself off at the knees. Look, let's try this. For the next six months, I'll work intensively with the bottom 20 percent in terms of sales figures. If business doesn't improve to the level you want, you won't have to fire me—I'll resign."

After much further discussion, and after extracting from Tom the promise that he wouldn't neglect his administrative duties, the owner of the dealership reluctantly agreed. And as Tom had predicted, sales steadily increased at the dealership. Even more significantly, the gap between the showroom's top and bottom performers narrowed dramatically, while the amount of staff turnover gradually stabilized. It may sound dramatic, but in fighting a self-defeating policy Tom probably saved the dealership from unstable performance and eventual self-destruction.

Fleeing the Organization

Less overtly heroic than those who fight the dysfunctional organization are the people who choose to flee from it. Like fighters, those who flee tend to hold firm convictions about how progress and growth ought to be achieved. But for one reason or another—a high degree of personal mobility, a minimal personal investment in the organization, or a long, wearing history of resistance to organizational policies—these people have come to believe that the best way to deal with a self-defeating organization is to leave it.

Lucille, for example, worked for five years as a designer for a firm of engineering consultants. In that time, she developed close professional relationships with several of the firm's major clients and established herself as one of its top designers. She managed to achieve this status despite her skepticism about the firm's ongoing obsession with increased billings and obscure ratios for measuring employee performance. This skepticism escalated to anger when the company announced its plans to install a software system that would track the number of hours each designer spent logged onto his or her workstation. The company contended that the data this software gathered would lead to more accurate billings and, as a result, higher profits.

"I saw that as the last straw," Lucille recalled with a mixture of bitterness and regret. "What it amounted to was electronic spying—they were treating us like third graders, or like drudges who slacked off at every opportunity. And when I said to Rolfe [the firm's managing partner] that they still wouldn't be paying me for the hours I spent thinking and worrying in the middle of the night, he just smiled and said, 'Well, that comes with the territory.' "

Lucille's reaction was abrupt and unequivocal. Within days she got in touch with one of the firm's competitors and announced her availability. Shortly thereafter, she was offered not only a job, but also a promotion and a 10 percent increase in salary. A month later, she was happily at work for a company whose management practices were more in line with her sense of personal worth and professional integrity.

Hiding Within the Organization

This brings us to the majority of people who find themselves surrounded by self-defeating organizational activity. For numerous psychological and economic reasons, these individuals have neither the will nor the desire to oppose counterproductive policies outright. At the same time, they don't see leaving the organization as a viable alternative, either because they fear change or because they haven't any other prospects. If these people are to remain part of the organization, they must either hide within it or adapt to its prevailing policies.

To hide within a self-defeating organization is simply to find an internal niche where a counterproductive course of action has only a minimal effect. Some people fashion entire careers from the ongoing process of hiding from employers or constituents: one computer executive told us—only half-facetiously—that he had been dodging a particularly tyrannical vice president for more than ten years, anticipating the man's next move and then changing jobs the minute he got too close. And though we couldn't help but wonder whether this executive's energy might have been spent in a more productive pursuit, we acknowledged the ingenuity of his method of dealing with an unhealthy environment.

As a result of its total quality management program, a manufacturing firm we worked with experienced a significant increase in business. But because it did not want to take on new workers to meet this surge in demand, the company made overtime hours mandatory for the people on the production line. A woman named Joanne—a quality inspector who had been instrumental in improving the firm's products—quickly discerned that it would be exceedingly difficult to enforce quality standards in this environment. But because she still thought highly of her employer and because, frankly, she needed the job, she arranged to transfer to the personnel department, where she would have to deal with subsequent quality problems only as numbers on a report. Rather than fight the company or leave it altogether, she simply distanced herself from the consequences of the misguided overtime policy. In effect, she hid.

Adapting to Self-Defeating Patterns

Unfortunately, most members of self-defeating organizations tend eventually to adapt to their surroundings. In varying degrees, they incorporate into their own attitudes and actions the dysfunctional beliefs their organizations seem to be advocating. They choose by default to neglect their healthy inner selves, simply because it seems too difficult to defy or escape from the self-defeating environment around them. If the environment remains fundamentally unhealthy, and if these beleaguered individuals continue to adapt to it, they eventually internalize the self-defeating messages they receive and develop unhealthy habits, fears, and obsessions of their own.

These individual self-defeating behaviors comprise a significant hidden cost for dysfunctional organizations. As a direct result of its failure to acknowledge this hidden cost, the counterproductive organization ends up granting bonuses to retain disgruntled members, paying increased health-care premiums, absorbing more sick days. In extreme cases, the dysfunctional organization finds itself subsidizing lengthy and costly "rehabilitation" programs designed to repair the damage that self-defeating organizational behavior has inflicted on individual members.

Consider the career of Norman, the assistant coach of a college football team that continually failed to meet the expectations of its fans and financial backers. The head coach Norman worked for was a mercurial but moody man who, by sheer force of personality, had managed to obtain what amounted to a life-long contract from the university. He maintained his position by continually promising improvements at the start of each sea-son—and, when they failed to materialize, by blaming and firing assistant coaches.

Because he had roots in the community and because he was by nature a self-effacing technocrat, Norman stayed with the team through its ups and downs and regular reincarnations. When the head coach announced one year that the team would switch to a run-and-shoot offense, Norman traveled around the country study-ing teams that had run the offense effectively. Ditto a few years later, when the coach became an ardent convert to the principles of the triple option. During this same period, Norman was also attempting to cope with the various motivational programs that the coach, a self-styled human dynamics expert, adopted and dis-carded on a regular basis.

"He put in a pass-oriented offense, and I coached and re-cruited for the pass," Norman subsequently lamented. "Then he switched to the veer, and I coached the veer. And when he an-nounced we were going to be Committed to Success, I became committed to success. After that, I had to become Goal-Oriented, Team-Focused, and Fan-Friendly—those were some of the slo-gans we had to spread, depending on what was in fashion. It may have been that we still weren't winning, but it all got to be too much."

It got to be too much because Norman's personal life was a shambles. He went through two marriages and an extended bout with alcoholism, all in part attributable to the difficulties he was experiencing on the job. It came to an end when Norman, weary and confused, found in cocaine a means of appearing upbeat and confident, his feelings and beliefs to the contrary. This led to fi-nancial difficulties and the collapse of a long-term romantic rela-tionship, after which Norman had to undergo treatment in a substance-abuse program.

"When the school offered me early retirement with a sever-ance bonus, I jumped at it," Norman ruefully admitted. "It was either that or die. I couldn't stay clean and sober in that crazy world. I just couldn't."

An extreme case of organizational self-defeat and its consequences? Possibly so, but the point remains valid. Healthy individuals in self-defeating organizations eventually develop unhealthy behaviors that parallel those to which they are regularly subjected. Individuals in dysfunctional environments often become dysfunctional in other aspects of their lives, with their organizations ultimately footing the bill.

Toward the Formation of Organizational Character

In organizations that persistently opt for self-defeating courses of action, individuals inevitably react in ways that further impede organizational performance. When people are fighting against their environment, they are expending energy that would be better directed toward other goals. When people flee, they deprive the organization of their expertise and experience, while at the same time undermining its reputation. Those who hide tend to reduce their commitment to the organization and—if only at an unconscious level—to limit their own effectiveness. And those who adapt gradually internalize negative beliefs and apply them to other phases of their lives. In each instance, the organization absorbs a cost that lowers its performance.

When a significant share of its membership is engaged in one or more of these reactions, an organization cannot possibly perform at a peak level. Too much of its energy and too many of its resources are consumed by the process of minimizing, rationalizing, and assigning blame for the cost of its actions. Worse yet, it may resort to additional expedient action to disguise or defuse the consequences of previous counterproductive actions.

At this point, the organization is in considerable peril. The ongoing practice of self-defeating organizational behavior patterns leads ineluctably to the formation of what we call a *self-defeating organizational character*. As core beliefs are eroded, the organization's principles are superseded by a set of counter-beliefs: cynical, negative, or deluded visions of what the organization is, what it stands for, and what its future holds. At the risk of simplifying complex phenomena, we'd like to look now at some of the more common manifestations of self-defeating organizational character. We'll look in particular at how each of these prototypical organizations systematically impairs its overall effectiveness, along with its potential for growth and ongoing success.

CHAPTER 3

Self-Defeating
Organizational Character

N ESTABLISHED retailer slashes its prices to the point of unprofitability, then reduces its staff, advertising budget, and in-store amenities to compensate for lost revenues. A public service agency spends so much time studying the financial implications of a project that cost overruns are virtually guaranteed. A major league baseball team mired in a decade-long slump suddenly launches into a frenzy of free-agent spending, wreaking havoc with its salary structure and internal cohesiveness. An insurance agency increases the price of its health-care and auto premiums by 30 percent, then takes urgent and expensive measures to add to its declining customer base. In each instance, you see a course of action that brings about the very consequences it sought to avoid. You see an organization working to defeat itself.

We see a similar pattern in individual people's behavior. According to the psychological principle of *cognitive dissonance*, each of us tends to accept only the information or evidence that supports what we have done or plan to do. If, for example, you've recently purchased a car at a bargain price, you'll tend to discount any crash-test or quality data that suggest you've made an unwise decision. At a subliminal level, you reconcile this "dissonance" between what you've done and what you know. You may rationalize your purchase on the grounds that you've saved thousands of dollars, that you're unlikely ever to be involved in a crash, or that quality data is notoriously unreliable. And then you'll fume about repair costs.

Groups work the same way. When an organization repeatedly puts self-defeating behavior patterns into practice, it eventually develops a self-defeating character. Where actions continually run counter to beliefs, the beliefs themselves must be modified if the organization is to maintain any sort of equilibrium. The need for internal harmony gradually forces the organization to develop core beliefs that seemingly justify its ongoing activity.

Because negative, cynical, or expedient beliefs cannot long serve as a basis for constructive action, the organization that has violated its original vision of itself must compensate if it is to continue to function. But the effort required saps the potential for growth and peak performance. As a result, the organization operates at a fraction of its capability, with the lion's share of its strength and creativity devoted to justifying its failure to perform.

How does an organization cope with the burden of working continually against itself? It may become dull and mechanized, lowering its performance standards and expectations in the interest of predictable functionality. Or it may swerve toward the opposite end of the spectrum and embrace the notion that because the environment is uncontrollable, all that matters is frenetic activity. Other self-defeating organizations rely on insincere optimism and empty slogans to mask an inner sense of desperation. Still others attempt to escape the present uncomfortable reality altogether, seeking solace in romanticized notions of the past and fantastical hopes for the future. And while variations on these reactions can be found within nearly all organizations, the majority of low-performing groups eventually settle on one predominant self-defeating organizational character.

ASPECTS OF ORGANIZATIONAL CHARACTER

Like the character of an individual, the character of an organization is defined by its beliefs and its actions. An organization's beliefs—or, more accurately, its core belief system—are based on the organization's past experiences. This system tells the organization what it must do to succeed and what will happen if it violates its own principles. In healthy organizations, this core belief system serves as a source of guidance. It helps the enterprise avoid both low performance and its consequences.

Actions are core beliefs put into practice. If both core beliefs and the actions they inspire are healthy, the organization will ultimately succeed in achieving its long-term goals. The collective experience of achieving this success validates the beliefs on which productive courses of action are based. This explains in part why successful organizations continue to be successful, or why, in other words, nothing succeeds like success itself. But when an organization pursues an expedient course of action *in spite of*—rather than *because of*—a long-standing core belief, a self-defeating pattern ensues. And while no single misguided policy or initiative has the power to distort an organization's core beliefs, a series of such activities eventually forces an organization to distort one or more aspects of its core belief system.

This happens because it is psychologically impossible for an organization to continue to believe one thing and do another. The organization that persists in a pattern of self-defeat has sooner or later to twist its core values into alignment with the kinds of policies, procedures, and goals it has chosen to pursue. (See our description of cognitive dissonance, pp. 43–44.) This erosion and distortion of core values has the effect of cloaking the organization's futile actions in a shroud of logic and consistency. At this point, they take on an aura of validity, but—and this is crucial—*only in the context of what has become a self-defeating organizational character.*

An organization with a long history of self-defeating activity may seem depressed or chaotic, stridently optimistic, perhaps even delusional. Although it may not accomplish much in the way of maximizing long-term performance, it is in fact working quite hard. It is toiling to live with a lie.

THE MAINTENANCE CREW

The members of the organization we've come to call the Maintenance Crew are collectively depressed. They go about their tasks with little enthusiasm, hope, or urgency. They know that they'll be doing the same thing today that they did yesterday and that—barring a catastrophe—they'll do again tomorrow. Petty rituals and procedures are paramount. Coffee breaks are taken at ten-fifteen every day, paychecks are distributed at twenty past four on the second and last Fridays of the month. Telephones are answered on the second ring. Rank-and-file members are allowed to have one small framed photograph on their desks or in their work areas. Senior members dress in dark blue suits. The Maintenance Crew seems to have an official or unofficial procedure for everything.

Often thought to be a relic of the past, the Maintenance Crew mentality is still very much with us. It's often found in large government bureaucracies, in clerical and data processing departments, on assembly lines, and in enterprises whose activities are subject to strict external regulation. A collective depression also tends to be the predominant characteristic of groups charged to provide essential services the rest of us take for granted: law enforcement, public utilities, transportation, and education. Often underfunded and underappreciated, organizations like these tend to hunker into their shells and to evolve in ways that are guaranteed to ensure consistent—and consistently low—performance.

As its preoccupation with routine and procedure suggests, the Maintenance Crew values *control* above all else. It seeks to function with a machine-like efficiency, which is often mistaken for true effectiveness. Its members take on the characteristics of mechanical cogs, performing their prescribed chores until they are worn out and replaced. This means that the role of any individual must be described in painstaking detail: every member must know precisely what he or she can and cannot do. If you find yourself in an enterprise that prides itself upon file cabinets filled with job descriptions, chances are you're involved with an organization that has become a Maintenance Crew.

Why do these organizations continue to put up with restriction, boredom, and stern limitations on their performance? The culprit, as usual, is fear: in the case of the Maintenance Crew, the specific fear of *change*. This organization fears change for two reasons. On the one hand, it has in the past experienced change purely as a negative phenomenon: it has been asked to take on additional burdens without commensurate increases in funding, staff, and other key resources. And on the other hand, the organization fears change as a threat to what it sees as its sole redeeming virtue: the sense of security that repetitive and clearly defined activity often provides.

In exchange for the illusion of security and control, members of a Maintenance Crew often impose limits on their own performance. They eventually strip their organizational roles down to the bare essentials—a handful of perfunctory tasks that will keep the wolves at bay. This gradual adoption of a survivalist mentality accounts for what outsiders often view as an anesthetized or robotic demeanor. Because spontaneity might lead to disruption and consume scarce resources, the Maintenance Crew is fundamentally hostile to emotionalism, excitement, and innovation.

We're reminded here of Mark, a social studies teacher at a junior high school in a beleaguered urban area. Having spent ten years in a depressed organizational environment, Mark had all but abandoned the idealism that had drawn him to education in the first place. And while not yet overtly cynical about the prospect of educating inner-city students, he had adopted over the years a perfunctory, low-performance approach to his job. It was an outlook, he claimed, that nearly all his veteran colleagues shared.

"To be successful on the job, I have to do four things," he noted somewhat sadly. "Number one, daily lesson plans. Number two, attendance reporting. Third, I have to maintain order in the classroom, and fourth, I have to document all behavior problems. Those are the key survival factors, and all of us—including the administration—know it."

When asked about the role that teaching played in a typical

day, Mark simply laughed. "Look, we're accountable to the public," he continued. "It's a matter of time and resources. The things I mentioned, they're what the taxpayers demand of us. To be honest, there just isn't enough money to do much more. We have our hands full trying to keep the kids safe and under control while they're here."

Again, *control*. It's the means by which many Maintenance Crews compensate for a lack of both tangible resources and a larger mission or purpose. It helps these organizations ward off external forces and the prospect of change. But it also diminishes individual responsibilities and all but guarantees that organizational performance will remain consistently low.

THE FUNHOUSE GANG

Where a Maintenance Crew organization is sternly governed by rules, policies, and procedures, the organization we call the Funhouse Gang seems not to be governed at all. It's a hotbed of chaotic, urgent activity, with people scrambling frantically to resolve problems largely caused by prior frantic activity. People seem confused, tensions run high, and constant crisis is a fact of organizational life. As our society has become more and more cost-conscious, and less and less patient, organizational chaos has become rampant. It's painfully apparent at the fast-food outlet where you have to wait twenty minutes for your order, at the service department of the auto dealership that returns your car with the air conditioner still not working, at the hotel that claims to have no record of the reservation you confirmed two weeks earlier. Retail stores—and in particular, large discounters—are thriving centers of chaotic activity, as are customer service departments and almost any business that offers drive-through service or "easy" pickup and delivery.

It's not that the Funhouse Gang doesn't work hard—usually it does, and it claims to be trying hard to improve its performance. But for all this effort, meaningful accomplishments are few and far between. Though few such organizations would admit it, a good portion of their time and money is devoted to correcting mistakes and hiding the consequences of counterproductive systems and procedures. The Funhouse Gang is very good at appearing busy. But it is not so good at getting things done.

At the heart of this organization's unimpressive performance is a formidable but unrealistic fear of *accountability*. This fear, which is often held at the uppermost levels of the organization, leads to hasty action and, subsequently, to a diffusion of responsibility among numerous departments, individuals, or internal functions. As a result, it's often extremely difficult for a Funhouse Gang to get a firm grasp on the problems that impede its performance. A store- or branch-level problem is blamed on corporate information systems; the management of information systems blames accounting; accounting blames senior management; senior management blames suppliers, consultants, or an ill-trained workforce. In the wake of yet another catastrophe, everyone in this sort of self-defeating organization blames everyone else—which, in effect, is the organization's way of telling itself that no one is really to blame.

Lately it's become increasingly fashionable for various organizations to blame their chaotic behavior on the volatility of the larger environment. According to this line of reasoning, organizational chaos is simply a reflection of the unpredictability of the world and the whims of public taste. The self-contradictory notion of "chaos management" has consequently come into vogue, as organizations try to convince themselves that internal chaos is a prerequisite for vitality, innovation, and technological breakthrough. But as problems persist and performance continues to lag, it becomes more and more difficult to justify missed deadlines, lost deliveries, and misplaced orders on the grounds that a revolutionary technique or insight might eventually come of it all.

In embracing trendy theories and refusing to establish internal accountability, the Funhouse Gang merely perpetuates its self-defeating patterns. At one large retailer, for example, the director of field operations ordered the installation of a computerized cash register system in the company's most profitable stores. The director acted on the advice of Management Information Systems, which saw the complex and technologically imperfect new registers as a means of centralizing data collection and reducing its overhead costs. Once installed, however, the new registers proved too complicated for the company's veteran sales clerks to operate. Even worse, the electronic cabling requirements of the new system made it necessary for checkout stands to be moved from their traditional locations to relatively obscure corners of the store.

The consequences of this misguided decision, though felt immediately among store employees, didn't come to management's attention until the next holiday buying season. At that time, management sent an executive committee to observe the rumored chaos on the sales floor. What they saw alarmed them. Exasperated customers were elbowing through the aisles in search of the cash registers. At the registers themselves, the lines were ten deep and growing longer; the cashiers were too confused to ring up sales rapidly. Even more disturbing was the method the store manager had developed to cope with the emergency. Jostling among the crowd were temporary employees with hand-held adding machines, totaling sales while customers waited to be checked out. The temporaries handed each customer a sales slip, which then had to be given to the cashier to be entered into the system.

"Talk about a retailer's nightmare!" a member of the committee recalled with a grimace. "You spend all year getting stock on the shelves, advertising it, putting up attractive signs, and there were customers who wanted to buy and literally couldn't get to the registers. I mean, there were shoving matches that Security had to break up. It was total chaos. The kids with the calculators were trying hard, but the fact was we were totaling every transaction twice."

Here he rolled his eyes: "They told us the new register system would double the productivity of store personnel. Sure."

Now, granted, there's no shortage of organizations that have been seduced by technology into disrupting their operations grievously. But in this case, the director of field operations, abetted by other headquarters personnel, compounded the problem. He consulted with the system vendor about changes to the equipment, only to be told that the system software would have to be rewritten at a cost upward of $1 million. The vendor assured the company, however, that the difficulties the stores experienced over the holidays were common the first year the system was up and running.

Things would go much more smoothly, the vendor said, once the bugs were worked out and store personnel got "up to speed" on the new terminals.

As it turned out, the store clerks were either particularly obtuse, or the vendor was lying, because in the years that followed, the scene in the stores continued to be chaotic during periods of peak sales activity. But that's neither here nor there. The point is that even while the flagship stores were experiencing losses at least in part attributable to the new system, the director of field operations forged ahead and installed the system in all of the company's other stores. In each store, managers reported problems and complained bitterly about the drain on profitability, only to be told that change is always difficult and that eventually things would settle down.

"But they never did," a company executive recalled, shaking his head. "We never faced up to the obvious—the system was a dog. Those damn registers were in the stores for three long years, until someone in Accounting decided they could be written off. We started pulling them out of the pilot stores then. We heard rumors of cashiers and store managers standing around and applauding as the terminals were hauled away and the cables were ripped out. I can't say I blamed them."

Although he was right in not faulting store employees for their reaction, this executive inadvertently touched on the source of the company's ongoing problems: no one was ever held accountable for misguided decisions. Such, unfortunately, is the rule for a typical Funhouse Gang. No one is ever to blame for anything. Ongoing problems seem to arise of their own accord, and then to spread through the ranks with no ostensible cause. Because accountability is never established, the Funhouse Gang seems doomed to struggle eternally with problems for which no individual, policy, or procedure can ever be held responsible.

THE PEP SQUAD

For all their productivity problems and internal conflicts, Maintenance Crews and Funhouse Gangs can be nice enough to work for and do business with. The Pep Squad only pretends to be—and woe to any member who might dare to suggest otherwise.

Our term for this kind of self-defeating organization derives from its resemblance to the athletic or civic booster groups whose sole mission is to impress upon the world the virtues of a particular institution, locale, or political cause. As the virtues of its sponsor are often not apparent, the Pep Squad relies on theatrics, flamboyance, and a relentless high-spiritedness to convey its message. The sponsoring group must insistently be portrayed as friendly, hopeful, welcoming, and benign. Any mention of the fact that city government officials are under investigation for violating environmental guidelines, or that a particular university has been on academic probation twice in the past decade, is hastily denounced as a symptom of "negativism" on the part of the observer—or, worse yet, as "wallowing in the past." In its own eyes, the Pep Squad is nothing if not forward-thinking and future-oriented.

Walk into this kind of organization and you enter a world of smile buttons, enlarged cartoons, and peppy slogans. The outer lobbies of these enterprises often feature murals depicting satellite launches, jet travel, or electronic laser shows. Interspersed among these panoramas are often grainy color photographs showing happy, healthy youths entranced by whatever technological marvel the organization manufactures or promotes. The people in the pictures seem to have been selected from the firm's own workforce, which at first glance seems to consist entirely of the young, the chirrupy, and the smartly dressed. If you were to ask any of these people to describe organizational life, he or she would likely respond with a glib but lengthy recitation of the company's innumerable virtues. The Pep Squad prudently supplies its members with canned responses to suit almost any occasion.

So far, so good. But as even a moderately discerning examination of the reality behind the facade soon reveals, no member of the Pep Squad believes a word of what he or she is saying—nor, for that matter, a word of what the company or agency publicly avows about itself. The entire performance—the futuristic physical plant, the folksy mottoes, the incessant paeans to the power of positive thinking—serve only to mask a diminished sense of organizational purpose and a byzantine network of internal fears.

What does the Pep Squad fear? At the most fundamental level, it fears the *truth*: the truth about itself and what it is doing, about its prospects for continued success, about its general attitude toward its individual members. It may believe that it is accomplishing or promoting nothing of value, that it is in business only to make money, or that its organizational policies are treacherous and demeaning. "People are our most important asset," this sort of organization might loudly aver, even as its board of directors contemplates the layoff of ten thousand employees. "We're only here to serve the public," the booster agency might cheerily proclaim, even as it tries to figure out ways to keep the public's nose out of its business. "Our team has a good chance of winning the conference championship," the coach of a basketball team might boldly announce, even as she and her assistants privately contemplate how they'll manage to keep their jobs in the wake of a fifth-place finish. In each case an insincere but rigidly prescribed optimism is trotted out to cover up the implications of dark, unspoken truths.

The Pep Squad relies heavily on slogans and so-called motivational training to perpetuate its self-defeating patterns. Now, there's nothing wrong with a good, snappy slogan, and specific, task-centered training is an ongoing necessity in today's competitive environment. But in a Pep Squad, the slogans of choice are either vapid ("The Most for Our World") or downright deceitful ("You Can't Be *Too* Overcommitted"). And what training these organizations provide for their members tends to have little to do with skill development and performance improvement. Rather, it's focused on "attitude adjustment," and thus might more accurately be viewed as the internal application of the organization's considerable public relations expertise, or as outright indoctrination.

You might think the Pep Squad phenomenon would be most common among organizations that depend heavily on sales and marketing activity: auto dealerships, insurance agencies, financial brokerages, and the like. Surprisingly, however, these enterprises tend to employ boosterism only as a last resort. The type of self-defeating organization we think of as a Pep Squad is much more likely to be found these days among the ranks of consultants and providers of various business and personal services. Perhaps because these organizations offer few tangible products, they seem especially prone to take on the attributes of boosterism and to hide behind smiling facades.

We once worked for a short time with a weight-loss center that claimed to provide its customers with a relatively painless way of shedding poundage. The value of the center's programs is, for our purposes here, a moot question—some customers lost weight, and others didn't. What was most notable about the company was the otherworldly good cheer that seemed to prevail at all of its organizational levels. As you might expect (and though the firm staunchly denied that it discriminated on the basis of appearance), there were few overweight people on staff. Employees were encouraged to attend quarterly motivational rallies at the company's headquarters and to avail themselves regularly of videotaped messages from its founder.

Although this weight-loss center was American born and bred, its members spoke a language that seemed curiously at odds with standard English. Company employees, for example, did not take coffee breaks, but instead stopped work at designated "alertness interludes." Customers weren't customers; rather, they were "friends." Even more bizarre was the terminology the firm used to describe its internal problems. If Mary loathed Joe to the point of physical violence—as, in fact, she did—well, Mary and Joe were said to be "negotiating their relationship tension." Slumping sales were "public awareness sags," and pity the employee who let slip from his or her lips the words *fat* or *overweight*. The firm seemed caught up in a collective effort to deny all unpleasantness or difficulty, to banish all traces of negativism from its operations.

The company's major problems? A lack of employee commitment, as it turned out, along with high levels of internal squabbling, territorialism, and backstabbing. Although a Pep Squad can sometimes fool the world, it can rarely fool itself.

THE ALUMNI CLUB

We come now to those self-defeating organizations that attempt to function productively in a sort of time warp. Faced with ominous present-day performance problems and clouded prospects for on-going success, these types of organizations seek refuge in other time frames. Depending on the specific nature of their current fears, they either dream of the past (and become Alumni Clubs) or fantasize about the future (and take on the attributes of what anthropologists call Cargo Cults). One way or another, they distract themselves from the policies, procedures, and repetitive activities that make unrealistic fears and prophecies all the more plausible.

The organization that dwells extensively on its storied past puts itself at risk of turning into an Alumni Club and constraining its collective imagination at key strategic moments. Well-established legal, accounting, and insurance firms tend to fall into this category, as do the top-level managements of vast corporate empires and dominant manufacturing enterprises. The Alumni Club typically enjoys a reputation beyond reproach. Its offices and physical plants reveal a deeply held respect for history: the walls are often decked with handsome portraits of founding fathers and other heroes, and with ornately framed letters of commendation and certificates of award. The atmosphere is subdued and clannish, like the aura inside an exclusive club. The intended effect seems to be to insulate organizational members from the untidy exigencies of the larger world.

This ambiance is revealing, for in its heart of hearts the Alumni Club feels threatened. Its prevailing fear is not of the present moment, in which things are going as well as can be expected, but rather of the *future*—of that unspecified time when the bills for its ongoing lethargy and self-regard finally come due. Though it claims to be functioning as effectively as ever, the Alumni Club senses at some level that it is coasting, living on inherited capital. Its typical response to this nagging discomfort is to conduct vague "strategic planning" sessions and announce broad but unfocused goals. In the end, the Alumni Club hires outside consultants to tell it what to do.

This is a shame, because of all the organizations we've discussed, the Alumni Club tends to have the greatest level of internal expertise and the clearest sense of its core beliefs. But this organization simply fears the future too much to deal with it effectively. In the eyes of organizational leaders, the coming years hold little other than the prospect of unpleasant or disruptive developments—increased regulation, closer public scrutiny, sweeping demographic change, perhaps even the obsolescence of the product or service the firm has long provided. It all flows together in a specter too amorphous and horrible to contemplate—which explains why, at crucial strategic moments, the Alumni Club habitually retreats into the kind of selective and clouded remembering that gives rise to self-defeating repetition and replication.

The Alumni Club's primary problem is that its main virtue (an adherence to core beliefs and tradition) has gradually atrophied into a vice (an unhealthy dependency on myth and legend). Myths are this organization's essential lifeblood. In the face of a current crisis, the Alumni Club dreams of how a hero from its past met a vaguely similar challenge, or of how the organization rose *en masse* to defend its stake. As with all such recollections, these memories are highly burnished: heroes have no tragic flaws, triumphs are invariably unqualified, foes are always utterly vanquished. The net effect is to paralyze the organization in the present. Worried that their own contributions will fail to measure up to the titanic accomplishments of the past, individual members become fearful and tentative. After considerable procrastination, they eventually settle on equivocal courses of action that serve only to postpone the long-dreaded day of judgment.

We witnessed some of the effects of organizational nostalgia while working with a company that manufactured automotive supplies. A shrinking demand for the firm's original equipment replacement parts had made it necessary for the company to look at ways of retooling several of its production plants. A management task force was formed to study the conversion and develop a budget and schedule. But after several months of deliberation, the committee had made little headway. The reason for this delay soon became apparent.

The company, as it turned out, had come into its own in the post–World War II period, due in no small part to the efforts of a legendary general manager named Henry. A former engineer, Henry was an almost prototypical corporate leader-behind-the-leader, the sort of cigar-chomping executive who would strip off his jacket and repair a piece of broken equipment on the production line. Henry was infamous for his impatience and his refusal to put up with nonsense. He told the company number-crunchers that their figures were ridiculous. He told difficult customers to find another supplier. He got things done.

Though Henry was long deceased, his name came up a lot at task force meetings.

"Henry would have gone in there, ripped the stuff out, and dumped it as scrap," said Al, the director of plant operations. Al had been charged with the responsibility of selling off the plant's outdated equipment.

"Henry wouldn't worry about getting everyone up to speed," lamented Herb, who'd been assigned the task of determining how long it would take to retrain plant employees. "He'd have walked the operators through it once, and those who didn't get it would be gone."

"You know, Henry had a problem like this when we opened the plant at Rock River," said Eric from Corporate Finance. "I think he figured it out one day at lunch, and drew up the solution on a napkin."

And so it went for hours, even days, at a time. Every tentative decision the task force contemplated seemed to recall a memory of Henry: what he had done, what he would have done, what he'd have said to headquarters. Meanwhile, the outdated plant continued to operate in the red, until finally the board of directors decided against conversion and ordered the facility closed. In its official explanation, the board said that company management had looked into retooling and had deemed it "unfeasible."

THE CARGO CULT

The term *cargo cult* isn't ours; we've borrowed it from the work of anthropologists who studied island cultures and the remote colonies of the great mercantile empires. These cultures—the earliest were discovered in the Melanesian Islands of the South Pacific— practiced a peculiar religion that combined attributes of both native and Christian theology. The basic belief of these cargoists, some of whom still exist in the highlands of New Guinea, is that a long-anticipated millennium will begin with the arrival of ships laden with equipment and supplies. To prepare for this golden era, the cargoists perform bizarre rituals and worship curious relics, among them old portraits of European kings. Anthropologists and military observers were fascinated by the degree of privation these isolated sects would endure, so long as they could cling to the hope that a ship bearing cargo might one day arrive. The longer the delivery was delayed, the more elaborate became the rituals and beliefs surrounding the eventual arrival of the ship.

These so-called cargo cults became bizarre, microcosmic societies that survived almost entirely on hopes and dreams that might never be realized. Among certain kinds of self-defeating organizations, we see a similar phenomenon at work. The modern equivalent of the cargo cult is an organization that justifies ongoing low performance and internal discontent on the grounds that circumstances will change dramatically once a distant goal is achieved— when, for example, a key patent is approved, a new product hits the market, or a crucial contract is landed. It really doesn't matter to this sort of organization whether its hope is realistic or whether its prolonged anticipation will in fact be rewarded. What matters instead is that the hope be kept alive, if only to distract the organization from its daily difficulties and ongoing performance problems.

This hope, we've found, is what differentiates the Cargo Cult from the Alumni Club. Although both are attempting to function in a distorted time frame, the latter acts out of a fear of the future. The Cargo Cult, however, is limited by a more immediate and more urgent apprehension. It lives in fear and dread of the *present*.

And often, with good reason. The Cargo Cult tends to conduct its business in unprepossessing facilities and in stark environments: individual members work in small cubicles, in converted storerooms, and at folding tables and chairs. While these spartan trappings may accurately reflect the organization's financial and spiritual health, they function also as subtle goads: they visibly impress upon individuals the necessity of continuing to work hard and to defer gratification. The Cargo Cult often prides itself on these signs of privation, believing they will be fondly remembered once the organization's metaphorical ship finally comes in.

Now it's probably true that every organization, in its formative years, takes on some of the aspects of a Cargo Cult mentality. At this stage of an organization's development, such attitudes are often realistic, appropriate, and even inspirational: they provide members with a source of motivation and keep operating costs down. But the mature organization that actively nurtures unrealistic or distant hopes as a means of disguising or minimizing the problems of the present may well be cultivating a counterproductive mystique. A low-performing organization that continues to devote scarce time and energy to the pursuit of remote goals is courting disappointment. More seriously, it is turning its back on actions it might take to improve its present circumstances.

In the tradition of successful research-and-development enterprises, the Cargo Cult allocates a portion of its resources to the ongoing work required to keep it afloat and another portion to its speculative projects. We think of the former as the organization's "real work." It pays the bills, keeps customers and clients happy, and generates profits. It also enables the organization to dedicate funding, personnel, and other resources to the "dream work" it does in pursuit of its ever-elusive deliverance from mundane daily activity. This system has worked well for some of our most successful business enterprises, particularly in the technological and medical industries. But it's viable only when "real work" and "dream work" are esteemed and supported in an appropriate balance. If an organization consistently devalues or underfunds the activity that accounts for its level of performance, it will eventually end up trying to survive on hope.

The founders of one software development firm, for example, had as their ultimate goal the development of a revolutionary, voice-activated system aimed at the medical accounting market. But because the hardware required for the product remained prohibitively costly, and because the software proved more difficult to develop than the founders had estimated, the introduction of the product was repeatedly delayed. To finance the delays, the company took on a series of routine programming and trouble-shooting projects, which proved consistently profitable. Before long, the firm acquired a reputation as a top provider of programming and debugging services.

Despite this development, however, the company founders continued to insist that they were not in the contract-programming business. Clinging stubbornly to their dream, they refused to reinvest the company's profits in better facilities, up-to-date equipment, and higher salaries for their employees. When a few key members of the staff began to complain about this policy, their loyalty to the firm's original vision was called into question.

"Do you want to spend the rest of your lives cleaning up someone else's mangled code?" the founders asked rhetorically. "Because that's what'll happen if we start thinking of ourselves as contractors. To be honest, we'd rather fail doing what we intended than succeed at the kinds of projects we've had to take on."

The founders eventually got their wish. After nearly ten years of delayed gratification and futile hope on the part of their employees, they sold their interest in the firm and took their self-defeating dreams of wealth and fame elsewhere.

FIX PROBLEMS, NOT PEOPLE

When an organization begins to experience the consequences of a self-defeating character like the ones we've outlined here, its first reaction is often to attempt to "fix" its individual members. This reaction accounts for the proliferation of executive seminars we now see, along with a majority of the unfocused "training" programs to which employees and managers are often dispatched. But such an approach is a classic example of treating symptoms of organizational dysfunction, rather than its root causes. Self-defeating organizational behavior patterns are both systemic and systematic: they affect teams, work groups, and businesses generally, and they do so in predictable ways. Until these patterns are identified and understood, repeated attempts to bring individuals into conformance are at best unproductive and at worst downright unhealthy.

A better response to ongoing low performance is for the self-defeating organization to understand its character and analyze the habitual techniques from which this character derives. The table on pages 62–63 can help you analyze the character and behavior of your organization as compared to the types described in this chapter. As you use this chart to evaluate the character of your organization, be aware of two important points. The first is that it's possible for an organization to have more than one of these characteristics. Although for the sake of explanation we've assumed that our prototypes are relatively homogeneous, we're aware that this level of purity is seldom found in the real world. It's entirely possible for an organization to be at once depressed and nostalgic, or to become chaotic as a consequence of a Cargo Cult mentality. So in diagnosing the character of your organization, don't be surprised if you find it doesn't fit clearly into one or another of these categories.

The second point to keep in mind is that in large organizations with many subgroups, one department, division, or functional area may have a character that differs from its counterparts. Depending on their level of isolation from the larger group, subunits may well develop characters entirely their own. Within a Maintenance Crew, for example, there may exist groups that behave like Funhouse Gangs, Alumni Clubs, or even Cargo Cults. And it almost goes without saying that pockets of high performance often thrive in the midst of organizations where self-defeating characteristics generally prevail. If you find these pockets, guard and nurture them; they are often the best possible role models for the enterprise as a whole.

As you'll discover in Part Three, the route to improved performance depends heavily on the telling of fundamental truths within the organization. An accurate appraisal of organizational character is a good starting point for this sometimes difficult activity. And the hardest truth a low-performing organization has to tell, we've found, is the truth about itself.

SELF-DEFEATING ORGANIZATIONAL CHARACTERISTICS

Organization	*Operating Principle*
The Maintenance Crew	This organization values control and procedure above all else. It's often part of a large corporate bureaucracy or a public service agency.
The Funhouse Gang	This type of organization equates activity with productivity, and mere motion with meaningful action. It spends a lot of time undoing the mistakes it has made—it always has time to fix things, but never has time to do them right in the first place.
The Pep Squad	Pep Squad members display a constant, strident, and sometimes eerie optimism. They can find a way to rhapsodize at the sight of a bomb crater. Unfailingly pleasant to the world, they are often quite unpleasant to each other. They are smiling, unhappy people.
The Alumni Club	The Alumni Club lives with constant regret. Its members are dimly aware that the world has changed and wish their old heroes were around to provide solutions to confusing new problems.
The Cargo Cult	In this organization, the virtue of eternal hope is transformed into an unhealthy vice. Members make a fetish out of deferring gratification, often to the point of thwarting growth.

SELF-DEFEATING ORGANIZATIONAL CHARACTERISTICS

Primary Fear	*General Behavior*
This organization is afraid of change, which may disrupt the ritual duties of members and destroy their sense of collective security.	The Maintenance Crew suffers from collective depression and performs its chores in a grim, functional way. Every task is defined by a rigid procedure, every form and document is carefully filed, and every moment of the day is rigidly scheduled.
The Funhouse Gang fears accountability, which forces people to think about what they are really doing. To see a Funhouse Gang in full chaotic flower, visit a typical fast-food restaurant or a discount store on a busy Saturday afternoon.	This organization specializes in confusion and mix-ups. If you ask a Funhouse Gang member to do anything slightly out of the order, he or she will claim to have to check with a supervisor—who will then have to check with someone else. If you complain, you'll be told that someone will get to the root of the problem. But no one ever does.
The members and leaders of this type of organization fear the truth above all else. Telling the plain truth—say, that the company is selling snake oil or that a proposed solution may drive a client to the brink of collapse—would spell disaster.	This organization frequently resorts to deceitful action to achieve its ends. Afterward, it finds a sanitized phrase to describe what it has done, thinking that no one is the wiser. Because the Pep Squad has no sound core beliefs, it is quick to adapt trendy new programs, vocabularies, and business models.
This organization fears the future, which holds unknown challenges that current members may not be up to. Company veterans dread the day when the costs of lethargy will come due.	Alumni Club members resort to reminiscing when they ought to be thinking about innovative solutions to today's problems. They burnish legends from company history to the point where any potential action or decision seems pale in comparison.
Cargo cultists are fearful of looking hard at their present circumstances. To avoid daily problems, they dwell on improbable future scenarios.	The Cargo Cult engages in rituals of self-denial. Its focus on the "dream work" that sustains its fantasies often leads to conflicts that inhibit performance. Young, high-tech organizations may fall into this pattern.

PART TWO

The Low-Performance Loop

We never reorganize without a good reason. Of course, the fact that we haven't reorganized in six months is a very good reason.

VICE CHAIRMAN, A FORTUNE 100 COMPANY

CHAPTER 4

Core Beliefs and Organizational Fears

YOUR ORGANIZATION'S character is the product of decisions it makes at key strategic moments. These moments arise when a combination of factors—internal resources, competitive challenges, new technologies, changes in regulatory policies or public opinion—force your company or department to choose among several problematic alternatives. Should you close an antiquated plant, retool it, or sell it? Should you maintain your staff during fallow times at the expense of bottom-line profits for the coming fiscal quarters? Should your firm comply with tough new legal regulations, or challenge what you view as antibusiness legislation in the courts? Should your management bet the company on a high-risk business strategy? Hunker down and attempt to weather the storm? Sell its name and assets to the highest bidder? Finesse the moment with a clever public relations ploy? Dilemmas like these can force your organization into some uncomfortable soul-searching, and equally uncomfortable self-revelation.

You can't avoid it: strategic moments are daunting, even for the most successful organizations and enterprises. But high-performing organizations have what seems to be an uncanny knack for transforming threatening scenarios into opportunities for insight, growth, and productive change. Low-performing organizations, in contrast, thrash about wildly in times of crisis, postponing the moment of truth until some shopworn strategy or knee-jerk reaction looms as the only possible response to the challenge. In both cases, the results are at first glance highly predictable. As if by destiny, winners continue to win and losers continue to lose.

The truth is, there's something much less mystical than fate or destiny at work here. That something is whether or not your organization has a healthy system of valid core beliefs and realistic fears. If your business or agency is healthy, it has in place and takes into account a variety of beliefs about its traditions, practices, and goals. Tacitly or explicitly, these beliefs provide your organization with guidelines and criteria for measuring success. They also serve as a source of the healthy fears your firm must heed if it is to avoid trendy, expedient, or downright dubious courses of action. The interplay between valid core beliefs and healthy fear guides the high-performing organization in moments of crisis, telling it what it should and should not do.

Low-performing organizations deny themselves this counsel. They dwell instead on invalid core beliefs and the kinds of mythical fear that such beliefs nearly always inspire. Time and again, they're confronted with an array of no-win options, any one of which promises to create at least as many problems as it solves. Caught in this dilemma, the self-defeating organization typically postpones the inevitable choice among unsavory alternatives as long as possible. Then, as tensions mount and deadlines loom imminent, the organization opts at the last minute for the most convenient, the most familiar, or the most plausible option at hand.

A MOMENT UNDER THE MICROSCOPE

As you're probably aware, making organizational decisions is a brutal business. The process brings to bear the experiences, hopes, and apprehensions of you and your colleagues, often in a highly charged context. More often than not, it plays out under pressures of time, limited resources, competitive threats, or various combinations of these stressful factors. It's no wonder that your organization may make decisions that later seem less than wise, prudent, or well intentioned.

Organizations with a recent history of high performance have a built-in mechanism for holding threats, trends, and ostensible urgencies at bay. As we indicated earlier, such an organization draws on a system of valid beliefs and a collective fear of low performance when it resolves matters of strategic importance. The beliefs point toward actions that should be taken; the fear, in turn, blocks any activities that seem rash, counterproductive, or otherwise unworkable. The organization subsequently chooses from among only those alternatives that fall between valid core beliefs and realistic fears. It acts, in other words, in its own best interests.

Consider, in contrast, the plight of the organization that lacks the collective confidence that a successful track record tends to inspire. Confronted with a crisis or challenge, this sort of organization finds itself trapped between invalid or insubstantial core beliefs and mythical or exaggerated fears. Like a deer suddenly exposed in the glare of onrushing headlights, the self-defeating organization at this point experiences panic and paralysis. It may, at the last instant, lurch reflexively out of the path of the crisis bearing down on it, but only at the expense of tumbling headlong into a ditch. But then—and here the counterproductive organization differs from the hypothetical deer—it ventures obliviously onto the roadway again, counting on dumb luck to save it from catastrophe.

Why does the successful organization behave so prudently, and its less successful counterpart so haphazardly? Conventional wisdom would have us believe that high-performing organizations respond to the dictates of principled and visionary leaders, while struggling organizations tend to be led by the whims of the stupid, the greedy, and the reckless. But in this case, the conventional wisdom is too simple. On the contrary, we've found the virtues of wisdom, charity, and patience to be more or less evenly distributed among organizations that regularly achieve their ends and those that habitually fail. (The same holds true for the commonly cited vices of ignorance, cruelty, and arrogance.) In terms of shaping organizational performance, morality and immorality play a suprisingly minor role.

The key factor in making better decisions is a careful analysis of what an organization believes about itself and its environment. This analysis often reveals why some groups regularly succeed and others regularly come up short. We've discovered that at strategic moments, both successful and unsuccessful organizations look into a mirror and act according to the image they see. Sound beliefs create images of strength, while unhealthy beliefs distort the reflection in bizarre, unattractive ways.

CORE BELIEFS AND ORGANIZATIONAL VALUES

As you're probably aware, the so-called values clarification exercise has become a common feature of organizational life. Caught between contradictory imperatives, your organization may bring together a select group of leaders, managers, and representatives of its rank-and-file membership, usually in a bucolic or luxurious setting. An outside consultant (or two) is usually on hand to moderate the proceedings. The consultant stands with folded arms and soulful countenance while you and the rest of the participants give voice to personal hopes, fears, dreams, and disappointments. The facilitator duly notes each comment, then asks your group to process and synthesize what you have heard. At the end of two or three days, these sessions yield a list of some three or four "values" that your group claims to hold dear.

Pardon the pun, but we don't see the value. A session like this may smooth ruffled feathers, ameliorate ancient hurts, or bolster a sense of hale camaraderie, but it does little to focus attention on the issues a troubled organization must resolve if it is to change its habitual performance patterns. It serves, in other words, like a glass of warm milk or a soothing bath. It provides momentary comfort, but does little to break a troublesome habit or cure a nagging infection.

This may sound unduly harsh, but most attempts at clarifying organizational values produce numbingly similar results. Almost unfailingly, the participants in this sort of exercise conclude that their organization places a high value on honesty, hard work, and loyalty. All well and good; but what organization *doesn't*? In our experience, we've yet to come across a company, agency, or team that cheerfully admits to holding deceit, sloth, or treachery in high esteem. Our point here is that at an abstract level, every organization values pretty much the same things. And you don't need consultants or off-site interludes to discover what they are.

Aside from their predictability and uniformity, we have another problem with using abstract values as a starting point for evaluating and improving organizational performance. Our difficulty stems from the fact that such values tend often to have about them an aura of smug morality. Now there's nothing wrong with this—provided your organization plans to make no other use of its exquisite values than to mount them on a plaque or engrave them on its letterhead. But if your organization tries to base its actions on moralistic sentiments, it's headed for trouble, often in the form of hypocrisy, duplicity, and cynicism. A bank or brokerage is better off admitting that it's in the business of making money than paying noble lip service to the virtue of prosperity. It's better, too, for a strapped school district to acknowledge the goal of imparting minimal literacy than to wax eloquent about the unquestioned goodness of learning and wisdom. Making money and turning out literate graduates are themselves formidable tasks, made none the easier when burdened with idealistic moral baggage. When it comes to accomplishing the *real* work of an organization, lofty values often inhibit choice and decrease the odds of success.

We've found, moreover, that there's little correlation between the values an organization champions and the way the organization collectively behaves. Self-proclaimed "charitable" organizations are often ruthless in their dealings with competitors; "honest" organizations lie all the time; and "loyal" organizations compulsively prune away at their memberships. We worked with one hotel chain that avowed to the point of dementia its commitment to customer service and comfort. Yet time and again we saw this organization opt for programs designed to increase profits or simplify internal operations, regardless of the impact on the much-esteemed customer. To cite another example, we worked during the 1970s with an electronics firm whose chief executive officer never passed on an opportunity to make public his distaste for communist and socialist governments. But even as he spoke, his company was lobbying for federal legislation that would allow it to trade with Romania and China.

Organizational values, in short, are invariably self-flattering and seldom based in reality. They provide neither a rationale nor a remedy for the low-performance patterns that continue to plague the companies, agencies, and even governments claiming to hold to them.

ANALYZING CORE BELIEFS

If collective values do little in the way of differentiating successful organizations from their unsuccessful counterparts, where does the source of the difference lie? We suggest that low-performance and high-performance patterns have their origins in organizational core belief systems. Unlike vague or euphemistic values, the beliefs that comprise these systems are grounded in the reality of an organization's experiences. They distill the organization's sense of what it is, what it does, and how well it does it—all the factors that come into play when decisions are made and courses of action are charted. For better or worse, core beliefs define an organization's character in the present, and at the same time shape its future.

All organizations have some sort of core belief system. Though it has become commonplace to assume that chronically under-achieving groups lack basic core beliefs, we've found that this simply isn't the case. In most cases, low performance is the result of acting in accordance with the wrong sets of group beliefs and, as a result, giving strength to the kinds of destructive mythical fears that make sound choices impossible. To see how this pattern develops, we need to take a closer look at the kinds of beliefs and attitudes that are typically at work within an organization. We need to examine how these beliefs differ in terms of their nature, their validity, and the courses of action they inspire.

Within any organization, ranging from the smallest clerical department to the largest corporate monolith, there exist in tandem two major kinds of core beliefs. The first type of core belief, the *descriptive* belief, reveals the organization's collective sense of what it does and what purpose it needs to serve. A luxury car dealer, for example, acts on the descriptive belief that it sells premium-priced autos to a selective group of buyers. Likewise, a wholesale bakery believes that it is in the business of making bread and desserts for grocery chains. Because they describe an objective reality, descriptive core beliefs are simply valid or invalid.

Evaluative core beliefs, however, are often highly subjective. They render either a positive or a negative judgment on an organization's general character. They reflect your organization's perception of how well it performs, how effectively it operates, and how fairly it treats its members. The luxury auto franchise may believe that it offers the best prices and most flexible leasing plans to its customers, and that it rewards its sales force well beyond industry norms. The wholesale baker may believe it is doing a good job of keeping its costs down, but not such a good job marketing itself. Your organization's core belief system is a combination of the descriptive beliefs that define its identity and the evaluative beliefs that appraise its performance.

These distinctions provide a basis for analyzing an organization's core belief system. In simple form, a core belief system looks something like the figure on page 74. Straightforward though it may seem, this model can be used to categorize virtually every belief, attitude, or perception that a significant number of organizational members share. Sorting through these various notions can provide an astonishing snapshot of an organization's character and potential for success at a particular strategic moment.

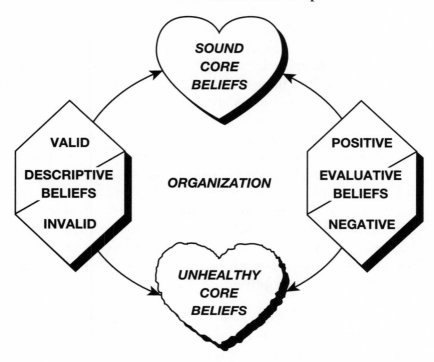

An Organizational Belief System

Descriptive Core Beliefs

An organization's descriptive core beliefs encapsulate its primary activity. Such basic beliefs may also include criteria that differentiate the organization from others: a description of a market segment, for example, or of a level of quality or service that must be provided. A company that manufactures photocopiers obviously holds to a descriptive core belief consistent with this empirical reality. It may further have as part and parcel of this belief the criterion that it produces photocopying equipment for home and small business use, thus differentiating itself from the Xeroxes and Kodaks of the world. Such beliefs, though hardly profound, have the salutary effect of encapsulating and clarifying an organization's purpose. In this way, they establish the basic parameters of successful performance, providing both guidance and a healthy sense of limitation.

Valid Core Beliefs In productive, high-performing organizations, valid descriptive beliefs are readily communicated and rarely in dispute. "We make the best car and truck tires in the business," a line manager at a manufacturing plant once told us in unequivocal tones. "The Big Three buy from us because we always deliver what we promise." In the table below, we've provided additional examples of the valid descriptive beliefs held by some of our organizational clients. Note how in each

VALID DESCRIPTIVE BELIEFS

Descriptive Belief	*Activity*	*Performance Criteria*
We produce state-of-the-art luxury automobiles.	Produce automobiles	State-of-the-art, luxury class
We provide prompt and effective electronic repairs.	Provide electronic repairs	Prompt, effective
We deliver letters and parcels the same day they are sent.	Deliver letters and parcels	Same-day delivery
We build the fastest computers for use in science and industry.	Build computers	Fastest, scientific/ industrial use
We market consumer appliances at the lowest price.	Market appliances	Lowest price, consumer use
We provide a wide range of accounting services for a business clientele.	Provide accounting services	Wide range, business clientele
We provide high-quality education at a minimal cost to the general public.	Provide education	High quality, minimal cost, public use

case, the belief statement establishes both an organizational identity and the general criteria for measuring effectiveness. Because valid beliefs like these seem self-evident, they are often overlooked when organizations evaluate how they view themselves. This is a mistake. An organization that takes for granted matters so crucial as its fundamental identity and criteria for successful performance is setting the stage for invalid descriptive beliefs to take root and, eventually, to distort strategic thinking when challenges and crises arise.

Valid descriptive beliefs tend to inspire sound decisions. In describing what an organization *does*, these beliefs exclude from the organization's outlook the kinds of things it *doesn't* do, or shouldn't be doing. When an organization is contemplating ventures outside its traditional range of activity, these sorts of beliefs give rise to healthy fears about the organization's identity and level of performance.

Invalid Descriptive Beliefs Valid descriptive beliefs are easily and readily identified. More elusive, though, are the fundamentally *invalid* descriptive beliefs that distort the thinking of numerous businesses, departments, agencies, and other groups. While at odds with reality, these invalid beliefs behave like viruses: they grow, mutate, and spread to the point where they inspire among members of an organization a sort of collective delirium. In the process, they weaken valid descriptive beliefs and give rise to the kinds of delusional fears that inhibit clear thinking and proscribe innovation.

An invalid descriptive belief is essentially a false perception of what an organization is and what kind of performance is expected of it. You can see the consequences of an invalid descriptive belief when, for example, a fast-food restaurant begins to seem more like an amusement park than a place to grab a quick meal, or when the customer service department of an insurance company seems more interested in selling policy add-ons than in answering questions or resolving complaints. You see it also when internal corporate training departments devote the bulk of their resources to the modification or correction of employee attitudes while providing little instruction about new products, policies, or job-specific skills. Once born, invalid descriptive beliefs take on lives of their own. They are often cited as the rationale for courses of action that steer a struggling organization away from effective performance and toward counterproductive strategies.

Invalid descriptive beliefs arise from two sources. The first is the ever-burgeoning complexity and compartmentalization of the modern organizational monolith. It's difficult for an employee of a corporate conglomerate involved in the food-processing, financial services, and petroleum industries to develop a clear sense of what the organization does and whom it serves. As a result, this employee will likely embrace a descriptive belief that is either too specific or too general to serve as a basis for sound action, or will grasp at fanciful notions that simply won't bear up under the test of reality.

We once worked with a trucking company that, in the course of computerizing its route-management activities, eventually created a sizable information services division. This division subsequently began to market the software it developed to other truckers and transportation departments. As a result, members of the information services group came to see themselves not as part of the motor freight industry, but instead as players in the field of vertical-market software.

"You just can't get those people to focus on moving the freight," complained Arthur, a vice president in the company. "They work hard, all right, but they insist on 'improving' the software we've got, on making it more 'elegant.' The problem is, the stuff they send over is harder and harder to use, and sucks up more and more of our resources. Someone needs to turn their heads around."

To be sure, complexity and fragmentation distract members of diversified organizations from valid core beliefs and give rise to invalid perceptions about goals and performance. Equally culpable, however, are the glib metaphors and grandiose rhetoric that organizational leaders loudly advance when in pursuit of the latest market or managerial fad. Included in this category are the alarmingly similar organizational "mission statements" currently in vogue, as well as the advertising or public relations slogans that organizations develop to justify whatever it is that they have chosen to do. Mission statements typically describe an organization's identity in terms of its devotion to the betterment of life for customers, members, shareholders, and in some cases all of mankind. ("At the ABC Corporation, we strive continuously to provide the benefits of our state-of-the-art products and services to an ever-expanding customer base and to our loyal employees"—a typical mission statement of the sort that no organization could resist.)

Slogans reduce organizational purpose to a snappy phrase or a sunny attitude. ("We believe in *life*"—believe it or not, a slogan actually adopted as a core belief by an insurance company experiencing a sharp decline in the sale of its whole-life policies.) Although neither slogans nor mission statements say much about what an organization actually *does*, both inspire whimsical and convenient interpretations of what the organization is really up to. These invalid beliefs, in turn, are invoked as justifications for the kinds of expedient and reactive behavior that so often undermines success.

Once instilled in the members of an organization, invalid descriptions like these tend to lead to all sorts of unanticipated and often counterproductive consequences. When a major banking institution decided that its tellers would serve as point-of-sale agents for new financial services and investment vehicles, a senior manager dropped in on the subsequent training sessions to convey the message. But his choice of words and his forceful tone turned out to be unfortunate. "From now on, don't think of yourselves as working for a *bank*," he admonished the assembled tellers, "because from now on, you're working for a *store*."

In response to this exhortation, the tellers returned to their stations imbued with both a fervent sense of purpose and a dubious new belief. To the best of their ability, they spent additional time with each customer, explaining new product offerings to every customer who seemed, in their judgment, to be a prospective investor in a certificate of deposit, an annuity, or one of several mutual funds. That the tellers only dimly understood these sophisticated financial instruments was a notion that management chose not to acknowledge. Nor did the movers and shakers behind the point-of-sale program take into account how the initiative might affect the bank's normal operations, and how customers might react if these operations were disrupted.

"I think 'fiasco' might be a charitable description of what went on during those first months," said Darlene, the manager of teller services, in the aftermath of the ill-starred effort. "To begin with, the average length of time per customer transaction tripled, which meant longer lines and increased waiting times. And even worse, the tellers, wanting to hurry on to deliver their pitch, started making mistakes when they keyed in transactions. After six months, we commissioned a survey to evaluate customer satisfaction." She paused, then shook her head. "You can imagine how the results came in."

What the survey revealed, in short, was that the bank's customers were less than thrilled with the new service the branch offices were providing. They resented standing in line while tellers explained money-market accounts and no-load funds to prospective investors. They felt harassed when, on visiting the branch office to make a deposit or cash a check, they found themselves subjected to the kind of aggressive sales pitch that many likened to a car dealer's spiel. As a result, more and more of them took to banking by mail, or conducting their transactions at the drive-through windows. There the auto-tellers, overwhelmed by the increased traffic, took to making mistakes, too. Through the communication of an invalid core belief (that the bank was now a "store"), senior management had set off a chain reaction of counterproductive events. They had ensured, in effect, that fewer customers would visit the branch offices, and that many who did would leave disgruntled.

Evaluative Core Beliefs

You can usually check your organization's descriptive core beliefs against reality. For this reason, you can readily identify them as valid or invalid. A processing plant cannot for long assume the identity of a servicing center, any more than a nonprofit agency can act as a viable competitive force in the marketplace. But your organization's *evaluative* core beliefs—its subjective judgments about performance, fairness, and collective organizational wisdom—are often harder to discover and more difficult to classify. Nonetheless, these subjective evaluations work hand in hand with their objective counterparts to shape organizational fears, which, in turn, determine how your organization will react in times of crisis or confusion.

In terms of collective behavior, it doesn't really matter whether an organization's evaluative core beliefs can bear up under the test of reality. The crucial distinction among evaluative beliefs is, as indicated in the figure on page 74, whether they are *positive* or *negative*: whether they convey healthy or destructive messages about an organization's character. A second critical characteristic of an evaluative core belief is how widely it is held throughout an organization. Evaluative beliefs that have achieved a sort of critical mass within an organization acquire the potency of objective truth, causing the organization to act in accordance with what it "knows." A small biotechnology firm, for example, may not yet have shown a profit. But if its members believe in the soundness of its products, the organization stands a better-than-even chance of survival, so long as its financial resources do not become depleted. In contrast, a gargantuan defense contractor may be an infectious bed of negative core beliefs, despite a quarter-century of uninterrupted profitability. For such an organization, the future might seem ominous, and justifiably so. Any organization that owes its success to negative beliefs and the toxic fear these beliefs engender is probably looking at a long-term crisis of confidence and performance, unless it takes immediate steps to change its collective thinking.

Positive Evaluative Beliefs

These core beliefs are the happy truths of organizational life. By "truths," we don't mean inviolable laws or points on which every member of your organization always agrees. Instead, we're talking about evaluations that cast the organization in a positive light that most individual members would probably acknowledge. If you were to ask these people to list their positive evaluations of an organization, you might hear one or more of the following:

- This organization is a top performer in its field.
- This organization reacts intelligently when challenged.
- This organization regularly pursues new opportunities.
- This organization treats its members fairly.
- This organization rewards hard work and high performance.
- This organization's goals are consistent with those of its larger environment.
- This organization has the ability to change when change is truly necessary.
- This organization will succeed in the long term.

To some extent, every functioning organization holds to positive self-evaluations like these. An organization without positive evaluative beliefs would be akin to an individual devoid of self-esteem, a person teetering on the brink of suicide. Like a suicidal individual, such an organization would find itself incapable of healthy action, and in dire need of some sort of external intervention to prolong its survival. To endure for any length of time, an organization must see some sort of virtue in its collective behavior or in the ends toward which this behavior is directed. Without any sort of positive self-evaluation, an organization is likely to wither and die early in its development.

An obvious question now arises: If virtually all organizations hold some sort of healthy self-conception, why do some organizations succeed while others fail? The short answer is that successful organizations act in accordance with their positive self-evaluations—or, more accurately, in accordance with the healthy fears these kinds of beliefs inspire. Low-performing organizations caught up in successive cycles of unproductive activity habitually choose to ignore these healthy fears, and to react instead to the mythical fears produced by invalid descriptive beliefs and, as it turns out, by negative self-evaluations.

Negative Evaluative Beliefs Just as both successful and unsuccessful organizations hold to certain positive self-evaluations, both also harbor among their memberships negative perceptions about organizational behavior, attitudes, and objectives. High-performing organizations, in fact, are among the most self-critical institutions you're likely to encounter. Here again, the analogy between individual and organizational attitudes and behavior patterns is revealing. Fashion models are relentlessly critical of minuscule imperfections in their appearance; star athletes dwell incessantly on weaknesses largely invisible to the spectator; intellectual giants brood endlessly over flaws or inconsistencies in their thinking. Similarly, the most technologically innovative companies seem to focus obsessively on the limitations of their products, just as the most esteemed universities search constantly for more stellar faculty and the best available students. This suggests to us that negative self-evaluations are not in themselves inhibiting or destructive.

Not, that is, until they become the sole or predominant beliefs an organization heeds when it makes decisions and embarks on a course of action. Among organizations that regularly fail to achieve their ends, this is precisely what happens. When faced with a crisis or a challenge, an opportunity or a fortuitous event, these organizations consistently make decisions based on the unhealthy fears born of the following kinds of self-evaluation:

- This organization never accomplishes what it sets out to do.
- This organization bungles every opportunity that comes its way.
- This organization always follows the path of least resistance.
- This organization rewards its members for conformity and duplicity.
- This organization is run by incompetent decision makers.
- This organization is motivated solely by greed.
- This organization's products or services are inferior to competitive offerings.
- This organization cannot succeed without lying or cheating.

Successful organizations are aware that negative evaluative beliefs inevitably arise among the ranks, and they do their best to keep them from achieving the critical mass of truth. At an international agribusiness firm, for example, senior and middle management discerned among the employee population the belief that advancement through the corporate ranks demanded a rigid conformity in dress, thought, and demeanor. Aware that this belief could potentially inhibit the kind of innovative thinking required in an unstable global economy, a vice president named Leon recommended that the firm begin to hire and promote mavericks and rebels, as well as people from different ethnic and social backgrounds. When this policy was approved and put into action, the negative belief in the virtue of conformity was effectively countermanded, and organizational performance began gradually but steadily to improve.

Consider, in contrast, a seemingly noncontroversial decision that fell in the lap of Craig, a purchasing manager for a sluggish real estate firm. An official policy dictated that the company purchase its computing equipment solely from a single approved vendor, regardless of price and performance issues. The policy originated in the mid-1970s, when a since-dismissed purchasing agent acquired a minicomputer from a manufacturer that subsequently went out of business. Craig was looking at a request for two dozen personal computers when a new vendor happened to call, offering superior equipment at a lower price than the approved vendor could provide. As he listened to the sales representative's proposal, Craig's mind wandered onto the legend of the unfortunate agent responsible two decades earlier for the acquisition of what executives still referred to as "the world's most expensive metal cabinet."

Craig knew he could save the firm money, and perhaps even give it a slight but crucial competitive advantage, by entering into an agreement with a new supplier of computing equipment. But his apprehension, born of a negative belief concerning the fate of those who bought from unapproved vendors, blinded him to the potential benefits of challenging established dogma.

"My hands were tied," Craig later explained. "I knew what

was right, but I wasn't interested in having my head mounted on a plaque in the lobby. So I ordered from the regular supplier." He shrugged. "It seemed right at the time."

A few months later, the regular supplier merged with one of its competitors, then announced that it would no longer support its earlier line of personal computers. The realty firm was left with two dozen near-obsolete personal computers that could neither be upgraded nor economically repaired, all as a result of an entrenched negative core belief.

There's no denying that negative evaluations can create an intense fear that sometimes spurs a temporary improvement in performance. But once they've enabled an organization to "succeed" in this fashion, they inevitably take on the aura of inviolable truth—the sort of truth that makes mythical fear the dominant feature of the organizational landscape. And the longer this fear goes unchallenged, the more credence the negative belief behind it assumes. Finally the organization becomes literally incapable of the kinds of action that are crucial to high performance over the long term: actions based on innovation, honesty, and the equitable apportionment of costs and benefits.

BELIEFS AND FEARS IN THE BALANCE

Within any organization, both descriptive and evaluative core beliefs are at work. The interactions among them define the organization's core belief system—its view of itself and the environment in which it functions. We can readily see how certain combinations—for example, valid descriptive beliefs supported by positive evaluations—lay the groundwork for successful action. Conversely, we can see that the unhappy coincidence of an invalid self-description and a negative evaluation creates a disastrous scenario. Consider the situation at Darlene's bank, where the tellers lost a clear sense of their duties but became convinced they weren't performing up to par. This is an extreme case. In the great majority of organizations, actions tend to be based on a shifting (and often ambiguous) balance between conflicting core beliefs and the collective fears these beliefs create.

Organizational fears are emotional responses to core beliefs. These fears are tacit apprehensions of the consequences that will result if core beliefs are in any way violated—if, for example, a manufacturer of luxury automobiles suddenly decides to start producing economy vehicles, or a nonprofit health-care agency sets out to maximize its earnings. When beliefs are in conflict with actions, there arises within an organization a collective tension, an anxiety that needs to be alleviated by any available means. Thus afflicted, the organization reacts instinctively. Often it resorts to the most expedient or familiar alternative at hand, at which point a cycle of self-defeat is set in motion.

Fear, as we all know, is a great motivator. It's also a natural and healthy response, one that keeps us from doing things we really shouldn't do. The fear of addiction has kept many a casual drug user from falling into a life of chemical dependency, just as the fear of imprisonment has no doubt stopped many would-be thieves in their tracks. And because healthy fear is both instinctive and prophylactic, it's futile and wrongheaded for an organization to attempt to drive fear out of its midst. So long as the human species remains at once sentient and vulnerable, fear will influence thoughts and actions. To pretend otherwise is naive and potentially destructive.

We're talking here about healthy fear, the kind that is an integral part of valid and positive core beliefs. But where valid descriptive beliefs and positive self-evaluations yield legitimate apprehensions, invalid perceptions and negative assessments give rise to mythical barriers that impede effective performance. This mythical fear is toxic and counterproductive; when it achieves a critical mass, an organization is little more than dry kindling awaiting the touch of a flame. It's this sort of exaggerated dread that a struggling organization needs to identify, defuse, and ultimately eliminate.

Healthy Organizational Fears

In one way, healthy organizational fears acknowledge the consequences of low performance. These kinds of fears derive logically from core beliefs. In the table on page 86 we've matched

HEALTHY CORE BELIEFS AND REALISTIC FEARS

Core Belief	*Healthy Fear*
This organization delivers letters and parcels the same day they are sent.	If we're late in our deliveries, customers may turn to our competitors.
This organization builds the fastest computers for use in science and industry.	Building computers for use in the home may compromise our position in the marketplace.
This organization provides high-quality education at a minimal cost to the general public.	If the cost of our service exceeds its benefits in the public mind, we'll have trouble surviving.
This organization regularly pursues new opportunities.	Passing on innovations or chances for growth will reduce our long-term effectiveness.
This organization treats its members fairly.	Unfair treatment of our members will reduce commitment and impair performance.
This organization rewards hard work and high performance.	Rewarding deceit, laziness, or mediocre results will undermine our organizational credibility.

some valid, positive core beliefs with the healthy fears they imply. While there's nothing extraordinary about any of these beliefs or their corresponding fears, in tandem they exert a powerful force on organizational decision making. Assuming that the decision makers are sensible and that no mythical fears distort the equation, *sound core beliefs and healthy fears make counterproductive decisions virtually impossible.* Healthy fears check the impulse toward rash, expedient, or destructive activities, while sound core beliefs point toward honesty, openness, innovation, and the sharing of rewards. These productive efforts, in turn, affirm the core beliefs on which they are based, creating a high-performance loop that can be endlessly iterative. As success follows on success, the beliefs and fears at the core of high performance are continually validated.

Mythical Organizational Fears

In our experience, few organizations have achieved this absolutely harmonious integration of beliefs, fears, and performance. The reason for this may be the dominance of destructive beliefs and mythical fears at the core of most organizational structures. And we note this with sadness, because in functioning organizations these toxins need never become potent enough to taint performance. Often illogical or insubstantial, they can be neutralized or eliminated with a minimal effort. Yet they continue to flourish, primarily because they either confirm some jaded view of human nature or because they're mistakenly viewed as effective motivators.

What, exactly, are these mythical fears that so regularly block the path to high performance? Like realistic fears, they derive from core beliefs. But as the table below suggests, they distort reality well beyond sensible limits. Do any of these mythical fears seem familiar? They should; they correspond quite closely to the characteristic fears of the various self-defeating organizations described in Chapter 3. As it turns out, the fears that govern such

DESTRUCTIVE CORE BELIEFS AND MYTHICAL FEARS

Core Belief	*Mythical Fear*
This organization never accomplishes what it sets out to do.	We can't be accountable for promises or commitments, because we won't live up to them.
This organization is run by incompetent decision makers.	We can't trust any of our leaders, because they'll lead us to disaster or betray us.
This organization always follows the path of least resistance.	We can't try anything new, because we'll abandon it the moment the effort stalls or becomes difficult.
This organization cannot succeed without lying or cheating.	We can't tell the truth among ourselves, because the truth is unpleasant and dangerous.

organizations derive in large part from invalid or negative core beliefs. In depressed, chaotic, booster, nostalgic, and cargo cult organizations, counterproductive behavior results almost inevitably from fears born of distorted belief systems.

The astonishing thing about this is that in the end, destructive core beliefs cause an organization *to fear the very qualities that can improve its performance*. This leads, over time, to what systems analysts refer to as a *closed loop*. A closed loop is a self-contained unit that has no identifiable beginning or end, like a circle or an integrated circuit. A circle, for example, has no beginning or end—any point on its circumference is preceded by another point and followed by yet another. In self-defeating organizations, poor performance comes to resemble this sort of eternally perpetuating cycle. Performance cannot be improved because the organization fears the very attributes that will bring about improvement. The organization develops these fears as a consequence of what it believes. But the only way the beliefs can be changed is by embracing what the organization most fears . . . and on and on, cycling through the loop again and again, until resources dry up, layoff notices arrive, and finally the lights go dim.

It's easy enough to dismiss destructive beliefs and mythical fears as so much cynical carping, or as run-of-the-mill grumbling. It's so easy, in fact, that it's downright hazardous to an organization's health. "Oh, that's just Vic down in Accounting, venting his spleen as usual," an auto executive shrugged when we apprised him of a growing discontent in the ranks. What this executive failed to acknowledge was that Vic was, in fact, an extremely fearful person, and that he was continually spreading his fear among others. And once this message took on the weight of truth, the organization as a whole would become fearful of the attributes it needed most. It would become a self-defeating system.

CHANGING THE BALANCE OF FEARS

An organization caught up in a self-defeating loop can choose one of three alternatives at crucial strategic moments. It always has the option of continuing to do what it has done in the past, and thus to guarantee precisely the kind of disappointing results it wishes to avoid. It can also take draconian measures to overhaul its entire core belief system, a course of action so daunting and complicated that only the brave and the desperate attempt it. (For those brave, desperate few, we recommend Chapter 13, where we outline some of the requirements for bringing about comprehensive organizational change.) In most cases, however, a less drastic approach will suffice. An organization typically needs only to alter the balance of fears and beliefs that lay at the core of its decision-making processes.

We say this in full awareness of the complexities and difficulties that are apt to be involved in any attempt at organizational change. But since the other alternatives are either self-defeating or even more formidable, most organizations would do well to look at their core belief systems and see what this analysis reveals. In all likelihood, one of the two pictures shown in the figure on page 90 will come into focus.

As should be clear by now, the organization's goal should be to take the steps necessary to replace mythical fear with its healthy, realistic counterpart. But how?

In Part Three of this book we offer several suggestions, which we'll mention here only in passing. Since all sound core beliefs are firmly grounded in reality, truth-telling is a good way to initiate the process of unmasking canards and freeing the organization from illusory apprehensions. It's also important for the organization to remain open to new ideas, methods, and people—but not to the point of grasping at every fad, trend, and buzzword that works its way into the headlines. Moreover, the struggling organization should strive constantly to legitimize its policies and procedures, and the decisions and beliefs behind them. To build its credibility, the organization must be diligent in making sure that the costs and benefits of its actions are equitably distributed among all its constituencies, so that every new initiative does not carry the taint of managerial self-interest. And finally, the organization must explicitly link improved performance to sound core beliefs, thus closing a new systematic loop—in this case, the right one.

We can think of no better example of a healthy shift in the

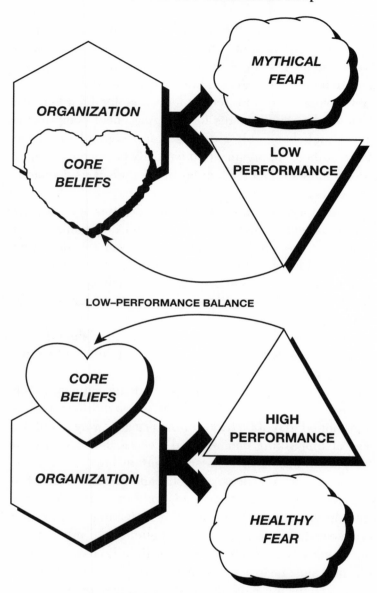

LOW–PERFORMANCE BALANCE

HIGH–PERFORMANCE BALANCE

The Balance of Beliefs and Fears

balance between healthy and unhealthy fear than the scenario that eventually played out at Darlene's bank. There, as you'll recall, senior management had, in a moment of exuberance, instructed tellers to function as salespeople, telling them that the branch office was to function more as a store than a service center. As a result, branch office operations nearly collapsed: transaction errors increased dramatically, and customers expressed indignation over the way they were treated during visits. Faced with an unfamiliar and ominous array of problems, the vice president in charge of the teller organization summoned Darlene and gave her *carte blanche* authority to restore some semblance of normalcy.

What Darlene chose to do was revealing. She called her tellers in for a meeting, where she concisely outlined the predicament. Then she assured the group that no member would be punished for any mistakes made during the implementation of the new program. Nor would they be punished, she added, for following the instructions she was about to give.

"For now, forget about making referrals and presenting new products," she then said. "If a customer inquires about a better interest rate or a tax deferral plan, by all means make a referral. But otherwise, concentrate on what you do best: completing and recording the transaction, accurately and pleasantly."

From one of the tellers came the predictable question: "But what about the teller referral program? The home office said we needed to get behind it 100 percent."

It was at this point that Darlene took what she later recalled as the biggest risk of her professional life. Aware that the tellers were looking to her for guidance, she simply told the truth.

"It's senior management's job to lead us—to set goals that will improve our overall profitability," she began. "And by and large, they do a fine job. But they can't always be aware of how a new program will play out in the trenches. It's our role to let them know when things go wrong, and to figure out how to make a program work.

"Sooner or later, we'll find a way to make teller referrals an effective marketing tool," she explained. "But until that happens, we owe our customers the best service we're capable of providing.

So unless you hear otherwise, go back to doing the job we hired you to do. In the long run, everyone—the home office included—will be happier."

These last words turned out to be prophetic. In the six months subsequent to Darlene's—dare we say the word—*courageous* reversal of a misguided directive, the number of transaction errors fell to an all-time low. Even more surprisingly, the amount of new business resulting from each teller referral soared dramatically, even though the number of actual referrals sharply declined. (Among other things, this suggested that consumer bankers were no longer wasting precious time and energy on unqualified—or largely uninterested—prospects.) Branch office performance, measured in terms of both profitability *and* customer satisfaction, climbed slowly but steadily toward a new peak.

A funny thing, the truth. Like a powerful adhesive, a little of it goes a long way. It often serves as a near-miraculous bonding agent. It can repair the shattered beliefs and, sometimes, the ailing soul of an organization gone awry.

CHAPTER 5

Reaction and Replication

INSANITY has sometimes been described as doing the same thing over and over, and expecting to achieve a different result. Substitute *ineffectiveness* for *insanity* and you have, in a sentence, the plight of the chronically unsuccessful organization. At once apprehensive and hidebound, the self-defeating organization resorts time and again to ostensible solutions that have failed it so often in the past. It's almost as if the leaders of these organizations are pinning their hopes on some quasi-divine intervention—or, failing that, on an extremely fortuitous turn of events. And when, predictably, the miracle or the lucky break fails to materialize, organizational decision makers scurry back to the drawing board, usually to sketch the outlines of a strategy remarkably similar to the one that has just failed.

Anyone who doubts the tendency of floundering organizations to replicate past activities need only consider the antics of politicians, particularly with regard to the problematic issue of taxation. When it is in control of the apparatus of government, one group typically seeks to enact a range of social programs designed to improve the lot of society's least productive members. Their reasoning is that once the targeted groups have more opportunities, they will become less dependent on government subsidies, thereby decreasing the public's tax burden. But more often than not, the programs fail, and the government must raise taxes to defray their cost. Those on the other side of this ongoing debate fare little better. When power shifts in their direction, their reaction is inevitably to enact widespread tax cuts in the belief that this measure will spur economic growth and offset lost revenues. But this rosy scenario never quite comes to pass. Deprived of expected revenues, the government simply operates at an ever-increasing deficit, until finally a tax increase becomes the sole means of maintaining national solvency.

Now a cynic might argue that politicians never have any real intention of lowering the long-term tax burden on the general public, and that those on both sides of the debate are interested only in advancing the interests of their major constituencies. But while cynics often serve as acute commentators, they seldom make for effective organizational leaders. Cynicism, in the end, is just another flawed core belief system. In assuming that no productive action is possible, it limits the range of available options to those that have proved marginally workable in the past. The cynic then chooses the most convenient or expedient alternative, and once that alternative has yielded predictably unsatisfying results, takes solace in the dubious notion that he or she has done all that could be done. Here again, we see unsound belief motivating counterproductive action, and the consequences of that action seeming to validate the belief behind it. We see a closed behavioral loop. We see a form of collective insanity.

There is, of course, a method to this madness. That method—an instinctive but systematic response to any perceived threat, challenge, or disruption—is our focus in this chapter. We'll attempt to explain why low-performing organizations continually flail about in a reactive mode when challenges arise, and how this reactive urgency leads inexorably toward strategies and decisions that replicate the failures of the past. Through a combination of reaction and replication, low-performing businesses, agencies, and similar groups all but ensure that their ongoing difficulties will be perpetuated. In the process, they cleverly defer the costs of counterproductive decisions until these costs can be effectively minimized and, ultimately, discounted.

STORE WARS

In the early 1980s, a medium-sized consumer electronics retailer faced the challenge of its decade-long existence. A national discount chain had opened several warehouse outlets in a geographic region the retailer had long dominated. Having established a foothold in this territory, the discounter proceeded to announce a lowest-price policy, offering to match or beat its competitors on any product in stock. The retailer correctly viewed the discounter's offer as ominous. Yet it reacted to this challenge in a curiously anemic way.

"Look, we have a loyal customer base," said Edwin, the company founder and president, to his senior managers. "They're not going to abandon us in favor of some fly-by-night operation that makes its money off extended warranties and impulse purchases. And what's more," he continued, getting to the crux of the matter, "we can't get into a price competition with these people. Our cost structure simply won't support it. Let's find another way to level the playing field."

The management group did as it was told. The firm eventually settled on a strategy of attempting to focus public attention on its superior sales staff and customer service. Through a series of televised and print advertisements, it touted the fact that its in-store staff were trained product specialists, as opposed to commission-hungry hirelings looking to pad their earnings at the customer's expense. And for a period of about a year, this strategy seemed to pay off. Although the retailer lost some of its sales volume to the discount chain, the decline gradually leveled off. For one brief, shining moment, Edwin and his managers basked in the glow of beating back a competitive challenge.

Then, alas, the recession hit.

It had been building, of course, for more than a year, and when it finally crested in middle America, it struck with a vengeance. As the news of layoffs and plant closings came to dominate the headlines and the airwaves, consumer spending dropped off sharply. Among the hardest hit were firms whose products were purchased with discretionary consumer income: upscale clothing boutiques, jewelers, and, naturally, sellers of nonessential electronic equipment. In a depressed economic climate, customers looking to purchase stereo systems, large-screen televisions, and videocassette recorders were relatively few and far between. And of those few, the vast majority flocked to stores offering rock-bottom prices.

How did Edwin's company respond to this crisis? The firm fell back on a tactic it had employed during earlier fallow times: it announced a round of layoffs. And who, exactly, did the company target as expendable? The senior and middle managers whose salaries contributed heavily to the top-heavy cost structure that ostensibly prohibited competitive pricing? Not a chance. The accountants who continued to divine clever ways of justifying this structure? Wrong again. The buyers who had repeatedly guessed wrongly about what customers would be likely to want and willing to pay? Not them, either.

As you've probably guessed, the company opted to dismiss many of its lowest-paid but most crucial employees: its in-store sales and service personnel. This left the stores undermanned and incapable of adequate customer service—*the very kind of service the company was still trumpeting in its advertisements*. These outlets thus found themselves in a position of total competitive disadvantage. Their prices weren't the best, and what service they could provide in the wake of the layoffs left much to be desired.

There is no happy ending here, no parable of back-from-the-brink resurrection. Within six months, Edwin announced that his firm would soon be merging with the discounter that had been its chief nemesis. At the press conference where the merger was revealed, Edwin spoke in mellifluous tones about the "creative destruction" of a capitalist system. And while we'd agree that considerable destruction had taken place, and that it was in a perverse way "creative," we saw an organization destroyed as much by its own behavior as by the force of immutable economics.

OF MATTERS REACTIVE AND REACTIONARY

Organizations and their core beliefs are, by nature, conservative. As we use it here, the term *conservative* has little or no political significance. It means simply that organizations tend to regard past events, and the beliefs drawn from these events, as touchstones for evaluating potential actions and policies. In successful organizations, this is a healthy state of affairs. A sound system of inherently conservative beliefs keeps the successful organization from chasing after windmills; from diversifying beyond the bounds of its expertise; from latching on to the latest management fad; from lusting after short-term gains that will result in long-term losses. The successful organization is conservative only in the sense that it is at once diligently self-evaluative and prudent. It regards its past as a source of valuable lessons about what works and what doesn't.

Self-defeating organizations are not so much conservative as *reactionary*—or, to use a more precise term, *reactive*. Much of their energy and resiliency is absorbed in a perpetual struggle with destructive core beliefs and mythical fears, or in an ongoing attempt to minimize the costs of recent disasters. This leaves few resources available for the critical chores of self-evaluation and innovation. As a result, such organizations are regularly caught off-guard by changes in their environment, as well as by new challenges and opportunities. And when shocked or surprised, the self-defeating organization does what comes most naturally. It replicates the less than optimal decisions and strategies of its own dubious past.

Why are self-defeating organizations so unfailingly reactive at key strategic moments? We've touched on the three fundamental causes of a reactive organizational mentality: an unsound core belief system, a preoccupation with illusory fears, and a diminishment of the collective energy required for a healthy response to change and challenge. If we look closely at each of these root causes, we can gain considerable insight into the peculiar logic at work inside an organization seemingly bent on self-destruction.

Inadequate Core Beliefs
We saw in the previous chapter how inadequate core beliefs—invalid perceptions and negative evaluations of how an organization operates—leave the organization ill equipped to deal with the

problems it encounters. These kinds of beliefs invariably steer the organization away from the measures it needs to take in times of crisis. They also tend to drive out whatever healthy attitudes are at work within the enterprise. Members of a self-defeating organization are, as a result of prior negative experiences, inclined to believe the worst. So when healthy core beliefs are advanced in times of crisis, those who advance them are often dismissed as naive or unrealistic.

Looking back at the scenario of Edwin's retail chain, we see an organization dominated by a corrosive, and perhaps inaccurate, core belief. It was a belief that Edwin himself articulated in his directive to senior management: that the chain *could not effectively compete on the basis of price*. With this belief established as a fact of organizational life, the chain was essentially denied a wide range of potential responses to the discounter's challenge. It could not even consider, for example, bringing its prices more in line with what consumers were willing to pay. Nor could it seriously entertain such possibilities as streamlining its operations in the interest of creating a cost structure that would support more flexible pricing policies, or accepting reduced profits in the short term so as to prevail over time. In this case, a single inadequate core belief had the net effect of excluding from consideration any sort of sensible response to the crisis at hand.

Heeding Mythical Fears

Mythical fears, as we discussed earlier, express an organization's apprehension of qualities that are inherent in high-performance behavior. An organization that fears truth, accountability, control, or change denies itself the kinds of strategic options it most needs to pursue. Among these options are truth-telling, innovation, and a clearheaded analysis of what kinds of results a proposed course of action will bring. This means that once mythical fear has come to dominate an organization's collective mentality, the organization becomes largely incapable of pursuing alternatives to its customary reactions.

Take the electronics retailer we've been discussing here. Believing that it could not effectively respond to challengers offering better prices, the organization reinforced the mythical fear that had come to dominate its collective outlook: the fear of competition. With the apparent blessings of its president and senior managers, the organization was essentially telling itself that it could not survive any sort of competitive threat—or, in other words, that it could prevail only in an arena where it was the sole, or at least the clearly dominant, player. But competition, as we all know, is a fact of business life; the vast majority of economists even view it as *healthy*. An enterprise that fears competition is like a fish afraid of water. It stands little chance of living a long, happy, and productive life.

Diminished or Depleted Resources

Another reason why unsuccessful organizations react badly to opportunities and challenges is that they simply lack the resources required to pursue more promising alternatives. High-performance behavior demands commitment, energy, and substantial funding. An organization lacking in any of these qualities—one that's unsure of what it should be doing, wracked by low morale, or short on available cash—is likely to resort to the kinds of ineffectual replication techniques described later in this chapter.

How, you might ask, can a sensible organization deplete its resources to the point where it can no longer implement sound initiatives? In certain cases, the organization bears little blame for finding itself in such straits. War, natural disaster, or political upheaval, as well as sudden market gluts or shortages, can all wreak havoc on an organization's balance sheet and, hence, constrain its flexibility. But in the majority of self-defeating organizations, resources are in short supply *because they are being drained in an attempt to minimize the costs of earlier misguided strategies.* This creates a vicious cycle, one where a struggling organization cannot adequately address today's challenges because it is still compensating for yesterday's errant decisions. But such attempts at minimizing the costs of organizational miscues are, as shown in Chapter 7, seldom effective. Not only do they consume precious time, dollars, and energy, but they also set the stage for blaming low performance on ostensibly uncontrollable forces and factors.

Among its many other problems, Edwin's retail chain simply lacked the funds to respond innovatively to the discounter's incursion on its territory. In the months preceding this competitive challenge, Edwin and his managers had decided to get into the personal computer business. (Leave aside for the moment the question of whether the company had the expertise to sell computers, or whether a viable consumer market for these machines even existed at the time: it was the early 1980s, and all things seemed possible.) The chain had entered into an agreement with a manufacturer of a relatively inexpensive computer, one that stored its programs on cassette tape and used a standard television set as a monitor. But the stores had no sooner taken delivery of large quantities of these units than the manufacturer announced that it would no longer support them; it had decided, prudently, to focus on more powerful and profitable computer systems. This left Edwin's chain with a huge inventory of machines, and little customer demand for them.

As it turned out, when the discounter announced that it was moving into the territory, many of Edwin's top managers, accountants, and buyers were scrambling to deal with the problem of the discontinued home computers. Even worse, the cost of carrying a largely unsalable inventory had drained away the firm's profitability. So at a time when the company's top marketeers and strategists ought to have been marshaling resources to meet the coming challenge, they were instead preoccupied with dubious promotions (for example, offering the discontinued machines "free" with the purchase of a marked-up television set) and attempts to fob off the essentially worthless computers on school districts and volume liquidators. Thus strapped for energy and capital, the chain could respond only tepidly to what emerged as the challenge of its organizational life.

FROM REACTION TO REPLICATION

Our major theme in this book is that organizational behavior is both cyclical and predictable. Faced with crises or opportunities, successful organizations behave in a way that replicates past success: they innovate, they explore, they evaluate, and they appropriately reward healthy initiatives. Unfettered by inadequate beliefs and illusory fears, they are, in the truest sense of the word, *free*: they can go wherever their ambition and expertise leads them. In contrast, self-defeating organizations enjoy no such freedom. Trapped between inadequate beliefs and unwarranted apprehensions, they find the path to high performance blocked. In microcosm, their dilemma might look like the figure below, where we see an organization on the verge of a disastrous decision. Looking inward for solutions to a threat or challenge, it runs headlong into its mythical fears—which, in turn, point back to beliefs that offer little solace. At this point, the organization ostensibly has available to it only two options. It can opt for the paralysis of inaction and, thus, remain trapped in a crisis of belief and fear. But this only causes the tension to build, until finally the organization is pressured into taking the only apparent route out of the circle. In a state of panic, it *reacts* convulsively to the problem at hand. And when it does, it embarks on the only course of action it

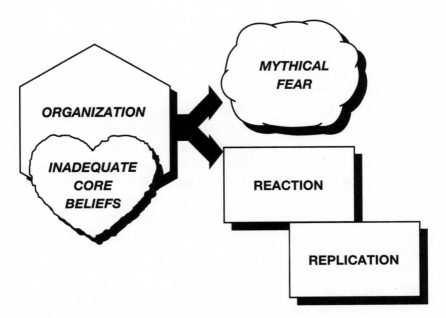

The Route to Replication

can conceive of in the frenzy of the moment. It *replicates* a course of action that has seemingly served its purposes in the past.

COMMON REPLICATION TECHNIQUES

You may often find that your organization replicates counterproductive activities or policies of the past. Under pressure, your business or agency may relieve the tension of a strategic moment by implementing decisions, policies, and programs that closely resemble past actions. Although your organization may have its own favorite technique, or may take several reactive measures simultaneously, these techniques often share two basic qualities.

To begin with, your organization's replication technique of choice is probably a strategy or program that has seemed to work in the past. The chances are good that if your facility has dealt with past quality problems by reorganizing its production line, you'll view reorganization as an apt response the next time trouble arises. Similarly, if your company has employed an austerity program to weather an economic downturn, you'll probably resort to retrenchment again and again. And if your organization weathers productivity or morale crises by "training" its members to accept harsh new realities—well, you can bet that you'll come to view "retraining" as a solution for all seasons.

That replication techniques have once proved workable points to the second quality they share: they are not necessarily evil, counterproductive, or ineffectual. In the appropriate context, an activity like restaffing, reorganization, retrenchment, or retraining may be an entirely viable solution to a perplexing organizational problem. But the key word here is *appropriate*. As it turns out, each technique that the self-defeating organization adopts as its panacea is truly appropriate only in a fairly narrow context or within a highly specific scenario. Reorganization, for example, may work when an enterprise has become fragmented, bloated, or operationally ineffectual. It usually will *not* work as a means of improving product quality, increasing organizational revenues, or bolstering morale. When applied under inappropriate circumstances, a replication technique is little more than a hammer in search of a nail.

Replication techniques, in short, tend to be specific remedies that are indiscriminately applied. The very names by which we know them—*reorganizing, retrenching, restaffing, restricting,* and *retraining*—suggest not only their reactive nature, but also the repetitive organizational behavior patterns they reflect. They are, if you will, the self-defeating organization's nervous tics—its habitual reactions to all signs of danger.

Reorganizing

In the epigraph at the start of this section, you read one corporate executive's pithy view on reorganization. In his jocular, minimizing way, this executive confirmed what we had suspected for a long time: that the majority of corporate reorganizations are cynical, pointless, *pro forma* exercises in futility. You've no doubt heard all the arguments in favor of reorganization as an effective management tool. Depending on the speaker, it's said to keep organizational members alert and wary, to centralize operations, to destroy factionalism, and to curtail the rise of "personality cults" under popular organizational leaders. More recently, it's been touted as an effective means of "flattening" hierarchical organizational structures, or of creating an "organization without boundaries."

Under optimal circumstances, reorganizing can help a struggling organization achieve any of these ends. But we believe that under the less than optimal circumstances of reality, repetitive reorganizing does far more damage than good. In the first place, it's inevitably disorienting for organizational members whose mental energies might better be devoted to improving their on-the-job performance. It reinforces the notion that individuals are mere pawns at the disposal of some disembodied, bureaucratic will, and thus discourages those hardy souls who value autonomy and self-direction. And most ominously, it often has the effect of crippling the performance of formerly productive work groups.

We saw an example of this in Gene's company, where senior management opted to reorganize a division for the most dubious of reasons: to reward a top-performing sales executive whom we'll call Mike. After a year during which Mike had been instrumental in capturing several major new accounts, management decided it was time to elevate him to a vice presidency, lest he sign on with a competitor. The problem was, there were no current openings at the vice-presidential level, and there was no sound reason to displace any of the incumbents. A committee of corporate elders mulled long and hard over this conundrum, then emerged with what they deemed an elegant solution: they decided to create a new division where Mike could reign supreme. To staff this rather amorphous unit, they drafted personnel from their current marketing, purchasing, sales, and quality assurance groups, none of whom were happy at being summarily reassigned. The architects of this plan weren't quite sure what function the new division would serve, but assumed that its role would become clear with the passage of time.

It didn't. None of the people assigned to the newly minted "Special Account Service" group ever quite figured out what they were supposed to be doing, other than following Mike around from one suite of offices to another. Mike, in turn, proved to be particularly inept in his new role as corporate ambassador; his specialty was closing deals, not holding the hands of current customers who had nothing better to do. (He eventually resigned to take a position as vice president of sales for the competitor that had been courting him at the time of his promotion.) Worse yet, his former group languished under his successor, a man loath to work the field with his beleaguered sales staff. Through its ill-conceived reorganization, divisional management had accomplished the neat trick of turning some twenty productive employees—among them a top sales executive—into a group of low performers.

In time, of course, they realized their mistake. And when they did, they dealt with the problem in their time-honored way. They reorganized.

Retrenching

With the possible exception of reorganizing, retrenching is the most popular replication technique among unsuccessful organizations. Whether it comes under the guise of cost cutting, layoffs, or divestiture of current assets, it comes repeatedly and indiscriminately in organizations bent on public displays of austerity. And while there's little doubt that such cutbacks are sometimes necessary—and, in the short term, effective—we have to wonder about the ultimate goals of an organization that views them as the solution of first resort.

There are two problems with retrenching, and they ought to give pause to any organization contemplating a new round of lay-offs or dramatic reduction in its operating budgets. The first is that the consequences of sweeping retrenchment—or the true costs of random cost cutting—tend to fall repeatedly on a single organizational constituency, whether it be low-level employees, customers, or harried line managers. (Recall that when Edwin's electronics chain found it essential to reduce operating costs, the five-figure salaries of store employees seemed a more inviting target than the six-figure salaries of those who loudly advocated the cost-cutting initiative.) Questions of fairness and morality aside, there's a very good reason why high-performing organizations ought not to let this happen. Over the long term, it simply doesn't work. As we discuss in Chapter 11, successful organizations are diligent in making sure that both the costs *and* the benefits of policies and decisions are distributed equitably among *all* their constituent groups. When one such group (say, senior management) continually reaps the benefits of success while another (say, plant employees) regularly absorbs the costs of failure, the organization is flirting with long-term disaster.

The other problem with retrenchment as a constant remedy to organizational ills is that it distorts the cause-effect relationship between problems and potential solutions. We once did some work with a software firm whose competitor had introduced a wildly successful new home finance program. An appropriate response, it seemed, would have been for the company to redouble its efforts to improve its own offering. But no: the firm decided instead to eliminate overtime pay for workers at its packaging and distribution center. No one ever explained, either to us or the affected employees, how a reduction in overtime costs might help the company meet the competitive challenge.

"When they start counting the pens, start counting your days." This from Steve, a former accounting supervisor for a major insurance company. In the late 1980s, when the company's profitable whole-life policies lost much of their luster to potential customers, its CEO launched a comprehensive cost-cutting program. As part of the program, accountants and other professionals had to obtain felt-tip pens from supply supervisors at the start of each day, and then return the pens at the close of business. In case anyone forgot, a clerical staffer came around in the evening to collect any pens that hadn't been returned. When we asked the CEO if he really believed that any savings thus realized could significantly improve profitability and performance, he mumbled words about the necessity of making a "symbolic" gesture.

The cost-cutting program was symbolic, all right. But we doubt it symbolized what the CEO meant it to.

Restaffing

Like dreamy adolescents, some self-defeating organizations seem to be caught up in a continual and wistful search for perfect men and women. These organizations tend to attribute their ongoing low performance to the personal and collective failings of lazy, ignorant, incompetent, and treacherous individuals among their ranks. When a new product fails to sell as expected, they summarily dismiss slumping sales representatives and replace them with fresh faces. If a backlog of orders results in a flurry of customer complaints and a loss of business, the organization cuts loose the allegedly responsible personnel within its distribution function, then brings in a new crew. Even more commonly, a slump in earnings per share prompts organizational ownership to topple a company president or CEO and replace the deposed leader with a perceived miracle worker possessed of insights and capabilities that will transform the organization overnight.

The problem with this approach is that it allows a troubled organization to look away from the systemic problems that are so often the source of its difficulties. While there are certainly scenarios where an organization's replacement of a tyrannical leader or its restaffing of a bungling work group is entirely justified, these situations are more often the exception than the rule. The modern world and the organizations that it comprises are simply too complex, and the sources of difficulty too widespread, for a single individual or group to be the sole source of low performance. To be sure, bad leaders or balky underlings can contribute mightily to a struggling organization's pattern of persistent failure. But under close observation, these so-called weak links turn out to be mere cogs in the metaphorical machine, functioning pretty much the way a malfunctioning organizational system has disposed them to function.

Where the consequences of such replication techniques as reorganizing and retrenching tend to fall disproportionately on low-ranking members of the organization, restaffing tends often to affect the organization's leadership and top management. Journalists and economists justifiably bemoan the obscene compensation packages awarded to corporate officers. Nevertheless, each paycheck these organizational leaders cash may be their last. Today's organizational shareholders are demanding an ever-increasing return on their investment, even as a turbulent marketplace makes this level of profitability increasingly more difficult to realize. Uneasy rests the head that wears the corporate crown—especially now, when organizational owners are apt, in times of crisis, to demand that head on a platter.

"Have you met 'Ms. Goodbar' yet?" Tim asked us one afternoon in the hallway of the public relations firm where he worked as an account executive. He was referring to Renee, the firm's new president and CEO—its fourth in a six-year period. Under the leadership of its mercurial founder, the company had prospered for nearly two decades. And when he sold his interest in the business and retired, the organization's board of directors did what it believed to be the right thing: it hired an executive search firm to find a suitable replacement. But that particular executive proved incapable of measuring up to the board's expectations. So, as it turned out, did the three unfortunates who succeeded him in short order. In each case, the board of directors duly prepared a detailed profile of the kind of executive it wanted, and just as duly retained the services of a well-regarded search firm. Yet in each instance, the results remained the same: operational problems persisted, and profits continued to decline until an increasingly impatient board of directors again let it be known that it was looking for new leadership.

Had the board taken a longer and harder look at its plight, it would have seen what even a cursory analysis of the firm's recent history revealed. For at least a decade prior to the founder's retirement, the firm had been relying on his charisma—his rhetorical skills, dynamism, and numerous business contacts—to mask a series of ongoing performance problems. Among them were a history of failing to meet commitments to both customers and suppliers, and an undeniable sameness in the public relations campaigns the firm developed for its clients. Now, with the founder gone, these ominous flaws lay glaringly exposed. Before anyone bothered to notice, the firm had acquired the reputation of a mediocre performer—a reputation that any new leader would need time and commitment to reverse.

We never got to meet Renee, the "Ms. Goodbar" to whom Tim so glibly referred. But had we sat down with her, we would have wished her good luck. She was going to need it.

Restricting

If you've seen it once, you've seen it a hundred times. Someone makes a mistake or a misguided decision, costing your organization lots of time, money, and goodwill. Your company or division responds by increasing the number of approvals required to put a plan into action, or by stripping away the authority of those deemed responsible for the disaster. Privileges and prerogatives are revoked; the iron hand of supervisory control is brought to bear. In response to a crisis, your organization reflexively *restricts* the behavior of its individual members, hoping vainly that such measures will inspire you to new heights.

Like retrenching, the technique of restricting behavior betrays a peculiar logic about performance and its root causes. Let's say that the research-and-development group of a computer company fails to come up with a new architecture for a machine the firm's marketing function has already promised to deliver on a certain date. As a result of this delay, several key customers cancel their orders, while others invoke penalty clauses that cost the manufacturer a good deal of money. Because of Research and Development's failure (which, for all we know, may have been entirely justifiable), the company announces that all employees will have to bite the bullet to compensate for lost revenues. Among the measures it invokes is the cancellation of its flexible-hours program, even for employees at a high-performing plant located a thousand miles away.

"I don't get it," says an assembler at the plant. "We've exceeded all our quotas, and our defects are way down. Why do we have to rush to beat the clock?"

"Headquarters says we all have to be more aware of meeting commitments," a supervisor answers without evident enthusiasm. "They want us to see that we're all in this together."

"Right," replies the assembler bitterly. "R & D screws up, so we pay the price."

And there, in a nutshell, is why restricting is so seldom an effective response to a problem brought on by low performance. To begin with, it treats hard-working organizational members as children who are best instructed by punitive example. What's more, it does little to address the root cause of a crisis. In the above scenario, there seems to be a somewhat bizarre assumption on the part of organizational management—namely, that the firm's research-and-development engineers might have met their deadline, had they only been forced to be at work by eight each morning.

Finally, restricting has the inevitable consequence of spreading unhealthy fear throughout an organization. Though the company employees in our example might indeed work harder in the short term, the chances are good that they'll do so without joy, innovation, or any sense of organizational loyalty. They'll become guarded and cautious; they'll refuse to commit to any deadline that can't be met with months to spare. In this atmosphere of fear, suspicion, and contracted horizons, long-term high performance is unlikely to be realized. When its members are working primarily to cover their own behinds, the organization as a whole is left naked and vulnerable.

Retraining

Today's organizations need to take whatever measures are necessary to make sure their members are properly and thoroughly trained in any skills that have an impact on individual and collective performance. Most organizations spend far too little to ensure that employees have mastered the latest tools, computer programs, and company procedures. That struggling organizations reflexively cut training budgets before pursuing other alternatives suggests that these organizations are myopically focused on short-term profits, rather than on long-term performance. Training, in short, is good, and the majority of organizations need more, not less, of it.

Nonetheless, we must admit to grave reservations about what passes for training in the typical self-defeating organization. And a good many of the human resources professionals we've worked with confirm our suspicions. When promised anonymity, one of them—we'll call him Wayne—admitted that most of the so-called training his company offered was conducted either for public relations purposes or to provide legal protection in the event of an employee lawsuit. Another training manager—let's call her Julie—inadvertently paraphrased George Washington Hill, the tobacco tycoon who couldn't determine which half of his advertising dollar went to waste. "I'd say as much as 90 percent of our training turns out to be worthless," she noted in an offhand manner. "The problem is, we have no idea which 10 percent actually works."

If even professional trainers confess these views, is it really any surprise that in self-defeating organizations, retraining is often deployed as a universal remedy for all that ails? The shocking thing here is that training, formerly the most earnest of organizational endeavors, has of late become a convenient and cynical means of replicating and perpetuating lethargic performance. It's come to be regarded as a simple and relatively inexpensive response to problems as disparate as redundant data entry and racial tension.

Why do the retraining efforts of self-defeating organizations tend to create at least as many difficulties as they resolve? In the first place, these initiatives are often imposed from the top down; the decision makers who authorize a new training program are careful to exempt themselves from it. As Wayne pointed out to us, the senior management of his company rarely participated in any of the seminars and workshops mandated for lower-ranking organizational members. When word of this got out, line managers and workers were justifiably cynical about the value and importance of the programs in which they were forced to participate. Hence all training, both good and bad, was viewed within the ranks as bread and circuses designed to distract the organizational masses from truly important issues and decisions.

Much current organizational training also fails for the most obvious of reasons, the one Wayne hinted at: it was never meant to be effective in the first place. Sound organizational training is designed to remedy a specific performance problem or knowledge discrepancy. It has clearly identified goals and outcomes that are readily measured. If, for example, a group of clerical employees is unable to use new software to perform a critical function, the success of any training they receive can be evaluated in terms of their subsequent ability to use the new program. But training intended to change attitudes or perceptions is seldom subject to this level of scrutiny, and for a very good reason—*it simply doesn't work*. Individual beliefs about race, gender roles, moral values, and human nature are formed over a lifetime of experience. It's either foolish or cynical to think that these beliefs can be significantly altered during the course of a two-day workshop, or even a week-long seminar.

Because counterproductive organizations so frequently design their internal training programs with an eye on the headlines, managers and employees are subjected over and over to sessions that reflect current trends, rather than organizational realities. One month the members of an organization may be instructed in the virtues of participative management, only to have these virtues contradicted in a round of workshops and seminars delivered just a few months later. This flavor-of-the-month approach to training leaves organizational members feeling skeptical about *all* the training they receive—including well-timed and informative programs actually targeted at improving individual and group performance.

Consider the case of Wayne's employer, a manufacturer of computer disk drives. Within a single eighteen-month period, the employees at one plant were subjected to a series of vague, hastily assembled training sessions on one-minute management, total quality improvement, and organizational reengineering. No one in the corporate ranks seemed to consider that the plant's production-intensive environment was singularly inhospitable to the kind of repeated interaction required to implement the "one-minute" approach, nor that the two subsequent initiatives—TQI and process reengineering—directly contradict one another. (TQI calls for the continual improvement and measurement of existing processes, while reengineering calls for the wholesale scrapping of existing methods and systems.) Apparently unsatisfied with the resulting level of confusion, plant management also mandated during this period compulsory seminars on the topics of diversity and sexual harassment. These sessions served little or no purpose, other than to inflame emotions at a facility that had been mercifully free of race- and gender-related conflict.

WHY ORGANIZATIONS REPLICATE SELF-DEFEATING ACTIVITIES

We've said it earlier in this book, and we'll say it again before we're through: your organization does not practice self-defeating behavior patterns because your leaders and decision makers are stupid, insensitive, incompetent, or deceitful. The staff of your organization probably consists of the standard mix of high performers, low performers, and a great number of individuals who fall between these extremes. Most are well-intentioned and reasonably competent souls forced to work under intense pressure and wrestle with decisions that would leave even a Solomon scratching his head. Like you, they toil hard and brood long on the problems plaguing their enterprises. More than anything, they need quick answers.

Replication techniques have the unfortunate quality of appearing to provide workable solutions to pressing dilemmas. They relieve the tension and anxiety that are so pervasive at strategic moments, and seem to grant the organization a temporary reprieve from the consequences it faces. They also tend to deflect and diffuse the responsibility for tough decisions throughout the organization, and to grant besieged decision makers a measure of control over the future. If we examine each of these dubious benefits, we can clearly see why replication techniques are regularly brought to bear in times of organizational crisis.

Replication Relieves Organizational Tension

Faced with a challenge or crisis, an organization experiences high levels of tension, anxiety, and internal confusion. If the organization cannot come up with a healthy means of dealing with the perceived threat, these internal pressures will build to an unbearable level and, ultimately, force the organization to react instinctively. Just as an individual surrounded by predatory animals or humans cannot indefinitely remain paralyzed, the besieged organization must eventually do *something*. That something, unfortunately, is almost always a replication of what the organization has done in the past.

Replication Buys Time

Because they are neither stupid nor insensate, self-defeating organizations are often fully aware that the replication technique they've chosen will not, in the long run, resolve the problems at hand. But they're also aware that in providing various short-term benefits, replication will grant them a reprieve from the urgencies of the moment. Hence they view reorganizing, retrenching, restaffing, restricting, or retraining as a stopgap measure that will give them the time they need to develop a healthy, innovative solution to their ongoing performance problems. The problem is, these organizations never quite get around to formulating such solutions in time to respond effectively to the next threat or challenge. Thus replication begets replication, until the costs of these counterproductive activities finally bring the organization to a long-delayed breaking point.

Replication Deflects and Spreads Responsibility

Having proved more or less workable at some point in the past, replication techniques seem eminently plausible to the struggling organization. An organizational leader who opts for replication maintains a measure of deniability. "Don't blame me," he or she can say when confronted with subsequent costs. "I only did what we've always done when times are tough." In this way, responsibility for unacceptable consequences is deflected away from the individual decision maker, and *onto the organizational system as a whole.* And as we demonstrated earlier, in organizations where everyone is to blame, no one is really to blame. The responsibility for low performance is spread so thin that everyone bears a bit of it. Thus the disaster that follows a counterproductive reaction falls not, say, on the CEO who slashed the workforce to dangerously low levels, but rather on the whole of his organization, whose habitual poor performance made this unwise course of action all but mandatory.

Replication Provides the Illusion of Control

Self-defeating organizations not only know that their replication techniques will not work—they also know *how* these unproductive activities will fail. This knowledge brings solace, because the organization is familiar with the inevitable consequences and believes it can effectively deal with them. Knowing that a series of expedient plant closures will lead to low morale and high turnover mitigates, in a way, the ominousness of these toxic consequences. Self-defeating organizations are nothing if not adroit at minimizing the costs of their destructive or ineffectual actions. These costs are the devils they know, and as such are infinitely preferable to the vaguely threatening shadows along the way to change and innovation.

In offering a ready escape from anxiety, self-scrutiny, and paralysis, replication techniques unfortunately enable an organization to act against its own best interests. In diffusing responsibility and providing the illusion of control, they put the organization in a position where it's all too easy to accept and minimize the costs of misguided actions. Replication fails not because it's inherently evil or wrong, but because it makes it nearly impossible for an organization to learn from its mistakes.

CHAPTER 6
Absorbing Costs

HE EMPLOYEES of a once-dominant data services corporation
had never seen anything like it. Only a few years earlier, their
company had been a prosperous (if somewhat sprawling) supplier of software and programming services for the federal
government and several of its major defense contractors. But
now, any visible signs of success were few and far between. Formerly influential managers and consultants brooded behind
closed office doors, accomplishing little other than to polish their
résumés and spread ominous gossip over the phone. Overburdened support personnel rushed from one temporary work assign-
ment to another, their ranks dangerously depleted by a recent
company-wide restructuring. Key field support teams were said to
be overtly impugning the reputations of colleagues within earshot
of customers. A number of key executives mused aloud on the
prospect of early retirement. Rumors of an imminent merger or
leveraged buyout circulated in the business press.

"You're looking at our new, 'flat' organization," said a marketing manager named Amanda. "Flat broke, flat on its back, and
flat-out dumb."

The company's predicament was hardly unique in the early
1990s. It had come of age in an era of rampant defense spending
and cost-plus contracts, adding layers of bureaucracy in the

manner of its primary government and private-sector clients. It had structured its operations around convoluted hierarchies and management matrices that lent themselves nicely to incessant tinkering and reshuffling. But the end of the Cold War, in combination with increasing taxpayer demands for accountability, had brought an end to all this. With demand for its products and services sharply reduced, and its customary sources of revenue drying up fast, the company realized it had to change. And the only strategies it could bring to bear were the time-tested techniques of reorganization and retrenchment.

But this time around, a committee of executives, planners, and consultants opted to do more than simply shift the names in the boxes on the corporate organization chart. In what they deemed a singularly bold stroke, these strategists abruptly shattered the firm's intricate management matrix. They eliminated scores of middle managers, then combined the disparate roles of project manager and lead project analyst into a single function. At the same time, they announced deep cuts in the firm's clerical staff and its field sales force. When questioned about these measures, company officials blandly observed that they were necessary to create the kind of lean, mean organization required for the '90s.

These officers were on the mark in one respect: in the aftermath of the sudden downsizing, the company was a mean place to work. The decision to merge the duties of the firm's project managers and lead analysts proved especially divisive. Many of the former had little interest in programming; most of the latter were at once bored and overburdened by the chore of monitoring schedules and budgets. Of the few who were willing to adapt to the change, many lacked the required skills to assume their new responsibilities. (For these hardy souls, the company offered helpful "retraining.") The organization was divided between those who seemed receptive to the new arrangement and those dedicated to resisting it. Key programmers and software designers shifted their loyalties away from the company as a whole, throwing in with individual project managers and analysts. Confusion and resentment suffused the depopulated corporate corridors.

The new spirit of meanness soon spread beyond organizational walls. Harried administrative assistants no longer knew where to direct customer requests and inquiries, and in any event had neither the time nor the energy to find out. Lacking the resources to resolve customer difficulties, the firm's marketing support teams offered excuses and blamed corporate headquarters for their inability to take timely action. As a result, the company lost one key account and found itself forced to renegotiate contracts with several of its remaining customers. The company's performance—not to mention its credibility and reputation—dropped to an ominous low.

What we saw here was an organization at the make-or-break point in its evolution. It was an organization forced at last to absorb the disastrous *costs* of its reactive and replicative behavior.

THE FRUITS OF REACTION

Organizations that react to challenge with shopworn techniques must inevitably deal with the costs of their replicative behavior. These costs are as predictable as the rain that follows hard on the rumble of thunder, as common as the weeds that spring up in a defoliated landscape. They are, in short, the natural consequences of self-defeating activities. And as we'll eventually demonstrate, the organization that ignores or minimizes these fruits of its misguided labor does so at the cost of contaminating its collective soul.

When we talk about organizational costs, we're not referring solely to the financial consequences of counterproductive actions. Although they often tax organizational resources, such consequences as reduced earnings, increased unemployment premiums, and legal and administrative fees are relatively easy to minimize. (Companies even have a name for the accounting legerdemain through which this is easily accomplished: they call it *cost justification*.) Quantitative costs are, for the most part, only momentarily problematic; the organization disposes with them handily, then moves on to more pressing concerns. But the *qualitative* costs of misguided decisions are not so easily dismissed. Once they take root within an organization's collective mentality, they are reflected in the behavior of individuals trying to cope with an untenable situation. As discussed in Chapter 2, these people tend to fight, flee, or hide from an oppressive new reality, or to adapt to the warped logic of a counterproductive system. Through the actions and attitudes of struggling individuals, the true costs of self-defeating organizational behavior are made manifest. And once these costs—territorialism, low morale, high turnover, low innovation, and lost opportunities—become established facts of organizational life, they displace sound core beliefs and pave the way to low performance.

Territorialism

Territorialism is the natural consequence of compulsive reorganization, retrenchment, and restaffing. When individuals are repeatedly jolted out of familiar surroundings and relationships, they react by shifting their allegiance away from the company, team, or agency as a whole, then casting their lots with a particular function, department, or individual. This explains why so many self-defeating organizations seem, on close inspection, to be little more than loose aggregations of dueling work groups, localities, and personalities. In extreme cases, even this marginal sense of collective purpose is stripped away, yielding a sort of oxymoronic "organization" made up of individuals who are working only for themselves.

In certain kinds of self-defeating organizations—for example, the chronically depressed or chaotic enterprise—territorialism is viewed not as a problematic cost, but rather a source of motivation. The thinking here is that mistrust, hostility, and insecurity on the part of fragmented internal groups will inspire these units to new heights of performance, with each trying to prevail over its counterparts. This viewpoint is both cynical *and* wrong. It's true that a spirit of internal competition can prove invaluable when an organization is faced with an urgent and daunting challenge. But the level of acrimony, blaming, and outright subversion that territorialism ultimately produces seldom bodes well for an organization's health. In elevating self-preservation and a grudging survivalism to the status of core beliefs, territorialism inevitably undermines any semblance of collective organizational purpose.

It's easy to fall into the trap of viewing territorialism through rose-colored glasses. When they first appear, internal rivalries and conflicts often seem a welcome alternative to the collective lethargy they have displaced. If, for example, a firm's product engineering and manufacturing groups have long enjoyed a dull but amicable symbiosis, organizational leaders may find it thrilling to see the two suddenly at fractious odds. But because the two functions are dependent on one another, neither will be able to achieve a conclusive triumph—and that, unfortunately, is when the competition is bound to turn nasty. Looking in on the rivalry six months or a year down the line, the same leaders who initially applauded it are likely to be shocked to learn that the two groups are working more to subvert each other than to make a positive contribution toward organizational ends.

Does this actually happen? You can bet on it. At the data services corporation we described earlier, the sales support teams under Amanda's charge were deprived of required personnel and financial resources, even as their responsibilities were increased again and again. For a while, Amanda told us, team members viewed this as a challenge; they began to compete to see which of them could best maintain their level of performance under the new conditions. When it became clear, however, that these conditions made success all but impossible, individual team members instead focused their efforts on making sure that none of their rivals had a chance to succeed.

"I know it's hard to believe," Amanda later told us, "but there were rumors—and evidence—of people destroying or misrouting customer requisition sheets. And one team leader was overheard telling clients that his group was the only one worth a damn, that the others had a reputation for screwing up."

It was around this time that Amanda's supervisor, one of the company's senior vice presidents, called her into his office and commended her for the "aggressive" and "cost-effective" performance of the downsized sales support teams. Knowing even as he spoke that some sort of explosion or implosion was near at hand, she derived little solace from this shortsighted praise.

Low Morale

Successive cycles of ineffectual activity erode the morale of all but the most resilient members of self-defeating organizations. For a short time, those disposed to fight the organization may bristle with combative energy, while those looking to hide or adapt may mask their distress beneath a pose of superficial good cheer. But if the organization does not frankly acknowledge and pay the costs of its counterproductive actions, this posturing will eventually have a destructive effect on the collective organizational character. It will cause the organization to become dispirited, fractious, unmanageable, or wistful in its thinking about the past, present, and future. And as we saw earlier, organizations with these characteristics are often at a loss to deal with new challenges and opportunities in productive ways.

The organizational malady summed up in the phrase "low morale" describes a scenario where destructive core beliefs have superseded healthy attitudes and perceptions. When misguided policies and decisions lead time and again to low performance, suspicions and rumors about an organization—that its management is incompetent, that it cares little about rank-and-file members, that it cannot succeed without treachery—achieve a critical mass and become operating principles of organizational life. Except for the few maladaptive sorts who thrive in an atmosphere of deceit and hostility, people who hold negative beliefs about their companies, departments, or teams seldom perform at their best. Instead, they become survivalists, lurking about in the shadows and peripheries of organizational activity in search of some means of making it through the day, month, or year. Unsure of the future, they hoard their individual resources, rarely offering more than what is demanded of them today.

Once low morale has taken root within an organization's character, it's not easily dispelled. Low morale is an expression of the unhealthy fear that accompanies destructive core beliefs. It's the product of a series of unpleasant experiences over a protracted period of time—experiences that have taught the wrong sorts of lessons about organizational life. Individuals find it extremely difficult to forget or set aside these experiences and the "truths" they have imparted. They cling diligently, sometimes even pridefully, to their psychic scars. The only long-term antidote to entrenched low morale is the kind of comprehensive organizational change that yields successful results and supplants the bitter wisdom of the past.

In the interim, the self-defeating organization must find a means of dealing with the low morale that results when individuals are stripped of their identities and sense of purpose. In the words of Chet, a once-esteemed project manager at the downsized data services firm, we heard unmistakable intimations of a deflated organizational spirit and a diminished capacity for hope.

"I've been with this company fourteen years," Chet told us. "I started out in the accounting department. I had a job to do and a boss to report to. I did the job, the boss was pleased, and I was promoted to accounting supervisor. Same thing: I knew what I was supposed to do, and I did it. Then I became a lead project manager and, I have to say, I was a good one. My boss seemed to agree—I received merit raises for six years running.

"But now they tell me I'm something called a 'lead account analyst,' " he continued, dourly. "I have no idea what I'm supposed to be doing, or who reports to me. As a matter of fact, I'm not even sure who *I* report to. Something called the 'status review board,' I'm told."

We asked Chet how he and his colleagues were dealing with the confused state of affairs. At this, he smiled.

"Well, I can't speak for the others," he said. "But me, I do my best to look busy. I take notes at meetings, chat with customers on the phone. And I sign up for every training program that's being offered. It's a way of passing the time, maybe even making a few new contacts."

We thought of Chet and dozens of individuals like him, sitting glumly in their offices and looking to get out. It was a prospect that boded ill for their employer, a company that had impulsively deprived its key members of their professional identities and, in some cases, of their personal pride.

High Turnover

Not much needs to be said about high turnover, one of the most predictable and underestimated costs of ill-advised organizational behavior. It's virtually a given that, in the wake of an organization's untenable or futile response to challenge, a sizable number of its members will choose to flee an environment in which they cannot function productively. Among the individuals most likely to take flight are those with highly portable or desirable skills, those with a minimal commitment to the organization, and those who are weary of fighting an endless battle against counterproductive policies and procedures. Their exodus not only drains away crucial skills and expertise, but also sends an ominous message to the friends and colleagues they leave behind.

It's somewhat alarming, therefore, that so many troubled organizations look on high turnover as a blessing in disguise (or, if you will, as an outright benefit of reactive and replicative behavior). They view the collective flight that follows counterproductive reorganization, retrenchment, or restriction as a convenient means of achieving desired staff reductions, ridding themselves of low and mediocre performers, and eliminating the big salaries they pay to erstwhile stars. To ensure that this systematic thinning of the herd occurs as planned, such organizations frequently extend an incentive to depart at the same time they announce a reactive change. Long-time employees are typically offered an early-retirement program or an attractive severance package as an alternative to reassignment, geographical dislocation, or a reduction in their status and level of influence.

"Sure, a lot of them are going to leave," said Naomi, a human resources consultant at the data services firm discussed in this chapter. "And of those who take advantage of our outplacement program, most are, frankly, earning more than they're worth to us. In today's environment, we simply can't afford to pay someone $60,000 a year when we can get more or less the same performance for $30,000. It all comes down to dollars and cents."

Does it really? Naomi and the corporate leaders who initiated her efforts seemed to be overlooking the fact that departing employees would take with them a significant amount of expertise and experience the company would no doubt need in the coming months and years. They'd also be leaving behind loyal friends and colleagues, none of whom could be expected to put much long-term trust in the company and its leaders. Moreover, news of a large-scale turnover in key personnel could hardly inspire confidence among the firm's investors and customers. Any organization looking to send a message by way of systematic high turnover should consider the grave implications of this cold-blooded approach.

Low Innovation

There are three requirements for the kind of innovation that leads to significant breakthrough and long-term high performance. First of all, individuals must have access to the resources—time, funding, and expertise—they need to transform ideas into innovative strategies, products, and services. Second, the organization must grant individual members the freedom to pursue their interests and test their insights against reality and established norms. And most importantly, the innovative organization must strive vigilantly to create and maintain a climate devoid of mythical or disproportionate fear. Individuals who are afraid of challenging the status quo or advocating new solutions are risk-aversive; they shun creative thinking as if it were a plague. When enough individuals feel this way, the organization as a whole becomes sluggish, dormant, and largely incapable of responding innovatively to problems.

Reactive techniques like reorganization, retrenchment, and restriction are the natural enemies of organizational innovation. Inappropriate or *pro forma* reorganization creates confusion, divides loyalties, and causes individuals to focus their energies on adapting to the changed environment. Retrenchment cuts deeply into the funds required to support new products and pilot projects, while at the same time increasing the burden on the employees who have survived the latest round of staff reductions. Restriction strikes hard at the sense of individual freedom that is essential to an innovative environment. Demanding adherence to arbitrary rules and regulations does little to encourage the kind of spontaneous exchanges and impromptu gatherings from which new ideas so often spring. And prohibiting individuals from taking any action without approval all but guarantees that they will propose only safe, sanctioned, and utterly predictable solutions to crises and challenges.

Like the other ongoing consequences of self-defeating organizational behavior, the cost of low innovation is difficult to quantify. Who can say, for sure, how much a company loses as a result of continuing to offer only shopworn products or services? Who can say, for sure, what sort of breakthrough idea a particular employee might have come up with, had he or she not been depressed, confused, or deprived of key resources? Low innovation is an organizational cost that's all too easy to ignore or minimize. At the troubled data services firm we worked with, for example, senior management largely subsidized its sweeping reorganization by drastically reducing the budget of the firm's research and development function. Renowned for its elegant vertical-market software, the company announced that it would no longer be developing these products, but would focus instead on customizing off-the-shelf applications. But the firm's customers had developed enough internal expertise over the years to perform this chore without assistance. Even more ominously, some of these customers soon discerned that if they needed this level of service, they could readily obtain it more cheaply from other vendors. In exchange for a tarted-up annual report, the firm in effect ceded the strategic position it held in the minds of several key customers.

Negative Reinforcement

When an organization is extremely young, or if it remains relatively small or homogeneous, it has a high level of control over the kinds of people it allows into its membership. But in large, diversified businesses and bureaucracies, this selectivity is impracticable and, in some cases, impossible. As a result, many organizations discover belatedly that they have admitted into their ranks a number of people who thrive on destructive or manipulative behavior. For the healthy, successful organization, this doesn't pose a significant problem. Over the course of time, these miscreants usually show their true stripes and are dealt with promptly and appropriately.

In a self-defeating organization, the issue of destructive individual behavior is far murkier and more difficult to manage. When cynicism and expediency have descended like clouds over the organizational landscape, the activities of opportunists and malcontents tend often to be obscured. Even worse, these activities may seem on the surface to be perfectly consistent with organizational goals and policies. A petty tyrant, for example, may find intoxicating the authority vested in him by a wholesale restriction of individual behavior. Likewise, the chronic schemer may view the machinations of compulsive reorganizing as a means of creating her own empire of insecure underlings. It's not at all difficult for a malicious or self-serving individual to masquerade as an organizational loyalist in times of acrimony and strife.

The tendency of self-defeating organizations not only to tolerate but often to reward destructive behavior is one of the less obvious costs of ongoing low performance. In reinforcing negative or counterproductive behavior, these organizations send out an ominous message: that promotions, raises, and accolades await those who wink at lofty goals and programs, then act in stealthy pursuit of their own dubious agendas. To cite but one example, it's common these days for organizational leaders to tout the significance of team spirit and cooperation. But it's equally common for these same leaders to settle partnerships, promotions, and pay raises on persons who have completed successful end-runs around group guidelines and procedures, or even the tenets of common human decency. When pressed to explain the inconsistency, senior managers often mumble that these people are "effective" in the short term, or that they possess qualities the organization needs to stir it from its lethargy.

Now while most people are fairly trusting, few are stupid enough to misread handwriting writ this large on the organizational walls. Soon enough, formerly well-meaning individuals take to emulating the actions and attitudes that the organization deems worthy of reward. Hence we see scenarios like the one Amanda described for us, where one member of a sales support team began to discredit other teams in conversations with the firm's customers. When this particular employee was subsequently recognized at a biennial communications meeting for the results he was able to achieve under stringent circumstances, his colleagues began to follow suit. Senior management viewed this "entrepreneurialism" on the part of team leaders as an encouraging development.

And so it was that one afternoon Amanda received a phone call from a perplexed and somewhat irate customer. "I don't know what kind of circus you're running over there," the customer complained, "but two days ago you sent over a crew that your own people had warned us about. We were explicitly told, and *by one of your guys*, not to let any of those people tinker with any of our mission-critical applications."

Although she had sensed that a fiasco like this was inevitable, Amanda fumbled for an appropriate response. She finally told the customer that these were confused and chaotic times for her firm, and that some field personnel had become a little too zealous in an attempt to put new organizational policies into practice.

The customer said that he understood. But there was no mistaking the damage that had been done and no convenient means of dismissing its root organizational causes.

Lost Opportunities

If pressed on the point, most organizational leaders will concede that such consequences as territorialism, high turnover, and low morale have some effect on bottom-line profits. They don't know what this cost is, but at least they're willing to acknowledge it. But few of the executives we've talked to have considered perhaps the most insidious cost of their misguided actions: the opportunities that are lost while the members of an organization struggle to survive amid untenable circumstances. And while we make no claim of being able to measure or quantify the cumulative cost of lost opportunities, we're convinced that in a self-defeating organization it eventually asserts itself with a vengeance.

There's no telling, for example, where a restaurant conversation between a sales manager and a prospective customer might have led, had not the manager needed to rush back to the office to plan yet another futile reorganization of the company sales force. And who can say what a caller put on interminable hold by a confused, overworked administrative assistant might have had in mind? Can a business or agency even hope to get a handle on the net effect of nasty rumors spread among the general public by disgruntled former employees? Or of the revenues lost because a promising idea never went beyond a production designer's desk, because the designer was certain it would be dismissed? Probably not. The impact of lost opportunity on organizational performance will always be problematic. There's simply no way of gauging *what might have been*.

Yet a few rare instances provide us with at least a general sense of the magnitude of this particular organizational cost. Consider what eventually happened to Chet, the distressed corporate veteran we mentioned earlier. After months of struggling to come to terms with his new role at the data services firm, he finally decided to accept the severance package the company was offering to its long-time employees. He used part of this financial settlement to pursue an idea he'd been kicking around during his idle office hours. With the help of his son and a friend, he developed a software product that performed a few simple file-transfer functions. Chet initially distributed the utility as shareware, handing out copies only to members of his local users' group. But the product proved unusually popular, and before long several software manufacturers had contacted Chet to discuss distribution rights. He eventually sold these rights for a six-figure sum to a major player in the software market. Better still, the buyer took him on as a consultant, a position he still holds.

Would Chet's former employer have benefited from his creativity, entrepreneurialism, and self-cultivated expertise? We can only speculate. Suffice it to say, though, that Chet had considerably more to offer than the data services firm might have imagined when it cast him and others like him so blithely aside. It's no secret that self-defeating organizations regularly drive away or alienate some of their most talented members. But seldom do these companies follow up on the true costs of counterproductive policies and decisions. They simply don't want to put a price tag on all they might have lost.

THE BENEFITS OF ABSORBING COSTS

So far, we've talked about absorbing costs solely in terms of its negative impact on the organization. This is the gloomy side of the story. But there's another way of looking at the costs of counterproductive action, one that reveals the healthy role these consequences play within organizational behavior systems. If we consider costs from this perspective, we can see how they help organizations avoid the unproductive minimizing and blaming activities that deplete precious resources and undermine sound core beliefs.

Systems theory suggests that a closed loop of activity, left undisturbed, will replicate itself over and over. This activity will continue until the system breaks down internally or is subject to an intervention from the external environment. Before a system collapses, however, it often displays signs that something is amiss. Users of computer systems are familiar with this phenomenon: a hardware or software component frequently behaves in an erratic or aberrant fashion before it finally fails. Organizational behavior systems perform similarly. When one or more of their internal elements has malfunctioned, they signal that something is amiss.

Costs are an ailing organization's symptoms of distress. They tell the organization that it has embarked on a misguided course of action, one it would be well advised to avoid in the future. Costs also provide an accurate picture of an organization's overall performance, making it difficult for a company or agency to derive solace from the short-term windfalls that self-defeating activity often yields. At this point, the organization has an opportunity to address and pay the costs it has incurred. In so doing, a troubled organization can effectively curtail its counterproductive behavior before it distorts or displaces sound core beliefs.

Costs Are Instructive

All behavior is ultimately governed by certain immutable performance rules. We're not talking here about finicky protocols or arbitrary restrictions, but rather about basic tenets of physical and human nature. These performance rules tell us, for example, that a raw material can be processed only within a certain temperature range, that a firm must spend money to make money, or that two people cannot consistently do the work of ten. They tell us also that people who are repeatedly deceived will eventually cease to believe their deceivers, that gratification can be deferred for only so long, and that without a higher purpose or loyalty, individuals will act only out of self-preservation.

Now it's perfectly natural for an organization to test established parameters. Without this pressing at the edge of the performance envelope, both technology and productivity would stagnate. New equipment and processes would never be tested in manufacturing environments; new strategies and theories would seldom cloud managerial horizons. Innovation demands risk, and risk brings with it the possibility of frequent failure. High-performing organizations understand this. They embrace the cost of experimentation, viewing it as an investment likely to pay off in the long run.

But the costs that self-defeating organizations typically incur seldom result from innovation gone awry. Instead, they're the predictable outcomes of the kinds of impulsive, reactive, and replicative activities that have failed the organization in the past. These costs tell the organization that if it resorts to hazardous or shoddy production processes, a catastrophe is bound to occur; that a reduction in capital investment will deplete resources beyond acceptable limits; or that restriction of individual behavior will stifle creativity and erode morale. In each case, the message is instructive, suggesting that counterproductive activities tend to create more problems than they resolve.

Costs Provide an Accurate Performance Picture

Through a combination of clever accounting practices and one or more of the minimization techniques we discuss in the next chapter, self-defeating organizations manage to paint a distorted picture of their actual performance. When costs are discounted or ignored, these organizations can bask in the short-term benefits that their ill-considered activities often afford. Ignoring low morale and a declining reputation among customers, the leaders of such organizations point with pride to the reductions they've made in labor costs. Oblivious to the chaos and internal fragmentation the latest reorganization has produced, they can boast about how "lean" their enterprises have become. If costs are acknowledged at all, they're viewed as the fleeting side effects of tough-minded organizational cures.

While even the most destructive policy or decision is likely to yield a few ostensible benefits, these benefits often cloud an organization's overall performance picture. Organizational costs have a way of bringing the scenario back into focus. A robust quarterly earning statement loses some of its ruddy glow when a firm acknowledges that these gains were achieved at the cost of thousands of jobs, or through the sale of one of its most profitable operating units. Increased productivity at an antiquated facility may look good to corporate officers, but not so good to the plant manager who must deal every day with increased absenteeism, turnover, and insubordination. All short-term gains have their price, and organizational costs firmly assert it. They tell the organization that it is courting disaster, and that its prospects for long-term high performance are not quite as rosy as last month's balance sheet would seem to suggest.

Costs Offer a Means of Escaping
Counterproductive Cycles

Costs provide a malfunctioning organization with a unique, last-ditch opportunity to curtail its counterproductive behavior patterns. In order to take advantage of this opportunity, however, the organization must acknowledge and pay these costs as soon as they emerge. Any attempt to set aside or defer the costs of reactive behavior will cause the organization to enter a cycle of minimizing and blaming—a cycle that inevitably plays out to its destructive conclusion.

In terms of our organizational behavior model, costs bring the fear of low performance immediately to bear. When such costs are taken seriously, the resulting fear effectively blocks the path to minimizing and blaming.

The diagram shown below hints at the healthy role that costs play within a self-defeating system. They focus organizational attention on such problems as territorialism, low morale, and declining innovation—*rather than on the measures required to justify these costs, minimize their impact, and blame them on forces beyond the organization's control.* The organization is thus forced to deal with a genuine and pressing performance problem, and not with the sanitized perceptions and revised history that often emerge from a cycle of minimizing and blaming. This effort consumes time, money, and energy. And when these resources are expended solely to remedy the consequences of errant decisions,

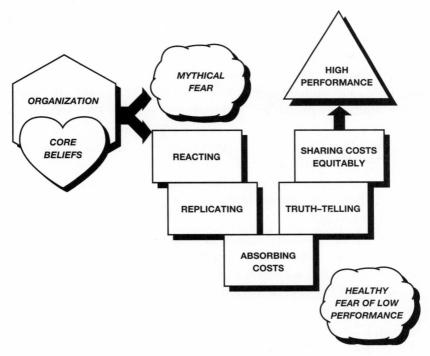

Paying Costs to Escape the Low-Performance Loop

the organization becomes motivated to identify once and for all the source of its difficulties. This process of acknowledging and tracking costs is both diagnostic and therapeutic. Not only does it discredit traditional replication techniques, it also steers the organization toward less costly ways of achieving its ends.

We're often asked what a single individual or group can do amid a sea of counterproductive organizational behavior. When this question arises, we think of Amanda, the marketing manager besieged by complaining customers and disloyal subordinates. After receiving a call about the devious antics of one of her staff members, Amanda sensed that she had reached a turning point in her career with the data services firm. But instead of throwing up her hands and blaming the problem on organizational chaos, she stepped back and analyzed the situation. She concluded that in demanding too much of its understaffed field support teams, the data services firm had encouraged territorialism without acknowledging its true cost. Her reaction was to call her team leaders together and announce that she'd no longer tolerate this sort of destructive behavior. But then she went a step further: she distributed copies of a memo she had submitted to the vice president of marketing. The document described her phone conversation with the irate customer. It also outlined what she felt were the minimum staffing and budget requirements for an effective sales support organization.

Amanda waited while the group read the memo. When they were finished, she said, "I've told management that unless we're provided with these resources immediately, I can no longer manage you folks effectively. If they don't give us what we need, I intend to resign."

During the days that followed, Amanda worried that she may have been too rash in forcing her firm to deal with the costs of its latest attempt at downsizing. She knew she stood a good chance of losing credibility, and perhaps even her job. Yet these ruminations led time and again to the same fundamental notion. Someone, she believed, had to make the company aware of the havoc its policies had wrought.

All this worrying proved for naught, because within the week senior management approved her proposal. Amanda immediately hired additional support personnel and reduced the number of calls each of her teams were expected to make each week. As a result, the performance of the sales support organization improved dramatically. Customer complaints dropped off sharply, as did the average cost of a typical call. Better still, Amanda received no further reports of sabotage among the ranks.

The alternative to dealing with costs in Amanda's bold fashion is to go with the organizational flow and minimize their impact. And while minimizing is convenient, it seldom works; the organization must subsequently blame its poor performance on uncontrollable fate or circumstance. But as we'll demonstrate, the organization that habitually takes this easy out may do irreparable damage to its core beliefs and collective character. Suffice it to say that minimizing and blaming link low performance not with preventable actions, but rather with some unsavory aspect of organizational nature. This closed loop seals the organization's predicament. It creates a paradoxical scenario in which the organization acts as both the perpetrator and the victim of its pernicious low performance.

CHAPTER 7

Minimizing and Blaming

ESTABLISHED organizations seldom fall from a single shot. Instead, they are diminished over time. A series of predictable actions and reactions gradually erodes their adaptive resources. When these resources have been depleted, the organization becomes rigid, tense, and all but incapable of innovation. At this point, the organization is well along the way to collapse. Having ceased to grow, explore, and change, it has mutated into a mechanical entity, grinding incessantly away at the grim chore of self-preservation.

How does a once-vibrant enterprise sink to these depths? The processes we call *minimizing* and *blaming* play a pivotal role in transforming an occasional performance lapse into an entrenched pattern of self-defeat. They enter the picture the moment an organization refuses to acknowledge and pay the costs of its misguided efforts. In offering a welcome respite from the recent turmoil, minimizing and blaming enable the ailing organization to maintain a facade of normalcy and health, even as its fundamental beliefs are under siege. These techniques smooth ruffled feathers, paper over cracks, subdue ominous rumblings. They serve, in short, as narcotics, and the organization that indulges in them flirts with long-term addiction.

Few struggling organizations are capable of resisting the

temptation. Minimizing, whether accomplished by way of clever cost justification or psychological manipulation, elevates to the level of profundity the trivial notion that things could always be worse. Then, once even the most sanguine members of the organization have begun to see through this threadbare fiction, there are any number of scapegoats—customers, suppliers, incompetent or recalcitrant colleagues—who can be blamed for a worsening predicament. And whereas minimizing always fails, blaming inevitably succeeds.

But this "success" comes at a high price. Once an organization has become convinced that uncontrollable agents or circumstances are responsible for its difficulties, it forfeits the power to alter or improve its collective performance. (Think about it. If treacherous competitors or disloyal customers are held solely responsible for an organization's poor performance, what can the organization do to change its situation?) In assuming the pose of powerlessness, however, the organization *becomes* powerless, a casualty of systematic self-defeat. The logic of minimizing and blaming establishes a cause-and-effect relationship between unwelcome consequences and a seemingly immutable aspect of an organization's character or environment. This connection effectively closes an organization's low-performance behavioral loop. It lends credence to the kinds of beliefs and fears that make victims of all who hold them.

BACK TO THE FUTURE

It's common these days for stagnant or problem-plagued organizations to embrace trendy concepts and programs without fully considering the potential consequences. This often leads to the kind of minimizing and blaming we witnessed at one medical products firm, where company officials had set about the difficult task of downsizing the enterprise and, at the same time, putting in place a just-in-time inventory system. An external provider of logistics management services had proposed a solution that would help the company achieve both these ends: a contractual arrangement under which the vendor would assume responsibility for the firm's order-processing and distribution functions. The vendor promised, moreover, to implement a state-of-the-art system that would shorten the ordering cycle and make the firm more responsive to customer requests. It was a deal that company management simply couldn't refuse. An agreement was signed, and shortly thereafter the firm announced the closing of its product distribution centers.

"Unfortunately, no one bothered to iron out a few of the minor details," recalled Avery, a senior official at the firm. "We were in such a rush to look like we were doing something that we never really established how much new equipment we'd need to purchase or who would be responsible for managing the transition."

The year following the elimination of the distribution centers was, by employee consensus, the worst the company had ever endured. A sluggish but functional enterprise was transformed within a few weeks' time into a hotbed of chaos, acrimony, and befuddlement. Under pressure to meet their quotas, the firm's field sales representatives refused to transmit their orders electronically to the vendor's computer systems; instead, they simply called company headquarters and delivered the information to anyone who happened to pick up the phone. That person was then forced to locate someone who had formerly worked at a distribution center—and who, in turn, had to contact the vendor and make the arrangements required to get the information into the logistics management system. As a result of this confusion, shipments were delayed, orders went unfilled, and the company was forced to absorb the cost of emergency deliveries. Many of the customers who had complained about the firm's old order-processing system now begged for its return.

"It was a very weird time, to say the least," Avery told us. "You had some people longing for the good old days, some walking around as if nothing had changed. And there were others—the folks who'd recommended the vendor's proposal—holding these gripe sessions and reminding everyone of how unworkable our old system had been.

"I sat in on a few of those meetings," he continued, "and what I heard was, frankly, incredible. Lots of talk about how wonderful things were going to be once we worked the kinks out of the 'new paradigm.' Someone would say, 'Hey, we can't wait until then, our customers are going to dump us,' and whoever was making the pitch would respond with some bizarre comment about the need to adapt to the 'contour' of the future."

But for this particular manufacturer, the future never came— not, at least, the future that company officials had been anticipating. Seven months into the new arrangement, these officials were forced to renegotiate the agreement with the logistics management firm and bring several key functions and responsibilities back in house. These duties were to be performed at four hastily established "order coordination" facilities, each with its own offices. To some members of the organization, these facilities bore a marked resemblance to the distribution centers the company had shut down a few months earlier.

"It's hard to say who was at fault, really," Avery replied when asked who took responsibility for the debacle. "Most of the people who pushed for the new deal either resigned or claimed they had only been following senior management's lead. And when management itself finally spoke up, it was mainly to announce that they were contemplating legal action against our so-called logistics provider. One vice president got up at a shareholders' meeting and said that in asking for off-schedule deliveries and faster turnaround, our customers had only been asking for trouble."

Avery went on to offer his assessment of the problem. "We work best as a sole supplier, which lets us take advantage of economies of scale," he said grumpily. "We're not some drugstore where the customer can pick up a little of this, a little of that, and two dozen of whatever happens to be on sale. We're not set up to work that way, and, if you want the truth, I doubt we ever will be."

For our part, we had never heard a more succinct summary of how blaming and minimizing contribute to the formation of unhealthy organizational beliefs. As Avery's words made unmistakably clear, these misguided efforts ultimately cause an organization to define its character not in terms of strengths, but rather in terms of perceived weaknesses.

EASING THE PAIN . . . FOR A WHILE

Minimizing comes naturally to all of us. When we've done something we know is wrong, harmful, or unwise, we instinctively take solace in the fleeting comfort that minimizing provides. After eating or drinking too much, we gulp aspirin or antacids to assuage the agonies of overindulgence. We buy houses we can't afford on the grounds that they'll appreciate in value, or that our opulent new surroundings will reduce the need for costly vacations. When bad behavior leads to the loss of a friend or lover, we alternately idealize or demonize the person we've lost. Under pain or duress, we do whatever we can to cope with the discomfort and justify its causes.

Organizational minimizing works much the same way. It provides the problem-plagued enterprise with a means of deferring, ignoring, or rationalizing the costs it has brought upon itself. If an organization simply denies these costs, uses surplus resources to quell the flames it has ignited, or shrugs off its losses and dreams of a better day, it can persuade itself that it has successfully weathered a crisis or met a challenge. But within the context of a self-defeating organizational behavior system, minimizing serves a larger and more sinister purpose. In combination with blaming, it enables a self-defeating organization to continue to indulge in its destructive habits while loudly proclaiming its desire to be rid of them.

There's only one problem: in the long run minimizing doesn't work. Like the various techniques we use to mask our individual maladies, an organization's futile attempts at minimization serve only to inhibit healthy change and postpone for as long as possible the day of final judgment. Sooner or later, even the most sophisticated minimizing schemes collapse, either because the organization lacks the resources to sustain them, or because a significant number of hardy souls face up to the truth and collectively decry the organization's floundering predicament. Unfortunately, it's usually too late for the organization to take effective or meaningful corrective action at this late date, which is why blaming follows on the heels of a failed attempt at minimization.

How does the self-defeating organization minimize the results of reactive and replicative behavior? The methods vary, depending on the organization's character and the nature of the costs that need to be defrayed. Cost justification, for example, provides an ostensibly "objective" rationale for the quantitative consequences of misguided policies and decisions. But this sort of accounting trickery is largely ineffective when it comes to ministering to the qualitative misery the organization is collectively experiencing. To ease this kind of pain, the self-defeating organization typically resorts to a set of minimizing techniques not unlike those that troubled individuals fall back on when their bills come due. The organization may encourage its members to deny that problems exist, or may employ the fruits of its latest dubious effort to reward selected groups and individuals. It may also distract its members from the present quagmire with legends of a storied past or promises of an ecstatic future. And if all else fails, the organization may systematically devalue any losses that it has incurred, nurturing among its ranks the notion that departed individuals and missed opportunities never really amounted to much in the first place.

Retroactive Cost Justification

Cost justification is a legitimate accounting technique that floundering organizations often use for the nefarious purpose of minimizing the quantitative costs of errant decisions. Without delving into the technicalities involved, this process compares the financial costs an organization is currently experiencing with the financial benefits it will allegedly realize as the result of a particular effort.

When used in its proper context—that is, *before* a precarious decision has been made, rather than in its unsuccessful aftermath—cost justification is often invaluable. It expresses the potential impact of a planned action in terms of dollars and cents. It can show an organization the true financial cost of dismissing experienced workers in favor of less costly replacements who will make mistakes, require training, and lack any sort of commitment to the enterprise and its goals. It can demonstrate the ultimate financial consequence of eliminating an ineffectual department or division, abandoning a stagnant market, or taking windfall profits that will shortly disappear. Clear-thinking organizations rely on cost justification to reveal these truths, even if they run counter to current plans and conventional wisdom.

Unhealthy organizations, however, use cost justification as an after-the-fact means of tidying up economic chaos. When the elimination of an internal function subsequently puts a firm at the mercy of price-gouging vendors, the company's cost accountants and financial planners are put quickly to work at the task of demonstrating the many benefits that will be realized at a later date. Similarly, the company that finds itself under financial duress after dropping a profitable product will undoubtedly present its ownership with a rosy scenario predicated on the resounding success of that product's successor. In its most despicable application, cost justification is used to demonstrate how savings realized through the use of inferior materials or components will more than defray any liability claims a company might eventually have to pay.

Even if it stops short of this extreme, retroactive cost justification is largely ineffective. It fails to achieve this questionable end for reasons that struggling organizations seldom understand.

It fails because it is usually based on fanciful or distorted comparisons. When planners and accountants develop financial projections, they typically look at both short- and long-term costs and benefits, and best- and worst-case scenarios. Accurate cost justification models take all these factors into account, assign probabilities, and legitimately assess what an organization stands to gain and lose from a planned course of action. Deceptive cost justification, by way of contrast, shifts time frames and circumstances so as to validate or recommend whatever the organization has done or plans to do. The picture that emerges often compares a low short-term cost with a high long-term benefit that will be realized only under the best and least problematic of conditions. When dreamy teenagers advance such scenarios, adults laugh. When planners and accountants advocate them, the leaders of self-defeating organizations all too often solemnly nod.

Retroactive cost justification also fails because it disproportionately distributes benefits and costs among organizational constituencies. It's not uncommon for a self-defeating organization to expound at length on how much ownership and senior management have benefited from a disruptive or unworkable decision, even though rank-and-file members and customers are struggling to cope with the associated costs. Conversely, an ailing organization may adopt and later justify a policy that bestows windfall benefits on workers or customers, while depriving management of the revenues and flexibility it needs to run the enterprise successfully. Consider the labor agreements that American automakers entered into during the 1960s and '70s, or the price wars that our major airlines waged against one an other in the '80s. This skewing of the cost/benefit balance may serve a short-term end, but sooner or later it undermines an organization's health and integrity. Just as a chain is only as strong as its weakest link, an organization is only as strong as its weakest constituency. Forcing that constituency or group to absorb the costs of failed initiatives is a slow form of organizational suicide.

Finally, retroactive cost justification fails because it never takes into account the *qualitative* costs that self-defeating actions inflict on organizational performance. We find it curious that during the due diligence investigations conducted prior to a corporate merger or sale, an organization's lawyers, financial officers, and accountants have little difficulty determining the financial value of what they refer to as "goodwill"—another term for a firm's reputation, visibility, and perceived strengths. But ask these same individuals how they determine the financial cost of territorialism, low morale, or reduced innovation, and they either shrug or claim that these factors are too subjective to be calculated. Organizational leaders readily acknowledge that qualitative costs make an impact on a company's bottom line; yet few express more than a casual interest in assigning a dollar figure to these lingering consequences.

See Chapter 11 for more on the need for accurate and equitable cost/benefit analyses.

Because cost justification cannot adequately defray the qualitative consequences of counterproductive behavior, the self-defeating organization typically resorts to other strategies and techniques. It encourages its members to deny troubling consequences, to divide the spoils of short-term success among themselves, or to focus their thinking on the past or the future.

Denying the Costs of Counterproductive Activity

The phrase "in denial" has become so ubiquitous that it has lost much of its original meaning. Yet we can think of no better way of describing what is perhaps the most common means of minimizing the consequences of self-defeating organizational behavior. You're no doubt familiar with how denial works in individual behavior: a person faced with an ongoing problem simply refuses to acknowledge its existence. The problem thus persists until it becomes overwhelming, at which time the individual either lashes out in a spasm of rage or seeks professional help.

Organizational denial works much the same way, albeit with a few odd twists. On the most superficial level, a company, team, or political group that has lost a preeminent position in its particular arena may continue to insist that it's still a leader in its field. In recent years, we've seen major players in the computer, retail, and automotive industries take refuge in this defiant pose. Ignoring fundamental changes in the economic environment, they've stubbornly adhered to policies and practices that have long ceased to serve any productive purpose. Most have teetered for years on the brink of collapse, clinging to the illusion that they soon will be restored to their earlier eminence.

When an organization as a whole is engaged in the process of denial, its individual members often follow suit. This leads to all sorts of bizarre behavior once the costs of misguided actions have begun to trickle down among the ranks. People who have been transferred from one department to another continue to seek work direction from their previous supervisors. When policies or procedures change, certain employees persist in doing their jobs as they have done them in the past: they fill out obsolete forms, they direct phone calls and deliveries to persons no longer on staff, they struggle with new equipment that fails to respond the way its predecessor did. Others claim to hold job titles that have changed or been stripped away. If confronted about their behavior, they offer the excuse that no one advised them of the change, or that they are confused about their new circumstances. This may explain why denial so often flourishes in depressed and chaotic organizations. In the former, internal communications are often sluggish; a change mandated in March may not be implemented until November. And in the latter, nearly everyone is perpetually befuddled, so confusion can be plausibly cited as a source of collective denial.

At the medical products firm we mentioned earlier, symptoms of denial were rife. You'll recall that this firm decided without thorough consideration to embrace the trend toward downsizing. To reduce staff and improve customer service, organizational leaders decided to contract out their distribution function to a specialist in logistics management. This decision soon proved unworkable. To deal with the disruptions it created, many employees simply denied that the change had occurred. Out of either ignorance, fear, or anger, members of the firm's field sales force continued to call their orders in over the phone, refusing to transmit them via modem to the vendor's computers. Managers and clerks who had been transferred from the closed distribution centers to corporate headquarters continued to spend their coffee breaks and lunch hours with their former colleagues, and, on the job, were loath to reveal "company-private" information to the third-party distributor. But the saddest spectacle of all, according to Avery, was the reaction of those employees whose friends and relatives had fallen victim to the cost-cutting ax. Many strolled the halls in an eerie sort of bliss, humming and joking as if they were on the way to meet their departed colleagues at the water cooler.

"You had to admire their resiliency," Avery recalled. "But at the same time, you had to wonder if they had any sense of what had happened. I worried for their sanity."

Dividing the Spoils

We have to admit it: the majority of reactive organizational activities tend to yield a flurry of short-term benefits. Plant closings, department mergers, and restricted budgets often provide an organization with a temporary surplus of cash and other resources. But these draconian measures also produce a good deal of anger and resentment among the members of an organization—particularly those members who feel strongly about what they do and are committed to high performance. As we pointed out in Chapter 2, these are the people most likely to put up a fight when faced with counterproductive organizational policies. For the self-defeating organization, they pose a definite problem. On the one hand, they are too valuable to be dismissed. On the other hand, their behavior is too incendiary to go unchecked.

In typical fashion, the self-defeating organization responds to this dilemma in a way that consumes valuable resources while failing to resolve its underlying performance problem. It divides the spoils of the latest reorganization or retrenchment among the angry and the wounded, in effect bribing them to hold their peace. If a plant manager protests that he can't meet his quotas with half as many workers as he had a year ago, the organization offers him a substantial bonus for persevering under adverse conditions. If a vice president vociferously complains that one of her peers has been terminated without cause, the company promotes her and grants her authority over her former colleague's division. If compulsory overtime leads to a sharp increase in absenteeism, the organization offers a financial incentive to those workers who make it through the year without taking sick days. In each case, the organization expends resources that could be put to more productive use, and in return receives only a show of cooperation or obedience.

"Sure, the outsourcing of our order-fulfillment operations ended up as a disaster," Avery told us. "But I'll tell you one thing: the whole episode made the careers of a lot of people around here. Even those of us who opposed the effort eventually got behind it, making speeches about how it was the 'right' thing to do, and how we all had to bite the bullet and make it work. Let's face it: we allowed senior management to buy us off."

Romanticizing the Past
This is the minimizer of choice for organizations that have become nostalgic or wistful in their collective thinking. As the prospect of future success, or even survival, comes to seem less

and less likely, the members of these organizations recall the glory or tranquillity of bygone days. Though they seldom admit it, they cling to the belief that all of their organization's performance problems could be solved, if only the firm could re-create or return to the circumstances of an earlier time. The more threatening the future looms, the more comforting the past seems. Talk to the members of an organization engaged in this form of minimizing and you'll come away believing that they once toiled in the service of Camelot, Incorporated, or dwelt amid the leafy confines of the Republic of Eden.

A respect for tradition and earlier successes can serve an organization well. But when this attitude is invoked to mask nagging fears of the future, it tends to mutate into a virus that can paralyze or kill. The organization that views its storied past as the sole model for performance improvement is, in most cases, doomed. For one thing, the earlier scenario that is so glowingly recalled often turns out to have been more the result of a historical anomaly—an epochal demographic shift, for example, or a long-closed loophole in tax codes or other government regulations—than the product of high performance.

What's more, objective scrutiny often reveals the storied organizational past to have been tumultuous, problem-plagued, and dysfunctional in its own right. Today's defense and aerospace contractors, for example, pine for the days of the cost-plus contracts. They conveniently overlook the fact that these risk-free arrangements served at once to encourage and cover up the kind of slipshod business practices that a struggling organization needs to eliminate, rather than replicate.

Though their firm was not, in the strictest sense, nostalgic, many employees at the medical products firm where Avery worked fell into the practice of romanticizing a situation that no longer existed. The company's closed distribution centers, which even in their heyday were sluggish, mistake-prone, and resistant to healthy change, came to be viewed as islands of tranquillity and virtual models of efficiency. This attitude soon spread beyond organizational borders, with even the customers who had demanded performance improvement now suggesting that the firm return to its earlier distribution system. Employees who had once worked at the distribution centers contributed mightily to this myth, pointing out at every opportunity that the problems the firm now faced had seldom arisen under the old system.

"You'd have thought we never lost an order or missed a shipment date," Avery reported. "And the customers who complained the loudest about late shipments and minimum ordering requirements . . . well, to hear them talk, it was like they had once lined up at the receiving dock to applaud the arrival of our trucks. But the fact is, our old system stank—it was costly and inefficient, and it was hurting our competitiveness. It wasn't that we didn't need to change. We just changed too drastically, and in the wrong way."

Fantasizing About the Future

Counselors and therapists often advise troubled individuals to "live in the here and now." The same advice might well be offered to the kind of organization that finds the consequences of its self-defeating actions so excruciating that only the future can afford any solace. When this method of minimizing the ongoing cost of low performance becomes entrenched among the ranks, the organization becomes what we've termed a Cargo Cult: it tempers its present pain with fantasies of the gala that will commence once its proverbial ship comes in. In so doing, it distracts its members from the drudgery and privation of daily organizational life. At times, this organization seems to be staffed by innumerable Little Orphan Annies, singing in plucky unison about the glories of tomorrow.

Like other minimizing techniques, fantasizing has its roots in a basically healthy impulse. There's nothing inherently wrong with hope, optimism, and the crafting of a grand vision or design; an enterprise devoid of these attributes would be a place grim beyond imagining. (For a glimpse of this type of organizational hell, visit your local post office or licensing bureau.) But when dreams of the future serve primarily to divert organizational members from the consequences of errant decisions and policies, the organization is headed for trouble. It is admitting that it can do nothing to address the performance problems that plague it in the present, and at the same time it is elevating the expectations of its members to a level where they can never be realized. The closing of a long-anticipated deal or the much-anticipated success of a new product often creates as many problems as it solves. Save for rare instances when luck or perseverance prevails over the odds, the ship that finally arrives brings cargo that seems, in retrospect, to have been hardly worth the painful wait.

More often, though, the future simply never arrives. That's what happened at Avery's company, where various "evangelists" ministered to organizational distress with promises of improved profitability, increased job security, and a wealth of new opportunities for individual advancement. "There's a fairly safe way of gauging how badly we've screwed up," he observed wryly. "When we succeed, we talk about how good things are today. But when the town criers spread the notion that our day of triumph is down the line, you can be fairly sure that we're in it deep."

Devaluing Losses

This minimizing technique serves as a sort of last line of defense for an organization that is struggling to defray the costs of a program or policy that has gone awry. Among these costs, as noted earlier, are lost opportunities: breakthrough product designs that never leave the drawing board, potential markets that are left unexplored, would-be clients turned away because of internal strife. And as discussed earlier still, many organizational members react to ongoing counterproductive activities either by fleeing the enterprise or by hiding themselves and their expertise amid the turmoil. The loss of lucrative opportunities, and of key members and their talents, exacts a dear price in terms of organizational performance. To minimize how this price is perceived, the self-defeating organization can avail itself of any of the techniques described here. And when all else fails—as, inevitably, it does—the organization can simply persuade itself that, in the grand scheme of things, its losses are largely insignificant.

The technique of devaluing losses is at least as old as Aesop's fable of the fox and the allegedly sour grapes. This may explain why, in the end, self-defeating organizations embrace it so regularly: it strips the mechanics of minimization to the bare essentials, insisting that what has been lost simply wasn't worth keeping. What about that beloved general manager who regularly achieved remarkable results, and who recently departed in the wake of an ill-timed reorganization? *Forget him; he was a renegade, a firebrand, an old-schooler who'd outlived his time.* The abandoned product concept that is currently swelling a competitor's earnings? *It's just as well that they did it, it's outside our core business, we'd have botched it, anyway.* The client deemed too "small" to bother with, now heading up a multimillion-dollar firm? *Only a fluke—and besides, the dollars weren't there, we can't be all things to all people.* If you've heard statements like these, chances are you've stumbled onto an organization in the final throes of an attempt at cutting its losses.

The senior managers at Avery's medical products firm, in close collaboration with their accountants, adopted this devaluing approach when it became clear that the new distribution arrangement wasn't working out. Its flaws and failings struck home when two of the firm's key customers canceled their standing orders, saying they simply couldn't abide the delays and mistakes that seemed to be occurring on nearly a weekly basis. They said they'd be glad to entertain proposals once the company and its logistics provider had worked the kinks out of the new system; for now, though, they'd be ordering medical supplies from a new vendor.

"But by this point, we'd moved into the Twilight Zone," Avery later told us. "We're talking a loss of six figures' worth of business, and some of our top execs are telling everyone it really doesn't matter, those orders weren't all that profitable, and, besides, the buyers were a royal pain to deal with. But here's where it got really crazy: those of us in management were instructed to tell the troops that *we* had canceled the contracts, on the grounds that those accounts weren't a 'good fit' with our new business mission. And when people suggested that for that kind of money we ought to have been able to work out an accommodation, all we could do was shrug and change the subject."

FROM MINIMIZING TO BLAMING

Although they may buy time or mask the symptoms of low performance, minimizing techniques never quite absolve the self-defeating organization of the costs it has incurred. These costs linger like radioactive fallout, contaminating core beliefs and inspiring additional replicative actions that demand further minimization. Finally, the organization reaches the point where it lacks the resources required to alter the perception of its performance. This is when the organization realizes that there's no shortcut to success. It belatedly discovers that actions rooted in unsound beliefs cannot possibly lead to long-term success and the formation of a healthy organizational character.

Minimizing leads to blaming because it changes the way costs are perceived while doing little to reduce the costs themselves. In creating a temporarily plausible fiction about organizational performance, it provides organizational leaders and members with a refuge from the harsh reality of lingering costs. But this reality remains unchanged; it smolders within the organization like a bed of embers, threatening at any moment to explode into flames. Cost justification, for example, may enable the errant organization to assure members, owners, and the general public that it is performing at a high level. But sooner or later, the costs that have been shifted from one column of the ledger to another, or deferred until some unspecified future date, are bound to assert themselves—often, with a vengeance. And while dividing the spoils of an errant policy may seem to alleviate a cost like low organizational morale, it consumes resources that could be better spent elsewhere. It also gives rise to the belief that bonuses, promotions, and pay raises will be doled out whenever morale takes a nosedive, an expectation the organization may not be able to meet.

This points to still another reason why minimizing is an ineffective means of dealing with ongoing costs. Simply put, it consumes too many valuable resources to be practiced indefinitely. The minimizing organization ultimately finds itself bereft of the funds or flexibility required to bury the costs of its ineffectual decisions and policies. The organization that continually encourages its members to fantasize about the future (see the discussion of the Cargo Cult in Chapter 3) needs deep pockets to underwrite the "dream work" on which the fantasy is based. Likewise, the Alumni Club (see Chapter 3) that fosters a climate of nostalgia must eventually come to terms with the fact that it is paying people to ruminate, rather than to innovate. Over the long term, minimizing is expensive—more expensive, usually, than paying the costs it seeks to defray.

In the end, minimizing fails because it violates the principles of behavioral logic. When an organization attempts to devalue its losses, it is essentially trying to maximize the benefits of an action that has yielded precious few. The devaluation of losses is a bit of alchemy through which the self-defeating organization attempts to transform costs into benefits. It's an attempt to prove that unhealthy beliefs and counterproductive activities can somehow lead to such sought-after consequences as high morale, improved profitability, and increased innovation. In this sense, minimization is yet another instance of a self-defeating organization's unending pursuit of a secret passage that leads from low-performance actions to high-performance results.

POINTING FINGERS AND CASTING STONES

You'd think that the failure of its minimizing techniques would motivate an organization to pay its costs, revamp its decision-making processes, and carefully evaluate the assumptions and beliefs on which its errant activities have been based. You'd think the organization would collectively vow never to repeat the counterproductive activities that have characterized its past, and would move forward with a healthier outlook and a renewed sense of purpose. You'd think, in other words, that the organization would behave in a conventionally rational manner. But bear in mind that self-defeating organizations function according to their own peculiar form of behavioral logic. And this logic takes a particularly bizarre turn when a malfunctioning organization sets off in search of culprits for its continual low performance.

Blaming assigns the responsibility for failed outcomes on agents, factors, and forces over which the organization claims to have no control. Ultimately, though, the self-defeating organization ends up attributing its failures to some unalterable aspect of its character. It embraces low performance as a fact of organizational life, and thereby denies the potential for healthy change and a better future.

Blaming Customers, Suppliers, and Competitors

When attempts at minimizing fail, self-defeating organizations often look beyond their walls for culprits. This search leads to customers, suppliers, or competitors. These external agents are beyond organizational control and, hence, ostensibly immune to corrective action. What's more, they can be easily—and in some cases justifiably—demonized. The organization can say all the bad things about them that it cannot say about itself.

Take, for example, customers. Everyone knows that they are fickle in their tastes, unpredictable in their actions, and self-serving in their motives. They demand change and, when change is offered, clamor for a return to earlier products or systems. They tell a firm that a particular set of features or level of quality is crucial—and then, once the firm has acted on their requests, take their business elsewhere. Books and consultants tell struggling enterprises that they must honor and heed the counsel of their invaluable customers—but when they take such counsel to heart, these same customers (or, in the case of government agencies, constituents) consistently betray them. It seems that customers are clearly to blame for most—if not all—corporate fiascoes.

The truth is that while customers are often a *source* of organizational conundrums, they are seldom the cause of the disastrous decisions that subsequently ensue. (We explain the difference in Chapter 10, where we discuss the inherent limitations of the customer-focused organization.) But this distinction is lost on firms like Avery's. There we saw senior managers blaming their ill-advised decision to contract out the company's order-fulfillment functions on the outlandish demands of a few fractious customers. The message sent out among the ranks was unmistakable. *Our customers are bad*, it proclaimed. *They lie and they cheat, making it impossible for us to serve them well. In many cases, we're better off without them.*

Hardly an inspirational notion, let alone a formula for improved customer relations.

Where customers can't be assigned the villain's role in an unfolding organizational melodrama, a firm's suppliers often serve in their stead. In some cases, contractual obligations or market conditions put suppliers in a highly favorable position, but also, as it often turns out, in a position where they can conveniently be blamed for any or all of an organization's miscues. During the late 1980s, for example, a medical report linked the consumption of oat bran with a reduced incidence of heart disease. (The report was later discredited.) This triggered an exploding customer demand for oat-bran products. At the time we were doing some work for a food-processing company that soon exhausted its supply of raw oats and had to look beyond its regular suppliers to feed its operations. Eventually the firm relaxed its quality standards and placed a huge order with a new supplier: in this case, a South American broker. But the low-quality oats subsequently decomposed under production conditions designed for the earlier quality standard. Yield per ton declined precipitously, customer demand went unfulfilled, and the manufacturer lost money when it ought to have been reaping windfall profits. And as you might expect, the firm subsequently put the blame on the South American broker, who ought to have known better than to sell a modern manufacturer a boatload of third-rate oats.

The members of a struggling enterprise may also cast blame on their competitors, and when they do, their aspersions come off sounding almost comical. While consulting with a computer company that was trying to enter the dog-eat-dog arena of direct marketing, we heard several employees of the new division complain bitterly about the predatory practices of competing mail-order firms. This competitor, we were told, bundled tons of valuable software with the machines it sold, while another firm was able to offer attractively low prices because it equipped its products with flimsy keyboards, cheap monitors, and failure-prone hard drives. Still another competitor, we were advised, owed its success primarily to deceptive advertising and bait-and-switch sales techniques.

"We can't compete with outfits that play the game that way," one marketing manager told us. "After all, we represent an established, *responsible* firm."

Our advice to this executive was fairly straightforward: his division could either emulate the practices of its competitors, wait for the buying public to pass judgment on their shoddily built computers, or develop an innovative way of packaging and marketing its products. Any of these alternatives would be preferable, we said, to blaming low performance on competitors who, after all, were simply doing what they deemed necessary to *compete* in a rowdy marketplace.

Fragmenting the Organization

You've undoubtedly known individuals who regularly blame their failings on something within their own makeup. If you believe them, they are regularly done in by the systematic malfunctioning of their minds, nerves, or various other internal mechanisms. "My mind goes blank when I have to take a test," they will tell you; or, to cite a common example, "My throat locks up at the thought of speaking before a group." Though part of an integrated whole, the treacherous muscle or organ is assigned what amounts to a will of its own. Under duress, it regularly exercises this will to sabotage the earnest efforts of its well-intentioned host.

In the context of individual behavior, we refer to this blaming technique as *fragmenting the mind and body*, and in organizations we've witnessed a similar phenomenon. When plagued by ongoing low performance, many an organization denies that it is an integrated enterprise and divides itself into a collection of unruly, and sometimes uncontrollable, components. The organization then adopts and cultivates the belief that one or more of these renegade elements bears the ultimate responsibility for an ongoing performance problem. At the same time, the culpable faction is viewed as exempt from organizational control. Its actions are therefore irremediable. The organization simply accepts them as necessary evils. They become its pet scapegoats.

Which internal groups or functions are typically blamed in an organization that has fragmented itself? Senior management is on the receiving end of much internal flak, and often with some justification: with authority comes accountability, and struggling organizations are more than willing to take their leaders to task. When low performance leads to an organizational crisis, rumors of executive malfeasance spread like wildfire among rank-and-file members. Senior managers are cast either as bumbling fools who are incapable of a single sound decision, or, conversely, as evil geniuses who have successfully managed to feather their own nests at the collective expense. But while some executives and boards of directors do act with dubious motives, the vast majority of organizational leaders are capable, hard-working people who are deeply concerned about the well-being of their enterprises. Trapped amid the conflicting demands of shareholders, customers, and their own employees, they often enjoy less latitude and flexibility than it pleases us to imagine. Like the rest of us, they do the best they can in trying circumstances; and, like the rest of us, they sometimes make mistakes. Unless these mistakes are repeated over and over, they rarely bring a healthy enterprise to the brink of ruin.

Where hard reality or organizational politics makes it unseemly to blame poor performance on senior managers, fragmented organizations seek out other culprits. Although any internal group or division can serve as a target for censure, personnel departments and sales forces seem to be the most common scapegoats for diminished productivity and declining profits. Personnel departments tend to be blamed within organizations that attribute their failings solely to the incompetence of their workers, even though they have hired precisely the kinds of people they were told to hire. And like football quarterbacks, sales forces are often assigned disproportionate credit for an organization's successes and disproportionate blame for its failures. In good times, they are cast as heroic frontline troopers; in bad times, as idle parasites living off the company dole. It's no wonder that sales representatives seem to change jobs and allegiances with the shifting winds.

"Salesmen are salesmen," the marketing manager at one brokerage observed with a shrug. "When they have a hot product, they make lots of money. When they don't, they make lots of personal phone calls."

Although self-defeating organizations regularly blame and excoriate their internal scapegoats, they are actually quite fond of them and wouldn't change or replace them for the world. The reasoning behind this paradox is simple: ineffective or supposedly intractable groups allow the organization to continue to practice its familiar habits, even as it claims to want to break free of them. This attitude is yet another hallmark of the self-defeating organization. Its insincere clamoring for comprehensive "change" masks a stubborn wish to persist in its counterproductive habits, but somehow to achieve high-performance results.

Embracing Low Performance as an Organizational Style

When your organization has struggled with related performance problems for a long time, your leaders and colleagues may throw up their hands and accept failure as an organizational style. Although you may at first see this as a step toward honest self-assessment, it frequently serves as a subtle—and devastatingly effective—blaming technique. Just as self-destructive individuals blame their reckless actions on psychic quirks, physical maladies, or genetics, self-defeating companies, agencies, and teams often end up attributing their difficulties to an inherent aspect of organizational character. *This is the way we are*, such organizations tell themselves. *We're weak, limited, and constrained by our history or internal structure, and there's not much we can do about it.* Too much of this kind of thinking over an extended period, and organizational character becomes permanently distorted, yielding an enterprise that is chronically depressed, disorganized, deceitful, or disoriented in time.

Consider the example of Avery's company. After the closing of its distribution centers led to organizational disaster, the firm did its best to minimize these consequences. When this effort proved unsuccessful, senior management blamed the calamitous decision on its customers and its logistics contractor. In the end, long-time employees like Avery came to view the entire episode as further evidence of the firm's limitations and of its inability to surmount its inherent weaknesses. These employees—and, eventually, the organization as a whole—lapsed into a state of depression, convinced that collapse was close at hand.

Now in some cases the organization may be right on target in reaching this sort of gloomy conclusion. Some flaw in its character may, in fact, doom all attempts at performance improvement to failure; the organization may have outlived its usefulness or become constitutionally incapable of adapting to a changing environment. But fortunately, these cases are few and far between. In most cases, the organization that seems to have embraced low performance as a behavioral style is simply buckling beneath the burden of its unhealthy core beliefs. It may believe, for example, that its management is corrupt. It may believe that its cost structure has rendered it uncompetitive, that its rare successes are more the product of luck than of innovation and perseverance, or that it cannot succeed without cheating one or more of its constituent groups. It may believe the worst about itself, hoping all the while that it is wrong.

Usually, it is. It's been our experience that even for self-defeating organizations, the future is seldom as bleak as it is perceived to be. But to improve its prospects, a struggling organization must avoid at all costs the temptation to accept equivocal results as the inherent consequences of its nature. It must take whatever measures are necessary to escape its low-performance loop and, subsequently, to shore up the healthy beliefs that lie dormant within its borders.

ESCAPING THE LOW-PERFORMANCE LOOP

When an organization disavows responsibility for the consequences of its actions, an unhealthy core belief is formed. This belief is, in essence, the behavioral conclusion that the organization has drawn from a failed decision, policy, or program. It confirms the self-defeating organization's worst image of itself; it tells the organization that its efforts must inevitably fail, and that it suffers from limitations that it cannot possibly surmount. This is the nature of unhealthy core beliefs: they are skewed, maladaptive, and often fatalistic.

Worse yet, they give rise to mythical fears within the organizational ranks. These fears convince the members of the self-defeating organization that they must shun at all costs the very qualities that the enterprise is most in need of: truth, openness, accountability, discipline, and hope. So the next time a strategic moment or opportunity arises, the organization is likely to find itself flanked by fatalism on the left and apprehension on the right. In this context, sound and thoughtful decision making is all but impossible; the organization ends up pursuing the most expedient or familiar course of action, which initiates still another cycle of self-defeating behavior.

How can a struggling organization escape this pernicious cycle of perpetual reaction and strife? We won't contend that it's easy, but then meaningful change seldom is. It requires a troubled organization and its leaders to acknowledge that a performance problem exists—or that business as usual is no longer good enough. It requires a receptiveness to new people, ideas, and procedures, and a willingness to learn from experiences that fly in the face of conventional wisdom. It requires the consistent and equitable distribution of costs and benefits among all who hold a stake in an organization's future, from the lowliest clerk or customer to the most eminent executive or shareholder. Above all, it requires the steady cultivation of healthy core beliefs that will shore up the organization when setbacks occur.

To escape the low-performance loop, an enterprise must cultivate and develop what amounts to a set of high-performance behavioral techniques. These techniques, which we'll discuss in the final section of this book, together form a behavioral model every bit as systematic, logical, and replicative as its self-defeating counterpart. We call it the *high-performance loop*. It's a system of thought and action that can provide an ailing enterprise with the strength to replace the yoke of low performance with the habit of success.

PART THREE

The High-Performance Loop

We succeed in enterprises which demand the positive qualities we possess, but we excel in those which can also make use of our defects.

ALEXIS DE TOCQUEVILLE

CHAPTER 8

A Model for Improved Performance

T HIS BOOK won't tell you how your organization can avoid every
pitfall waiting in its path. It will not tell you how to micro-
manage your business or agency, how to make sure all the
members of your organization remain content and happy, or
how to rise to a position of leadership and influence in
twelve easy steps. Chances are, you've already taken such
counsel to heart—only to discover, as we have, that today's
organizational dilemmas seldom yield to simple solutions or
artful panaceas. After following to the letter any number of
these schemes, you may have come to realize that your organization's fundamental problems still persist. You may have
learned through trial and error that the roots of your firm's difficulties lie beyond the reach of even the most carefully designed
programs for change. You may have despaired of ever improving your organization's collective performance, directing your
efforts instead toward the more pressing goal of mere survival.

If so, read on. In the remaining chapters, we describe a set of
techniques that, in our view, cannot help but improve the future

161

prospects of a beleaguered enterprise. While they don't guarantee success, these techniques can displace the unhealthy attitudes and actions that so often taint the performance of the struggling business, agency, or work group. What's more, the high-performance techniques we'll be discussing tend to have a cumulative effect on organizational behavior. They complement one another in unexpected ways, creating a *system* that thrives on its own success.

The implications of this notion are at once obvious and profound. They tell us that we can identify the conditions under which high-performance behavior patterns most often arise, and that we can take a close look at these conditions and determine how they were created. This allows us to track organizational success back to its origins; we can identify the actions that a high-performing enterprise has taken at strategic moments in history, and how these actions have played out in the face of numerous challenges. We can see how a thriving organization has taught itself the techniques of success and how it continually applies these techniques to bolster the strength of its collective character.

High performance is not some gift that the gods have arbitrarily bestowed on the fortunate few. Just as low-performance patterns stealthily entrench themselves within ostensibly thriving enterprises, high-performance patterns often arise amid the most stricken organizational environs. The reason for this is that dire circumstances often demonstrate to an organization the error of its ways. This grants it the freedom to pursue alternative strategies, allowing for the kind of honesty and innovation that can work performance wonders.

BROKERING SUCCESS

This book began with a discussion of the events that transpired at one brokerage during the reign of George, an organizational henchman deployed throughout his company to whip sluggish branch offices into shape. George, as you'll recall, favored the Monday morning sales meeting as a means of confusing, humiliating, and generally terrorizing his department heads. Soon the entire branch became focused on these weekly sessions, with managers and support personnel neglecting their normal chores in order to prepare elaborate presentations that George typically ignored. The results were predictable: the level of productive activity at the office fell off sharply. At the same time, absenteeism soared, top managers and brokers resigned, and customer orders were either lost or mishandled with an alarming frequency. The branch nearly ceased to function, a fact that company headquarters seemed willing to overlook in light of the cost reductions that George had managed to achieve.

This was all by misguided corporate design. The company had fallen into the habit of using George to administer a sort of organizational shock therapy. But once his punitive and restrictive measures had extracted the last drop of profitability from a low-performing branch, the company replaced him with a low-key administrator charged with maintaining performance at its stricken level until a shift in market conditions occurred. And that's just what the firm did in this situation. It recalled George from the field and dispatched a relatively undistinguished middle manager named Dave to serve in the role of branch caretaker.

Dave arrived at the branch with few illusions about what he was meant to do. But a few weeks on the job convinced him that mere maintenance was not, in this instance, a viable option. A series of informal interviews with department managers, brokers, and administrative personnel soon persuaded him that unless dramatic changes were made, the branch seemed destined to collapse in a way that would reflect poorly on the corporation as a whole. Before he acted, though, he set about gathering information. He read dozens of books—not only about organizational development and microeconomic theory, but also sociological and historical treatises. In addition, he met with several consultants; and while none provided a solution he could wholly embrace, each supplied him with valuable insights. One dealt with the concept of "intrapreneurialism," an approach under which company employees are granted the latitude and resources of an independent business proprietor.

Piece by piece, the elements of Dave's strategy fell into place.

But he realized that he needed a stopgap measure, a sort of symbolic gesture that would buy time while signifying that change was on the way. To that end, he called his managers, brokers, and their administrators together and announced that Monday morning staff meetings would no longer be held. When asked why, he replied that, insofar as he could tell, they no longer served any productive purpose.

"But how will we keep you up to speed on our sales figures?" blurted one confused department head.

"Drop me a one-page memo whenever you have time," Dave answered. "I'll get back to you if there are any problems."

"Well, that's certainly a change from what we're used to around here," said another department manager in a challenging tone.

"Look, I know there have been abuses," said Dave. "They won't be repeated."

In the next few months, Dave held both individual and group meetings with key branch employees, working out the details of his plan for change. Relieved of the burden of preparing for the Monday morning sessions, these people suddenly had time and energy to contribute to the cause of improving their collective performance. With their help, Dave refined a system under which all nonadministrative employees would act as the owners of their own "businesses." Each would prepare a business plan that included sales projections, budget requirements, and net profitability. Once this plan had been approved, each individual would operate without interference or close supervision. The compensation for these individual operators would be calculated using a formula that would take into account not only standard commissions, but also the performance of the branch as a whole.

When Dave announced these intentions, they met with the usual mixture of confusion, alarm, and skepticism. Many of the brokers, still bearing the scars of George's manipulative practices, submitted sales goals so low that they could easily be met without contributing much to overall branch performance. In response, Dave met with each broker, explaining that the revenues projected in the combined business plans would be inadequate to keep the branch running.

"Try to do a little better," he advised them. "For this to work, we have to keep headquarters happy."

The revised business plans contained figures that exceeded Dave's own estimates of how much growth the branch could expect to achieve. He approved them immediately, then busied himself with the mechanics of calculating compensation and measuring each broker's effectiveness.

Within a few months, the results of the new approach began to trickle in. As a whole, sales steadily rose, with no abatement in sight. While analyzing these numbers, Dave could not help but be amused at how much of the increased sales volume was attributable to the timely booking and processing of customer transactions that, less than a year earlier, might not have shown up on the books for the appropriate fiscal period.

Still, there were problems. Word reached corporate headquarters that Dave had turned renegade and, worse yet, was practicing a form of "socialism" within the struggling branch. The rumors grew so exaggerated that the firm sent a team of financial officers and analysts out into the field to see what, exactly, Dave had been up to—and, if necessary, to set him straight on company policies and procedures. The summit meeting took place in Dave's office, less than a year into his tenure.

The management team's initial inquiries all had to do with the alleged socialism that Dave had installed at the branch. He parried these objections neatly, pointing out that treating each broker as an independent business agent seemed consistent with the principles of capitalism. A corporate financial analyst then pointed out that the compensation formula Dave had developed would be impracticable on a company-wide level. Dave replied that it wasn't intended to be applied throughout the corporation: it had been designed to address only the specific problems of one particular branch.

When still another company official launched into a meandering discourse on corporate image and the potential consequences of "wildcat" management, Dave cut him short. "I think I can save us a lot of time here," he said, distributing a single sheet of paper to each attendee. "If you'll look at what I'm handing out, you'll see three different scenarios. I ask only that you determine which bodes best for us as a company."

The document that Dave had prepared consisted of three simple graphs. The one on the left, indicating branch performance prior to George, showed a steady decline in both profits and total revenues. The middle graph, which covered the period when George ran the branch, showed a slight increase in profitability, even as revenues declined. The graph on the right, representing branch performance under Dave's leadership, showed a gradual but steady increase in *both* profits and revenues, with additional growth projected into the future.

After perusing this document and muttering a few comments about the need for "consistency" and "improved communications" between headquarters and the field, the leader of the management team brought the meeting to an end. Although the visitors stopped short of an enthusiastic endorsement of Dave's approach, neither did they attempt to impose their will upon him. The numbers told the story: the management delegation couldn't argue with success.

THE HIGH-PERFORMANCE MODEL

Organizations that have struggled for long periods of time come to view high performance as a distant and ever-receding goal. They believe they can achieve success only when they have perfected all their internal processes, or when a fortuitous combination of brute diligence and good luck drops the prize at their door. This outlook makes the prospect of high performance seem unduly remote, a far-off destination the organization can only hope to reach. And where no clear connection between success and daily activity has been established, individuals are left with the notion that they can do little to help their organization achieve its lofty ends.

Our discussions with members of successful businesses and work groups have led us to believe, however, that high performance is far more systematic than it might first appear. The experiences of these individuals—leaders, consultants, managers, and workers— suggest that thriving organizations achieve their success through the diligent application of a set of clearheaded practices and beliefs. Such actions and attitudes come together to create a *high-performance system*: a pattern of thought and action that serves as the healthy organization's instinctive response to dilemmas, challenges, and perceived threats. The figure on page 168 shows how this pattern can work. Note that in terms of its structure, this high-performance model resembles its low-performance counterpart. It indicates, for example, the alternative paths an organization can follow once it has arrived at a strategic moment, and it suggests the role that core beliefs and fears play in shaping organizational decisions. But that's where the similarity ends. Techniques like truth-telling, open-mindedness, and the sharing of costs and benefits stand in sharp contrast to the replicating, minimizing, and blaming found in so many self-defeating organizational milieus. The former are proactive practices designed to help an organization live up to a healthy self-image; the latter, reactive quirks that unintentionally confirm the organization's worst suspicions about itself.

Although we've depicted these high-performance techniques in linear sequence, each can be applied at any point in a decision-making cycle or a business campaign. Truth-telling, for example, is a basic prerequisite for any successful initiative. But this doesn't necessarily mean that an organization, having faced the truth at a strategic moment, is subsequently free to dissemble or to evade reality. On the contrary, the techniques that define high performance must be continually brought to bear on organizational plans, decisions, and policies. They can even be employed in the midst of a self-defeating cycle, where they can effectively counteract an organization's tendency to react, replicate, minimize, and blame.

Like individuals, organizations fall into bad habits and ineffectual behaviors more or less by chance. They tend to replicate what has seemed to work for them in the past, and to continue to repeat this behavior until it leads to a dramatic—perhaps even catastrophic—failure. But there's no reason why this same behavioral logic should not apply to the formation and cultivation of healthy habits and behavior patterns. The organization that has somehow learned how to do things wrong can just as readily learn

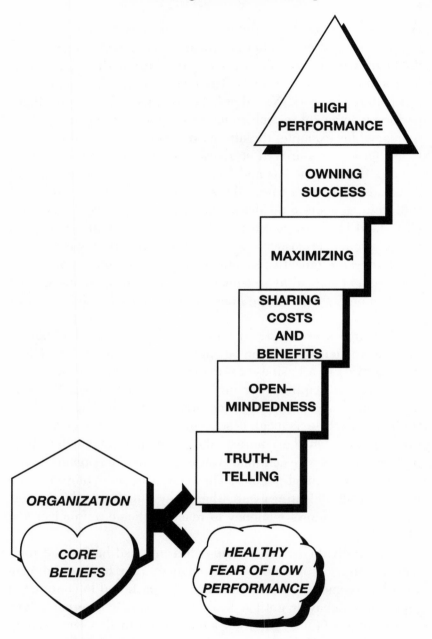

A High-Performance Organizational Behavior System

how to do them right. It can systematically replace each component of its counterproductive pattern with a healthier alternative;
it can break the habit of low performance. And once an organization has rid itself of corrosive beliefs, fears, and tendencies, it
seldom seeks to return to its earlier state of systematic dysfunction. It draws strength from its core beliefs, and uses this strength
to ward off expedient or trendy solutions to the thorny problems of
organizational life.

Sound Beliefs and Healthy Fears

The previous section of this book explained the role that beliefs and fears play in the shaping of organizational decisions,
policies, and practices. Successful organizations, like their low-
performing counterparts, act in accordance with their beliefs and
fears in moments of crisis. But where the unsuccessful organization struggles with fears that often prove to be illusory, the thriving
enterprise is guided primarily by an abiding fear of low performance and its consequences. This healthy, realistic fear helps the
organization resist the temptation to take the easy way out of a
problematic situation. And when such readily available solutions
are eschewed, the organization has little choice but to look within
itself for fresh, innovative answers to the pressing questions at
hand.

Think, for example, of the dilemma that Dave faced when he
replaced George at the low-performing brokerage. Having abandoned any hope that the branch might flourish under existing market conditions, senior management had tacitly instructed Dave to
maintain performance at an acceptably low level—and, if possible, to heal the more serious wounds George had inflicted. But
Dave correctly saw that these instructions would be impossible to
follow. He could not embrace management's belief that low performance was inevitable and, at the same time, restore hope and
enthusiasm among the members of his staff. So he made what
turned out to be a momentous decision. His firm had long claimed
to hold the qualities of individual initiative and independent
thinking in highest esteem. The time had come, Dave decided, to
put these claims to the test.

"I could have done as I was told, I guess," he later recalled. "Headquarters had more or less given up on the branch, so it wasn't as if I'd be held to blame if things didn't turn around. I was supposed to be a caretaker, charged with setting the branch back on an even keel. But, frankly, I'd played that game all my working life. It was time, I guess, to try something a little different."

When asked if he had been afraid of criticism or retribution from corporate headquarters, Dave smiled and said, "Sure, there was always that. But I was more afraid that we were on the verge of losing our spirit. I'd invested fifteen years in this company, and I didn't want to believe that time had been wasted."

It seems that Dave had come to the conclusion that both he and his firm had reached a sort of crossroads. He saw an organization in danger of incorporating low performance into its collective character, despite professed beliefs in progress, innovation, and growth. And he knew that until the company started practicing what it long had preached, it would remain trapped within successive cycles of fear, reaction, and recrimination.

Truth-Telling

There are few absolute requirements for improving organizational performance. One of them is truth-telling. It's the bedrock necessity for improving performance and sustaining success. In the absence of a collective commitment to honesty and integrity, none of the other high-performance techniques is likely to prove effective. An ailing organization can open itself to new ideas, develop innovative and popular products, and share the fruits of its labors equitably among its members and constituents. It can take full credit for the success it has achieved, establishing a clear connection between results and core organizational beliefs. But if it continues to dissemble, speak in euphemisms, and withhold key information from concerned members, these efforts seldom make a lasting impact on an organization's long-term performance. When acknowledged, the truth can serve as a source of organizational strength. When denied, it can undermine any or all of the measures an organization has taken in pursuit of healthy change.

The benefits of truth-telling are obvious. It enables an organization to assess its options accurately at strategic moments and to evaluate honestly the potential consequences of any course of action. It serves as a sort of clarifying lens through which core beliefs and counterproductive patterns can be viewed, analyzed, and frankly discussed. Most importantly, it provides organizational members with a basis for trusting one another and committing their energies to the collective good. In this way, truth-telling subdues the cynicism and self-interest that feeds on and perpetuates patterns of self-defeat.

For all this, truth-telling remains the most controversial of the high-performance techniques we typically propose. When we suggest to an organization that the route to healthy change begins with the truth, we often meet with an incredulous reaction. "If we told the truth, this whole operation would fall apart in a month" is a typical response—one which, we're sad to report, reflects the attitude of all too many of today's organizations. This aversion to truth-telling is expressed in several ways. Some organizational leaders protest that the truth is simply too unpleasant to be told; some argue that the truth is far too complex for rank-and-file members to understand. Other executives and managers maintain that there's no point in trying to tell the truth, because no one will believe them. Still others claim that they lack the rhetorical or interpersonal skills to communicate honestly and openly.

Under closer scrutiny, these objections turn out to be little more than manifestations of the mythical fears at work within a troubled enterprise. These will be analyzed in the next chapter. Unless an organization can set aside its mythical fear of truth, it will be apt to revert to its low-performance activities whenever they seem expedient. When a well-intentioned program yields unwelcome results, for example, a truth-aversive organization will seek to minimize or disguise these consquences. In the process, it will inevitably begin to tell itself plausible lies. The denial and disorientation that subsequently ensue may well undermine whatever progress the organization has made, confirming the unhealthy notion that productive change is all but impossible.

Organizational leaders who are committed to performance improvement are well aware of this pitfall and take stern measures to avoid it. This may explain why Dave took prompt action to deal with the duplicity, evasiveness, and mistrust that had deformed the collective character of his troubled brokerage. First, he conducted extensive informational interviews with representative employees, ranging from managers to brokers to support personnel. He encouraged these people to speak freely and, as a result, obtained an accurate reading of the attitudes, beliefs, and procedures at work within the branch. This pointed him toward a symbolic gesture intended to restore sanity at the office and establish his personal credibility; in canceling the Monday morning sales meetings, he effectively dispelled the fiction that these sessions made any sort of positive contribution to branch performance. And finally, he offered a forthright acknowledgment of the grave error the company had made in giving George free reign to prey on the fears and insecurities of the office staff.

"That was a tricky point," Dave later admitted. "On the one hand, I didn't want to hold a group grievance session—I'd heard all the horror stories in individual meetings, and I didn't see the benefit of airing them. But on the other hand, I couldn't honestly endorse the kinds of practices I'd been hearing about. I wasn't there to apologize for George."

How, then, did Dave deal with this dilemma? He didn't dwell on negativism or harsh reality, but neither did he deny it. Instead, he frankly acknowledged that abuses had occurred, then moved on to promise that they wouldn't be repeated. He told the members of his staff that the company had done wrong, and that he planned to make things right. He told no more—nor less—than the truth.

Open-Mindedness

Self-defeating organizations tend to be closed systems. They adhere rigorously to policies and procedures that they themselves have developed; they are suspicious of ideas, methodologies, and business practices that cannot be traced to internal origins. In some cases, they may even go so far as to restrict their memberships to certain kinds of people—not only in terms of race, gender, or appearance, but also in terms of temperament and ideology. This wholesale rejection of all that is foreign to, or different from, the prevailing organizational character often robs an enterprise of its capacity for innovative action. When confronted with a challenge or an opportunity, the organization has at its disposal only a limited range of options, all of them products of standardized and formulaic thinking.

Just as incestuous families breed themselves into disease and out of existence, the self-defeating organization eventually acquires a collective character that is skewed in the direction of its least savory attributes. The organization that has made it a practice to hire only conformists may, for example, find itself saddled with an employee population that conforms resolutely to counterproductive patterns of thought and action. The organization that has long operated according its own exquisite vision of how the world works may be at a loss to respond when, abruptly, the world begins to work quite differently. There's a fine line between constancy of purpose and stubborn closed-mindedness, and self-defeating organizations often fall on the wrong side of it.

High-performing organizations, in contrast, look upon new people, ideas, and methodologies not as contaminating influences, but rather as the very stuff of their ongoing success. These organizations are aware that if they draw exclusively on their own intellectual and spiritual capital at strategic moments, they will eventually consume the adaptive resources required for growth and change. With this in mind, the successful organization is seldom reluctant to consult outside experts, to hire people from different backgrounds, and to encourage its members to imagine wild alternatives to problematic scenarios. From time to time, the healthy organization is even willing to entertain the notion that its way of doing things is utterly wrong, and that it needs a dramatic shake-up to set things right. In this way, the growing organization continually renews itself, much as the healthy human body continually generates new cells and sloughs off those it no longer needs.

However, don't take this to mean that the successful organization is in a perpetual hurry to incorporate or embrace every new management theory, strategy, or trend that comes its way. The fact is, organizations that indiscriminately chase after fashionable solutions are often engaged in an ostentatious display of what we view as "false open-mindedness." It's a strategy that floundering organizations frequently employ to camouflage what amounts to a survivalist mentality. When questioned about stagnant performance, these organizations are quick to point to all the new approaches—quality circles, process reengineering, sensitivity training, downsizing—they have pursued over the past few months or years. They cite these initiatives as evidence of their willingness to try anything to bring about healthy change—neglecting to mention, of course, that they seldom stay with a program long enough to realize its potential benefits. They will, indeed, try anything—so long as it doesn't interfere with business as usual.

The leaders of high-performing organizations, however, are highly selective when it comes to introducing new operating procedures and methodologies. Although they remain open to a wide array of possible options, they adopt only those that seem likely to yield the desired results. They borrow, they shape, and they synthesize, always with an eye on organizational attitudes, traditions, and goals.

Take Dave, for example. When he agreed to take over the problem-plagued brokerage, he had little or no firm notion of what he might do to restore the productivity and morale of its dispirited staff. In search of a workable approach, he looked beyond his organization and its traditional dogma; he read widely and consulted with numerous outside experts. And though he rejected much of what he read and heard, a single notion stayed with him: the importance of striking a balance between the needs of individual employees and those of the branch as a whole. It was an idea that Dave's brokers initially stigmatized as "socialistic," and one that he himself would formerly have dismissed out of hand. But he came gradually to see its viability and to contemplate ways of putting it into practice. He began to see the broad outlines of a strategy that would not only promote individual initiative, but would also help realize the larger goal of improved group performance.

Sharing Costs and Benefits Equitably

Innovative programs and strategies are not panaceas. Rarely do they provide an organization with a cure-all solution to all the

problems that it faces; often, in fact, they give rise to new challenges, yielding consequences the organization would prefer not to
deal with. These consequences are the *costs* of healthy change,
which is bound to bring with it some measure of uncertainty, dislocation, fear, and deprivation. Dropping an established product in
favor of a more promising alternative can wreak havoc on the
careers of designers and engineers who have put lots of time and
energy into the discontinued line. Facing the truth about a misguided decision can cause senior managers to lose a good deal of
sleep. New procedures and equipment can disturb the comfortable
habits of administrators and operators. What's true in the larger
world holds true for the modern organization: there can be no gain
without some degree of pain.

High-performing enterprises seldom embark on a course of
action without first evaluating all of the potential costs and benefits it might yield. These organizations are not caught off guard
when the costs of change emerge; they know what is coming and
are prepared to deal with it. They formulate detailed plans for
managing both the quantitative and the qualitative costs they are
bound to incur. As much as possible, they seek to distribute costs
and benefits equitably among their primary constituencies. They
are aware that if any one of these constituencies—owners, senior
and middle managers, employees, customers, or clients—is forced
time and again to absorb the cost of errant policies and decisions,
the performance of the enterprise as a whole will ultimately suffer.

The merits of this approach seem obvious. It not only builds
trust among constituent groups, but also promotes accountability
within the ranks. Once workers have ceased to believe that they
will be taken to task when performance drops for whatever reason,
they become less defensive and more productive. And when managers are no longer compelled to equivocate about how costs and
benefits have been distributed, they acquire the credibility and
status of true leaders. The same holds true for the owners of the
organization. In sacrificing short-term windfalls, they demonstrate
their concern for an organization's long-term viability. They become *partners* in the project of maximizing organizational performance. Customers and clients, in turn, benefit from the improved

products and fair prices that only a high-performing organization can consistently offer. They also gain peace of mind in knowing that today's unbelievable bargains are not the result of practices that will cause a valued supplier to fold its tents six months or a year down the line.

How does an organization go about achieving this harmonious blend of conflicting interests? One way is to acknowledge that such interests are, inherently, *in conflict*; and that, more importantly, no one of them ought ever to achieve total dominance over its counterparts. Organizational stability depends on an equitable give and take between competing constituencies, and the business or agency that serves any one or two of them at the expense of all others is headed for trouble. Another effective means of balancing internal interests is to factor *qualitative*—as well as *quantitative*—costs into the performance picture: a business or agency should avoid the trap of viewing rosy numbers as an infallible sign of robust internal health. A third (and particularly innovative) approach is to structure and manage an enterprise so that some of the arbitrary divisions between constituent groups are blurred or dissolved. When individuals see themselves as part of more than one constituency, they are likely to see more than one side of an issue, problem, or potential solution, and to view the associated costs and benefits from a wider perspective.

Dave employed a combination of these techniques to ensure that the costs and benefits of change would be shared among all members of his staff. As we mentioned earlier, he worked with his department managers and accountants to develop a formula that factored overall branch performance into each broker's compensation. While brokers remained accountable for the projections contained in their individual business plans, each also held a stake in the aggregate success or failure of the branch. This effectively discouraged many of the less savory practices—poaching on one another's accounts, hoarding sales leads, and writing up bad orders—to which brokers had resorted while George was in charge. The brokers were smart enough to see that these kinds of activities would ultimately make a negative impact on the collective bottom line and, hence, on how much each stood to earn.

Still another of Dave's decisions proved, in retrospect, to have served the branch especially well. Aware that brokers would need extra time to develop and revise their individual performance plans, he asked his department managers if they'd mind working the phones during the transition period. At first, two of the managers were reluctant.

"They said it had been years since they'd done any cold calling," Dave remembered. "To be honest, they weren't sure if they still had what it took. So I had to reassure them that they were still going to be paid to run their departments, not to meet any strict sales quotas."

Because Dave had already established his credibility with the department managers, they were willing to take him at his word. They dutifully took to the phones, calling on key accounts and prospective customers while the brokers were at work on their business plans. The results, according to Dave, surprised even the two managers who had balked at the notion of filling in as sales representatives.

"It turned out that neither of them had anything to worry about," he recalled with a smile. "Together, they wrote up more orders than the people they were filling in for. One said that calling on customers brought back memories of his early days in the business and made him feel ten years younger. And the other told me he'd never realized the kind of competition our people are up against. He even went so far as to suggest that all of us in management spend a few weeks each year in the trenches, if for no other reason than to get a feel for what customers might be thinking."

Maximizing Results and Owning Success

Maximizing and owning comprise a high-performance alternative to the cycle of minimizing and blaming that unsuccessful organizations use to perpetuate their patterns of self-defeat. Having equitably distributed the costs of innovation and change, the healthy organization has little or no need to deny them, nor to expend its energies in futile attempts to cover them up. On the contrary, the organization is at this point free to focus on the future, rather than on the past; and, better yet, to capitalize on its strengths and make a persuasive case for the kind of thinking that has yielded the benefits it now enjoys.

The concept of maximizing strikes many executives and managers as implausible. They claim that their organizations have yet to achieve the kind of smashing triumph or breakthrough performance that this technique seems to presume. But such objections are based on a distorted notion of organizational success and how it is achieved. In the vast majority of cases, high performance is the result of a series of incremental steps: the organization makes a sound decision, evaluates the consequences, then incorporates the lessons it has learned. But where the self-defeating organization compulsively dwells on the costs it has incurred, the high-performing enterprise focuses on how it can benefit from less than optimal results.

Even in the wake of a setback, the healthy organization seeks to identify signs of progress and evidence of innovative thinking. It singles out individuals or groups that have performed admirably under duress, encouraging others to emulate them. It builds on what it has done well, drawing strength from small triumphs and symptoms of gradual improvement. This explains why so many instances of "overnight" success turn out, on closer inspection, to have been years in the making.

Success is a boon to any organization, regardless of how it has been achieved. Most analysts agree, though, that until a business or agency demonstrates the ability to maintain performance at a high level, the question of its long-term strength is open for discussion. It's not enough for a firm to earn record profits during a given fiscal year, or to rise to market dominance with a single breakthrough product: the organization has to be able to do it again. And to repeat an episode of success, an organization needs to understand *how* and *why* it has come about, and then incorporate into its character the patterns of thought and action that have brought about the performance breakthrough. It must, in other words, *own* its success, rather than regarding it as an accident, a fluke, or the product of a unique set of uncontrollable circumstances. And often, this means that a business, agency, or work group must be willing to embrace attitudes and actions that run counter to some of the practices and procedures it holds most dear.

That's what happened, more or less, at the financial services firm where Dave worked. You'll recall that in introducing a new approach to calculating broker performance, Dave seemingly violated several of the firm's established tenets, foremost among them the belief that its best brokers would survive any assault that the market dealt them. To an extent, Dave's compensation system robbed individual stars of some of their luster, leaving him vulnerable to the charge of subverting company policy. Only when he was able to make a solid business case for the measures he had taken did the firm's senior management allow him to persist in his efforts—and then, only grudgingly.

But as sales figures at the branch continued to improve, the thinking at corporate headquarters gradually started to come around. Senior executives began to receive discreet phone calls from their counterparts at competitive firms who wanted to know what was going on at Dave's branch office. It seemed that a few of their own top brokers had resigned their positions and signed on with Dave's team.

"Oh, we're trying a little experiment out there," one corporate vice president allegedly told a rival executive. "Nice to hear that it's working out."

Not long afterward, Dave received a memo from headquarters asking that he "write up" the measures he had taken in the form of a corporate white paper. Senior management was interested, the memo said, in learning how the ailing branch office had managed to thrive in the midst of a protracted market downturn. More to the point, management wanted to know what Dave had done to lure star performers away from rival brokerages.

"Answering that question was easy," Dave said later. "I just wrote down what the folks who had come over told me: that they were tired of working without a net, constantly afraid of falling off and ending up on the pavement. But when it came to describing my 'management philosophy,' at first I was stumped." He laughed. "I mean, I'd never thought there was any kind of method to my madness."

As it turned out, there was. In the short document that Dave subsequently submitted to corporate headquarters, he described some of the steps he had taken to turn the branch around. Among them were the following:

- On arriving at the branch, he had assessed its predicament honestly and had acknowledged the mistakes the company had made in the past.

- In planning his course of action, he had consulted a wide range of resources, borrowing what he could and looking for a proper fit between potential alternatives and the particular needs of the branch.

- He had evaluated the advantages and disadvantages of each solution that he considered, and had factored these pluses and minuses into the approach he eventually settled on.

- He had assumed responsibility for the policies he had implemented, defending them against internal skepticism and objections from headquarters.

- Once his plan started to succeed, he had made sure that his employees were aware of the connection between his formerly controversial approach and the positive results the branch had achieved. He also used these results to bring established brokers into the firm, and with them a number of major new accounts.

At the conclusion of his document, he thanked senior management for its trust and cooperation. He said that the firm had lived up to his expectations and, in granting him the latitude to try a new approach, had fully justified the faith he had placed in it.

Do any of Dave's methods sound familiar? They should. His somewhat ironic closing aside, the process Dave described closely resembles the high-performance model outlined in the figure on page 168. Throughout this process, he unstintingly told the truth. He opened a closed organization up to new ideas and new people. He calculated the costs and benefits of each decision he made, avoiding those approaches that unduly penalized any internal group or individual. He took responsibility for, and ownership of, the approach he put into practice, deflating the notion that he and his organization had simply been lucky or uniquely blessed. In the end, he effectively replaced a system of counterproductive thought and action with a model for improved performance: a systematic approach his company used in lieu of the punitive methods it had come to rely on.

SHAPING CORE BELIEFS THROUGH SUCCESS

Beliefs are shaped and transformed through experience. Both individuals and the organizations they comprise are motivated primarily by their perceptions of what will happen if they behave in a particular way. These perceptions, in turn, are shaped by memories of what has transpired in the past. But memory is highly selective, particularly within an organization that has weathered numerous crises and moments of extreme duress. This sort of organization recalls what has been done in the past to meet critical challenges, but conveniently forgets any negative consequences that have ensued. Banished from the official organizational history, the memory of these unpleasant side effects lingers in the form of unhealthy core beliefs. Though often unacknowledged, they continue to exert a pernicious influence on organizational thinking, all but ensuring that an enterprise will persist in conforming to its worst image of itself.

The ultimate goal of any high-performance system, therefore, is to establish within an organization's collective mentality the kinds of beliefs that enable healthy change and growth. This often requires the transformation of an entrenched cluster of negative—but, nonetheless, valid—notions about an organization's fundamental character. These are the kind of beliefs that cause organizations to become depressed, chaotic, deceitful, or disoriented in time, and they pose a vexing problem to anyone looking for ways of improving organizational performance. If beliefs are grounded in experience, and if an organization's recent experiences all lend credence to its negative self-evaluations, how can the organization possibly break out of the cycle of bad belief and counterproductive reaction? This is the eternal conundrum of the closed behavioral loop: the success an organization or individual most needs to escape an unhealthy pattern is seemingly unattainable *because* of the pattern.

All we can offer in the way of an answer is that an organization in this predicament must somehow find the wherewithal—call it hope or courage—to break with its troubled past. Many organizations see this as a blind leap of faith, and rightly so. To make it less precarious, we'll describe some of the techniques that an organization can use as milestones for measuring improvement or as a means of navigating an uncharted abyss. They're designed to do no more nor less than alter what an organization believes about itself: to reveal to even the most stricken or hidebound enterprise its latent capacity for self-renewal.

CHAPTER 9

Telling the Truth

RGANIZATIONS lie. They lie in good times and bad, for the best reasons and the worst, and with great expertise and gross ineptitude. They say that they plan to do one thing, then proceed to do another; they claim to hold a particular virtue in the highest esteem, then proceed to reward the opposite vice. They indulge not only in small equivocations that preserve the peace among warring internal factions, but also in grand deceptions aimed at manipulating the masses or achieving an unfair advantage. Some organizations even look on their bent for duplicity as a strategic asset that grants them a level of flexibility that their truth-bound competitors lack. They believe that they can finesse their way past any crisis or dilemma, and that it is indeed possible to fool all of the people all of the time.

In this, of course, the untruthful organization is totally mistaken. No organization that relies primarily on deceit to achieve its ends can ever hope to achieve long-term success: sooner or later, the truth *does* come out; and when it does, the results aren't pretty. The problematic issues the organization has successfully skirted, as well as the residual costs it has attempted to minimize, come thundering down like an avalanche. It's a phenomenon that, in recent years, has become all too familiar: the political landslide that rousts an entire slate of complacent incumbents; the winless football season that sends coaches and general managers packing; the CEO abruptly fired by a board of directors under pressure from shareholders to achieve short-term gains. This or a similar fate awaits the organization that stubbornly refuses to acknowledge the reality of its circumstances. It ultimately collapses beneath the weight of its deception.

Self-defeating organizations are, by definition, averse to the truth. If we look closely at each of the steps that make up a counterproductive behavior pattern, we see that each entails some measure of equivocation or outright deceitfulness. The cycle begins when the organization fails to act in accordance with its healthy core beliefs—when it talks all the right talk, then walks in the opposite direction. At this point the organization must effectively persuade itself that the familiar or expedient course of action it has chosen to follow is, in fact, the best and most appropriate solution to a problematic set of circumstances. Then, as the onerous consequences of this decision become obvious, the organization must deny that they exist, buy the silence of dissident members, or put a fanciful spin on the losses it has incurred. Shortly thereafter, the organization evades reality and responsibility by blaming its troubles on either scapegoats or the hazards of fate. The organization thus succumbs to the greatest falsehood of all: the notion that it cannot change its behavior to bring about better results.

High-performing organizations, in contrast, are firmly committed to telling the truth. Although they may tolerate any number of little white lies—the equivalents, say, of dinner guests telling their host that a leathery lamb chop is broiled to perfection—there are certain ethical boundaries they always honor. First and foremost, they never knowingly lie when the credibility of an enterprise or its leaders is at stake. They never, for example, dispatch their managers to tell the troops that no staff reductions are planned, knowing full well that within six months they'll be handing out pink slips. Secondly, they never withhold important information from those it will affect, *unless revealing the information will unnecessarily jeopardize profitability, security, or a crucial plan or strategy*. A commitment to honesty does not compel an organization to share the specifications for its latest breakthrough product with every temporary clerical worker on its payroll.

Most importantly for our purposes here, healthy and successful organizations are always unstintingly honest when it comes to evaluating performance, either of an enterprise as a whole or of individual members. In assessing a recent downturn, they refuse to resort to the dissembling language of corporate reports and quarterly statements. And only rarely do they allow their managers to couch frank appraisals in canned legalese and innocuous psychobabble. When an employee isn't doing the job, his or her performance evaluation says so in terms that are at once honest and nonjudgmental.

If the case for truth-telling is so strong, why, you might ask, do so many organizational leaders and managers argue against it? Later in this chapter, we'll analyze the kinds of objections we typically encounter, showing how each is, in its way, an expression of entrenched mythical fear. For now, though, let's turn our attention to a scenario that illustrates how effective truth-telling can be, and how a lone truth-teller can enhance the prospect for healthy organizational change.

THE POWER OF TRUTH

Let's call him Tyler. During the early '90s he worked as a district manager for an established chain of retail stores that had been gradually losing its market share over the course of several years. Tyler had been charged with reversing this trend. But his hands were somewhat tied; he had been directed to make changes that would lure patrons away from a variety of competitors, yet at the same time maintain the traditional identity of each of the stores in his district. It was the classic dilemma that established enterprises have faced in recent years: how to innovate without alienating an existing customer base.

There were other problems, too. The staff at the major stores in the district—cashiers, stock clerks, and commissioned sales personnel—had become nostalgic in their approach to the business, calling for a return to the practices and procedures they associated with past successes. For years, the stores had managed to be all things to all people. Veteran employees didn't see why the chain couldn't return to its former prominence; they viewed the current slump as a product of the company's obsession with quick fixes and voguish solutions. They pointed with some justification at the failure of a series of ill-conceived initiatives: the installation of malfunctioning cash registers, the closing of store cafeterias, and an employee empowerment program that never quite got off the ground. These failures, in combination with declining profits and a hiring freeze, had caused store employees to lose confidence in their leaders—and, to an extent, in themselves.

Tyler had to find some means of turning this situation around. Although he had sensed from the start that the process would be painful, he didn't realize *how* painful it would be until he paid a series of informal visits to the chain's major competitors. He walked the aisles of discount retailers, warehouse outlets, and even a few specialty shops. What he saw did not encourage him: the competition had better or equivalent prices and, in many instances, a friendlier shopping environment. He came to believe that to attract new customers in an increasingly specialized and price-sensitive market, his stores would have to offer better deals on a wider range of products. And no matter how you looked at it, that meant reducing the operating overhead at each store.

Wary of imposing the required reductions by executive decree, Tyler put the case to his store managers in a series of meetings. He asked them to identify areas in which operating costs could be brought down without significantly affecting store revenues. The results of this approach were, at first, unremarkable. The managers came back with suggestions that were cosmetic in nature or short term in scope: laying off younger, part-time employees; closing the stores on Sundays; increasing the number of items offered as loss-leaders. One manager contended that his employees needed yet another customer service training program. Another suggested eliminating certain in-store amenities—optical services, portrait photography, and key duplication—even though each was successfully and profitably operated by an outside contractor who leased floor space from the store.

This last recommendation struck Tyler as particularly ridiculous, closely akin to advising a dieter to have a limb amputated to
lose unwanted weight. He didn't say as much, though, opting instead to address the larger issue.

"Look," he began, regarding each of the store managers seated
around the conference table, "none of what you're proposing is
going to get us where we need to go. You're talking about trimming
a few dollars here, a few dollars there. But no one has brought up
any of the areas where we're really weak." He gestured to a chart
on the overhead projection screen behind him. "Sporting goods,
for one. A dud for most of the year, with peaks at the start of the
school year and at Christmas. And decorative jewelry—a full-time
clerk and two part-timers in each store, with average sales of less
than $100 per normal weekday. You could say the same for lug-
gage and stationery. Let's face it: people can get those items elsewhere, and usually at a better price."

Here Tyler paused, allowing the assembled store managers to
brood in silence.

"And I haven't even mentioned the auto centers and the home-
and-garden shops," he said when the silence had become uncomfortable. "They're both housed in freestanding structures, and
they're both overstaffed and underutilized. Frankly, folks, they
take a lot from the table, and they don't bring much back."

This drew a rumble of protest, as Tyler had expected it would.
He knew that store managers held these two operations especially
dear, viewing them as crucial to the company's position as a provider of a comprehensive range of services and goods.

"What you don't seem to understand," said one disgruntled
manager, "is that without Auto and Home and Garden, we'd be
just another store."

This was the opening Tyler had been waiting for. "I know
that," he said evenly. "But what you don't seem to understand is
that in the eyes of the customer, we *are* just another store."

Tyler spent the rest of the session talking about how the stores
had for years operated under the assumption that they occupied a
special and unique place in the public mind—that, all things being equal, customers would continue to flock to their aisles. But

now that things had, in fact, become more or less equal, many traditional and potential customers were choosing to take their business elsewhere. Modern consumers evaluated the store not on the basis of its vaunted reputation, but on what it offered them *today*. And with an ominous regularity, they seemed to be concluding that other retailers served their needs better.

"We have to think and act as if we opened our doors last week," Tyler said pointedly. "We have to behave as if headquarters won't continue to subsidize falling performance, because I don't think headquarters will."

What Tyler had done in this meeting was use the power of truth to strike at an entrenched, but no longer valid, core organizational belief. And in this case, the truth proved to be powerful indeed. Disabused of the notion that their stores enjoyed an inherent and unassailable competitive advantage, the managers subsequently presented Tyler with a jointly developed plan for reducing costs and maximizing profitability. Included in this document were provisions for eliminating the overhead associated with the auto centers and home-and-garden stores. The former were to be sold to an outside firm that seemed willing to pay a premium price for proximity to an established retailer; the latter would be shut down, with their top-performing products then offered through in-store departments. A plan similar to this one was eventually adopted, and as a result even the marginal stores in Tyler's district—two had been targeted for closing—gradually transformed themselves into stable profit centers.

TRUTH-TELLING BASICS

Moral and legal considerations aside, the leaders and managers of successful enterprises have a very good reason for telling the truth. They know that unless they are honest with themselves and organizational members, they will not be able to achieve the level of credibility required for high-performance organizational leadership. They're aware that deception is a difficult habit to break and, worse yet, that in the long term it undermines any steps an organization might take in the direction of healthy change. In other words, they know that truth is the bedrock of organizational success.

But for all this, truth-telling is often problematic, particularly in scenarios that involve large numbers of people and that play out over extended periods of time. The matter can become even more complicated when organizational leaders are themselves in doubt about the wisdom of a decision or policy, and when rank-and-file members have good grounds for disbelieving what they are told. In these kinds of situations, it may not be enough for an organization simply to do what it has said it will do. Complex circumstances demand a more systematic approach. In the sections that follow we present such an approach, showing how it can help organizational decision makers build their credibility in a step-by-step manner.

Deciding What to Do

It should come as no great surprise that the process of truth-telling begins well before a policy, program, or change is announced. It starts when organizational leaders, planners, and consultants are contemplating the alternatives available to them at a strategic moment. If these individuals are less than honest with themselves and each other, chances are they'll end up making a decision that will be difficult to implement, hard to justify, and ineffectual in terms of its ultimate results. When it comes time to make a decision, you have to ask, and answer truthfully, questions about whatever action you're considering:

- Is it an effective or innovative solution to the problem at hand, or is it simply the most convenient or familiar approach available?
- Will it reinforce a healthy core belief or run counter to a set of assumptions that is inhibiting organizational effectiveness?
- What are the costs and benefits of the alternative under consideration, and how will these costs and benefits be absorbed?
- Which organizational groups or constituencies are likely to win and lose as a result of your decision?

- Will the action you're considering provide a foundation
  for additional growth and innovation, or will it serve
  merely as a stopgap measure to resolve the current
  problem?

You need to formulate your answers to these questions carefully,
taking care to avoid glibness, euphemism, and the ever-present
temptation to base strategic decisions on best-case scenarios.
Keep in mind that the case you're developing will eventually have
to be sold to the organization as a whole, and that rank-and-file
members will be quick to spot the weak links in any jerry-built
chain of reasoning. You must persuade yourself of the viability of a
decision before proposing it to rank-and-file members, lest the
organizational masses later roll their eyes and go on with business
as usual.

This is easy enough to say, but not that easy to do. It often
involves hard choices, not to mention extensive data gathering and
analysis. When, for example, Tyler looked at alternative ways of
improving the profitability of his stores, he sensed early on that he
would need to pursue a course of action that flew in the face of a
fundamental core belief: the notion that his stores could somehow
overpower the marketplace on the strength of their reputation and
accumulated resources. To do this, he needed facts—not only
about sales volumes and trends, but also about how his stores were
perceived by prospective consumers.

"You're always going to hear the 'first in the heart of the customer' line when you try to make a change," he later explained.
"So I called in a market research firm and commissioned a survey
of the district. The results came back pretty much as I'd expected—we were first in the hearts of our oldest customers, folks
well beyond their prime purchasing years."

These data aided Tyler immeasurably as he evaluated potential options. They freed him from the limitations imposed by an
outmoded core belief. Because this belief was no longer serving
any healthy purpose, he saw little need for his organization to
continue to behave according to its dictates. What's more, he now
had at hand hard evidence that seemed to support the course of

action he had in mind. He believed that this evidence would enable him to make a persuasive but dispassionate case for the kind of changes he wanted to make.

Explaining Why Change Is Necessary

Once an organization has decided how it intends to respond to a crisis or challenge, it must explain why it has chosen to pursue a particular course of action. This is no time for waffling, hedging, or invoking executive privilege. Organizational members need to be told in plain and simple terms what has been decided, why the decision makers believe it will work, and how various groups and individuals will be affected. It's not enough to assert, as many businesses and agencies do, that a potentially disruptive policy will be put into effect "for the good of the organization." Nor is it sufficient simply to sketch the broad outlines of an impending decision and leave the troublesome details for later. Organizational members need specific and accurate information about changes that will affect them, and they need as much of it as possible.

This brings up the problem of maintaining organizational security, and here the waters grow murky. Obviously, no organization can adhere to an approach that requires it to divulge the details of sensitive negotiations or cutting-edge research to anyone who asks about these matters. But in some cases, withholding this information can make the organization seem secretive or duplicitous, undermining the level of trust that leaders and managers are trying so hard to build. It's a dilemma, frankly, and like all dilemmas it entails a measure of risk taking. In determining how much sensitive or volatile information to reveal, you need to balance the benefits of total honesty against the cost of breaching organizational security. You may determine that it's simply too risky to share all that you know with rank-and-file members; like all other strategies, truth-telling has its time and place, and the current situation may not lend itself to absolute candor. Or you may decide that the best way to gain trust is to grant it—that the credibility you'll gain through full disclosure might, in the end, outweigh the consequences of an information leak. Either way, your organization stands to benefit; it's strictly a judgment call.

Tyler found himself faced with precisely this dilemma when it came time to visit each of the stores in his district and explain the changes that were in the works. The sale of the auto centers was a key element of the plan he and his managers had developed; without the revenues and expense reductions realized through this sale, his figures simply wouldn't add up, and his case for change would seem flimsy at best. So he decided he had to tell store employees that the auto centers would probably be sold, even though negotiations had not yet been completed.

"They had to know," he said later. "We'd misled them so many times in the past, like when we told them the cafeterias were losing money. That was a canard—the truth was, headquarters didn't want to upgrade the fixtures and equipment to comply with new regulations. And besides," he added, "some people were going to lose their jobs, and they could all read and do arithmetic. Our projections didn't include any revenues from Automotive and Home and Garden. You can't keep that kind of secret from your people—not if you expect them to keep on believing you."

Explaining Detours and Setbacks

We're all aware of what often befalls even the best-laid plans. In the course of implementing a plan or program, it's common for difficulties to arise. A new piece of equipment may not function as promised, a product may fail to sell as expected, or the behavior of groups and individuals may take an idiosyncratic turn. This doesn't necessarily mean that failure or catastrophe is imminent, or that organizational leaders have been mistaken, naive, or cynical in their thinking. But it does mean that executives and managers must, in the spirit of truth-telling, describe and explain any detour or setback that has occurred.

The members of an organization—and, for that matter, the members of the public at large—have every right to expect a business, agency, or political group to do what it has said it will do. They do *not*, however, have a right to expect unerring judgment, clairvoyance, or any other manifestation of infallibility. For an organization to innovate and grow in a way that sustains high performance, it must be allowed to make an occasional mistake.

When the members of an organization or the general public demand perfection, most organizations—our major political parties come immediately to mind—are apt to pursue safe but ineffectual strategies, and then to cover up, minimize, or disown the predictable consequences. This virtual formula for self-defeat helps explain much of the cynicism currently targeted at government, big business, organized religion, and so many of our once-venerated institutions.

Truth-telling is an effective means of ensuring that a single instance of errant decision making does not ultimately flower into a pattern of self-defeat. But for truth-telling to serve this purpose, organizational leaders must be forthright in acknowledging both its miscues and any unforeseen developments that have come up. The organization that fails to tell the truth on this score leaves itself open to suspicions of incompetence and deceptiveness. Rank-and-file members are left to conclude that their leaders are either blissfully unaware that their plans have gone awry—or, worse yet, that they are trying to cover up their mistakes and avoid responsibility.*

Think back for a moment to Tyler's strategy for improving the profitability of the stores in his district. This plan, which had seemed eminently workable in its conception, ran abruptly aground when the prospective buyer of the auto centers had second thoughts about the deal. Negotiations broke off, leaving the stores still responsible for the cost of operating their automotive departments. In that the company had already shut down the flagging home-and-garden centers, this created a potential morale

---

*There's no rule saying that all detours and unplanned consequences must yield negative effects. It may, in fact, be necessary for an organization to deviate from a plan or schedule because circumstances have changed for the better. A product or organizational unit may, for example, have performed much better than expected, making certain planned activities unnecessary. Signs of health and innovation may abruptly spring from a most unlikely source; a group or individual deemed incapable of creative activity may come up with a breakthrough or insight that brings about a stunning reversal of organizational fortune. Under these happy circumstances, the high-performing organization takes full ownership of the windfall success that has come its way. More on this in Chapter 12.

problem among store employees. Many of them viewed the collapsed sale of the auto centers as yet another example of the company's failure to follow through on its grand designs.

"I had to do some fast talking, all right," Tyler recalled. "What made it more difficult was that the negotiations had broken down over some fairly esoteric business points, the kind of nits you can't really simplify. I did my best, though: I went to each store in the district and reassured the staff that our goal hadn't changed, and that we were still planning to sell the auto centers or work out some sort of franchising agreement. And I also told them that we may well have been caught off guard by a negotiating ploy, and that the sale might still come off as planned."

Which, eventually, it did. As a result, both Tyler and the managers of the stores gained stature in the eyes of store employees. But without the forthright explanation that Tyler was quick to offer—and the subsequent sale of the auto centers—these employees would probably have looked on the new profit-improvement program as yet another of the "paper miracles" for which management had become notorious.

Describing Results

Many of the executives and managers we've talked to complain that they get little or no credit for the successes they achieve and disproportionate blame when their organizations come up short. There's some truth to this: in today's winner-take-all world, modest improvements tend to draw little acclaim, with relatively minor setbacks triggering loud and plaintive cries of alarm. A lot of the time, though, gaps between an organization's actual performance and how that performance is perceived can be traced to a collective failure to communicate the results of new policies and programs. This can lead to an environment where individuals and groups are asked to bear the costs of change, but are not subsequently told about the benefits achieved through their sacrifices. And such conditions, as noted previously, are an ideal medium for the cultivation of skewed or corrosive organizational beliefs.

Truth-telling can help an organization close or eliminate discrepancies between the reality and the perception of its collective performance. It works like this: in deciding on a course of action and explaining why it is necessary, organizational leaders establish a set of expectations among their employees. This obligates executives and managers to let their people know when these expectations have been achieved—or, as the case might be, when and to what extent they have not been realized. Unless these results are explicitly and honestly described, rank-and-file members are left to wonder how well the organization is performing. They may even assume that a much-heralded change or initiative has failed to live up to its billing, and that their leaders are loath to admit it.

It's crucial, therefore, for a truthful organization to describe the results of any plan or strategy they have put into practice. And it's essential that these results be described honestly, plainly, and in terms of the goals or objectives the organization has set. As stated earlier, successful organizations almost never equivocate about individual or collective performance, and here this principle comes starkly to bear. The healthy organization takes a clear-eyed measure of what it has accomplished, then tells the unvarnished truth about it. It shuns the obscure or cleverly coded vocabularies of sluggish bureaucracies and glib booster groups. Its leaders and managers refuse to speak a polyglot language derived from the patois of lawyers, accountants, and pop psychologists. Nor does it yield to the temptation to manipulate performance and financial data in a way that obscures hard truths.

This temptation is always present, as Tyler discovered when it came time to meet with store employees and present the outcomes of his cost-reduction program. Though the program had for the most part been successful, the figures showed that overhead costs hadn't dropped as dramatically as he had anticipated. Nor, for that matter, had profits climbed to the extent he had projected: at some stores, profitability soared, but at others there had been only slight gains. And the performance of individual departments within each store varied more than Tyler would have liked, suggesting that these outlets were still carrying dead weight. All in all, it was a performance picture marked by ups and downs, pluses and minuses, good news and bad—in short, a fairly typical organizational scenario.

"For a while, I considered talking about the results on a relatively high level, where it would seem like we'd accomplished what we set out to do," Tyler recalled. "That would have given our people a boost in morale and—let's be honest—made the managers and me look good. There was a problem, though: we were already considering additional changes, such as merging certain departments that weren't pulling their weight. So what I ended up doing was going over the figures department by department for each store, noting where we were strong and where we were weak.

"I won't say this made everyone happy," he added. "Some of the managers advised against this approach, and with good reason: after a year of playing the villain, they wanted their moment in the sun. But I convinced them the glory would be short-lived, that we'd be looked on as heroes today and—there's no other word—liars before the month was out."

THE CASE FOR TRUTH-TELLING

Truth-telling works. Although it may be inconvenient or disruptive in the short term, over the duration of an organization's life truth-telling validates a basic and time-honored notion: honesty is still the best policy. Better still, it doesn't require a huge capital investment or a burdensome commitment of organizational resources: it's a technique that even the most underfinanced or overworked enterprise can bring to bear on its problems. We'd be less than honest, though, in claiming that all—or even most—problem-plagued organizations embrace the notion of telling the truth with unbounded enthusiasm. As we mentioned at the start of this chapter, low-performing organizations are by nature aversive to the truth—and often, we've discovered, for what seem to be good reasons.

The objections to truth-telling we most frequently encounter fall into four general categories. Many executives, managers, and consultants contend that their organizations cannot tell the truth because it is unpleasant, or because it is far too complex for rank-and-file members to understand. Others maintain that attempting to tell the truth would be futile, because no one would believe it,

while still others are unsure of how and when the truth ought to be
told within organizational ranks. But if we analyze each of these
objections to truth-telling, we can see that they are often little
more than manifestations of invalid or unhealthy core beliefs—the
kinds of beliefs a troubled organization ought to be trying to dispel, rather than to reinforce through ongoing dissimulation.

Unhealthy Belief: "The Truth Is Unpleasant"

This is far and away the most common protest we hear when
the topic of truth-telling comes up. You'd be amazed at how many
organizations labor under the assumption that their motives are
base, that their policies are hypocritical, or that their methods are
outmoded and ineffectual. Once these kinds of beliefs have gained
a foothold within the ranks, it's not surprising that organizational
leaders are loath to give voice to them by telling the unvarnished
truth. No one wants to be the bearer of bad tidings, or the herald of
impending doom.

Some businesses and agencies fear that truth-telling will create a climate marked by perpetual acrimony and confrontation, a
powder keg ready to explode at any moment into verbal or physical violence. It seems to us that they don't fully understand what
organizational honesty means to accomplish. The kind of truth-
telling we're talking about here is always based on objective evidence and *is always directed toward the goal of improving performance*. A commitment to truth-telling is not a blanket license to
berate, abuse, and censure individuals or groups that have fallen
into disfavor. Nor does it provide a rationale for people with questionable motives to vent their hostilities or express their idiosyn-
crasies. When truth-telling turns vituperative, something other
than the truth is usually at work.

On close inspection, the unpleasant truths an organization is
afraid to tell often turn out to be not all that abhorrent. Nor should
they come as any great surprise to members of an organization,
save for those individuals inflamed with a rigid idealism that
serves little purpose in the compromised world of modern gover-
nance and commerce. Self-defeating organizations are fearful of
admitting, for example, that their primary purpose is to make

money, that they'll do whatever it takes to survive, or that their leaders are ambitious and acting with an eye on career advancement. Are such truths inherently odious or destructive? It depends on your perspective. From ours, they are little more than statements of the obvious—facts of life that most organizational members have probably long since come to terms with. We seriously doubt that the employees of a financial services firm would be shocked on discovering that their company is in the business of achieving ever-increasing profitability; or that the staff of a high-powered intercollegiate athletic department would be dumbstruck on learning that its coaches are out to win at all costs. The leaders of these organizations risk little in admitting the obvious, and in many cases stand to gain credibility in acknowledging the plain truth.

There are, however, those organizations who are rightfully fearful of owning up to the truth about their attitudes and actions. These are businesses and agencies that base their operations on negative notions that also happen to be accurate. Take, for example, the engineering firm we talked about in the first section of this book. Believing that the members of their design staff were lazy and irresponsible, the managing partners responded by installing software that tracked how much time these designers spent at their workstations. For obvious reasons, they were reluctant to reveal why they had resorted to this measure. So they dispatched John, their computer services consultant, to spread the word that the new software was designed to improve the efficiency of the firm's billing system.

But the design staff immediately saw through this transparent ruse. Some left the firm at the earliest opportunity; others flogged away like galley slaves at their terminals, accomplishing little; and still others employed the ingenuity they might better have applied elsewhere to developing computer programs that tricked the software into reporting inaccurate data. Needless to say, the installation of the so-called productivity management software had the net effect of lowering productivity and eroding trust within the firm.

What to do, then, if your organization cannot tell the truth because it expresses a hostile or sinister core belief—and, in the worst case, a bad belief based on demonstrable fact? If you happen to be in a position of leadership, you can dedicate yourself to changing the noxious beliefs at the root of so many unmentionable truths. This means refusing to fall back on negative assumptions when it comes time to make a strategic decision and, as a result, making decisions that can be justified without resorting to deception. But if you're a worker or a person of minimal authority, your options are more limited. It comes down to this: you can either adapt to your organization's self-defeating character and hope for improvement, or you can choose to go elsewhere. Although drastic and precarious in today's job-poor environment, the latter alternative isn't as outlandish as it might seem. You need simply to decide whether your personal interests will in the long term be served by an enterprise that you do not trust, and that doesn't trust you.

Unhealthy Belief: "Our People Won't Understand"

Another common refrain, and one we heard in the words of Martin, the vice chairman of a consumer goods conglomerate. He was talking about his company's plans to reduce the workforce at a plant that made a highly successful line of snack foods. The firm's financial planners and market research experts had determined that these products had matured to the point where their sales would soon begin to decline, and that the company would be better off cutting back on production and investing its resources in new, improved brands.

"This is a strategic decision," Martin explained, "and it's based on MBA-level management concepts and statistical analysis that even I don't fully understand. How can you explain a proactive staff reduction to a group of assembly-line workers who know that their plant is operating at full capacity?"

It seemed that Martin was acting in thrall to a belief common among organizational leaders who want to avoid telling the truth. Probe beyond the surface, and you'll soon discover that such executives and managers hold to the ominous notion that most of their employees are stupid.

But the vast majority of them aren't. Although it's absurd to expect rank-and-file workers to comprehend the intricacies of complicated corporate mergers, leveraged buyouts, and advanced technological research, most have little trouble understanding the concepts of supply and demand, profit and loss, and sacrifice in the long-term interest. (They may not necessarily *like* what they hear, but that's another problem. Suffice it to say that no organization can grow and prosper if it insists on telling the truth *and* maintaining a state of uninterrupted bliss for all of its members.) When it comes right down to it, there are relatively few organizational truths that cannot be honestly expressed in terms that sentient people have little difficulty comprehending.

"But you don't understand," Martin countered. "We're talking about real bottom-of-the-barrel types here, unskilled laborers for the most part. There's no way they'll see the wisdom."

Again, a problem having little to do with the need for truthfulness. That's why truth-telling is such a powerful technique: it's not only healthy in its own right, but it often forces organizations to look at other issues that are inhibiting performance. In Martin's case, a contemplation of the truth quickly pointed at the source of many of the company's ongoing problems. The firm needed to be more selective in its hiring, and to abandon the belief that diamonds can be had at zircon prices.

Unhealthy Belief: "No One Will Believe Us, Anyway"

Having long since abandoned truth-telling as a means of improving performance, some organizations see little or no point in trying to build credibility among the ranks. They believe that they have cried wolf so often in the past, and doled out so much insincere lip service, that anything they say will be viewed as suspect. This circular logic creates a miniature self-defeating loop within a larger counterproductive pattern: the organization believes it cannot tell the truth because it has seldom (if ever) told the truth, and as a result, continues to equivocate in a way that renders truthtelling ineffective for the present and well into the future. These kinds of organizations attempt to remedy a history of deception with even more deception, fooling no one but themselves.

We're reminded here of Julia, the sales manager at the weight-loss center we discussed in Chapter 3. Her most pressing problem was the number of customers who defaulted on their contracts, claiming that they weren't receiving the kind of service or results they had been promised. This difficulty was directly traceable to the alarming number of instances where sales representatives had made claims the center couldn't possibly live up to—which, in turn, harkened back to the company's practice of promoting sales personnel who sold the most memberships, regardless of how they achieved these ends.

"We've tried telling them to go soft on the promises," Julia claimed. "But then they see who gets ahead in the company, the people who are given their own franchises, and the next thing you know, we're back to square one. So I call a meeting and announce a new policy on defaulted contracts, and I get these knowing looks. I feel like a weak parent, saying, 'Here's how it's going to be—*and this time we really mean it!*' "

Obviously, this organization had a severe credibility problem of the sort that often emerges as the *bête noire* of truth-aversive booster groups. Julia's objection to truth-telling derived from her firm's reluctance to stand by its claims; because the company failed to follow through on its pronouncements, these edicts were consistently disregarded. An enterprise in this predicament needs to make a frank evaluation of its goals and beliefs, and test these beliefs against the characteristics associated with long-term high performance. But at some point in this process, it must ultimately make an unequivocal commitment to truth-telling—and, at the earliest opportunity, to demonstrate through its actions the premium it now places on honesty.

Unhealthy Belief: "We Don't Know How to Tell the Truth"

Of all the objections to truth-telling we've encountered, this one strikes us as the most credible. Some organizations—those that are content to muddle along at a less than optimal level of performance—have never been faced with a pressing need to tell the truth and, hence, have never really learned how to go about it.

We wish these groups well, but warn them that middling performance is apt to become more and more difficult to sustain in today's environment of intense global competition and rampant organizational restructuring.

How can a business or agency learn to tell the truth about its identity, its collective attitudes, and its actions? We're aware of at least a couple of alternatives. One is the four-step process we discussed on pages 189–196: a system of forthright decision making, explanation, and follow-up that can effectively counter any tendencies toward reaction, replication, minimizing, and blaming. We encourage organizations to give this approach a try before looking elsewhere. Be aware, though, that this methodology works only when an organization is willing to be honest with itself at key strategic moments; one of its primary benefits is to steer an enterprise toward decisions that will not subsequently require rationalization or equivocation. These are the kinds of decisions on which viable performance improvement is ultimately based. Organizations that make them often find themselves settling happily into the healthy habit of regular truth-telling.

A second alternative is to hire outside experts for the purpose of disseminating uncomfortable but crucial organizational truths. There are numerous consulting firms that specialize in taking an honest measure of an organization's performance patterns and communicating them succinctly to leaders and rank-and-file members. Consultants can bring to bear on a problematic scenario a credibility that internal agents might lack; in theory, at least, outside experts speak for no particular constituency and are largely immune to charges of interest-brokering. We advise, however, that an organization choose its performance consultant carefully and that executives and managers be firmly behind the effort. Consulting firms are, after all, in business, and most are acutely capable of reading between the lines of whatever directive they are given; many will do what it takes to please their sponsors. They may end up telling management what management wants to hear, or engaging in the counterproductive activity of diluting or sugarcoating the truth they have been hired to tell.

That said, we've nonetheless seen consultants work wonders

in organizations where truth has traditionally been a rare or absent commodity. One glass manufacturer, for example, had been subsidized for years by its parent company, a major automaker. This had enabled the glass company to maintain a cost structure well out of line with the marketplace. As a result, performance at its plant had been allowed to stagnate. Under no pressure to improve, management had itself ignored the reality of the situation. In the early 1980s, however, the parent corporation began to demand higher productivity and lower prices, making it clear that offshore competitors could provide both. The subsidiary organization suddenly found itself in need of administering shock therapy to its members. It required the sort of abrupt and blunt truth-telling that its low-key managers couldn't effectively bring about.

After interviewing numerous consultants, the glass company selected a firm that specialized in systematic performance improvement. Management instructed these consultants to develop a business plan for change, and to be unstinting in their evaluation of company strengths and weaknesses. The consulting firm undertook a top-to-bottom analysis of the company's performance and delivered a report that backed its recommendations with production data and the available information about industry norms. With management's approval, members of the consulting team held a series of meetings with plant employees, describing the situation in clear terms and backing up what they said with hard facts.

"This is scary stuff," a production supervisor wrote in his evaluation of one such meeting. "Up until now, I had no sense of what bad shape we were in. Management always talks about increasing productivity and improving quality, but to most of us it seemed like just so much talk."

These sessions had the desired effect of driving home the urgent need for change. As a result, plant employees became more receptive to policies and programs they might well have otherwise winked at or rejected. The key to this success was the company's commitment to telling the truth, as well as to an ongoing program based on unequivocal evaluations of performance, growth, and progress.

THE IMPORTANCE OF HONEST COMMITMENT

Truth-telling is powerful. Once unleashed, it tends to rumble through an organization like a seismic wave, causing atrophied patterns and structures to collapse and mythical fears to crumble. It can transform depressed Maintenance Crews into energetic seekers of change, challenge chaotic Funhouse Gangs to figure out who is doing what, and force Pep Squads to strip away their glib but deceptive facades. It can startle Alumni Clubs and Cargo Cults out of their disoriented time frames, forcing them to come to grips with present reality and legitimate prospects for the future. In each case, performance inevitably improves, with each small improvement restoring a measure of organizational credibility and self-respect.

To reap these benefits, however, an organization must commit to truth-telling in all of its actions and at all levels of operation. A flagging enterprise cannot expect to change if it tells the truth only when it is convenient or when the truth conveys an uplifting message. Its self-defeating patterns derive much of their impetus from precisely this kind of selective honesty, and these are the very patterns it needs to eliminate. Neither can it expect to thrive if, in the interest of building trust, its leaders encourage rank-and-file members to tell the truth at all times while reserving for themselves the right to dissemble.

Truth-telling is the foundation for each of the high-performance techniques you'll be reading about in the pages that follow. In the absence of complete candor, these techniques soon mutate into their self-defeating counterparts and yield, in the end, strikingly similar results. Let's consider for a moment what might happen within an organization that attempts to avail itself of our other high-performance techniques in a climate of less than total honesty.

- Such an organization may claim to be open to new people, ideas, and methods, knowing full well that it will reject any alternative that has not originated inside its walls. Or it may hide behind a pose of false open-mindedness, introducing a flurry of fashionable programs to distract members from the fact that it continues to do business as usual. When a crisis or dilemma arises, such an organization will resort under duress to its customary self-defeating practices. Result: reaction and replication.

- This sort of self-deceiving organization may claim to have based its decisions and policies on frank and accurate appraisals of the potential consequences. But because these evaluations will, in the absence of truth, be inevitably skewed or distorted, the organization will continue to make decisions that repeatedly afflict particular constituencies while working largely to the benefit of a favored group or set of interests. Result: an ever-accumulating backlog of consequences that demand redress and, consequently, distract the organization from key goals and opportunities.

- This pressing need to back and fill makes it difficult or impossible for an untruthful organization to take full advantage of any of the benefits its actions have yielded. The business or agency that tries to maximize its performance under these conditions must largely ignore or deny the troubling consequences of an ill-advised decision or policy. Result: minimizing, a systematic means of propagating blatant fictions.

- Honest ownership—the critical link between sound decision making and the formation of healthy core beliefs—is by and large impossible for organizations that are aversive to the truth. Because they know that shortsighted decisions and policies seldom result in significant improvement or change, they are apt to view any triumph they achieve as a fluke, an accident, or the result of an action or attitude that violates organizational norms. This makes it difficult, at best, for the organization to learn from its successes—or, for that matter, from its failures, which must be attributed to factors the organization cannot control. Result: disowning and blaming, both of which confirm suspicions of organizational impotence.

There's a reason why courts of law demand that witnesses tell "the *whole* truth and *nothing but* the truth." Partial or selective truth-telling serves little productive purpose, and often leads to more harm than good.

Is your organization honest in its desire for healthy change? How you answer this question is a matter of paramount importance. Far too many self-defeating enterprises want it both ways: they want to persist in their counterproductive patterns, but somehow to achieve dramatically improved results. This simply can't happen. A self-defeating organization can no more behave in its customary ways and achieve a performance breakthrough than a dieter can continue to gulp down rich food and expect a miraculous weight loss. So answer this question truthfully, lest your smart organization fall into the trap of continuing to outsmart itself.

CHAPTER 10
The Open-Minded Organization

THE LOW-PERFORMANCE loop is a closed behavioral system. Like the problem-plagued individual—the compulsive job-hopper, say, or the chronic procrastinator—an organization caught up in this cycle finds itself again and again in situations where it must choose between two ultimately unsavory options. On the one hand, it can continue to do what it knows best, taking comfort in illusory promises of protection and control and enjoying whatever short-term benefits it realizes through expedient action. On the other hand, it can cast caution and habit aside and enter uncharted territory, exposing itself to the predatory forces that may await it there. It's no wonder that so many self-defeating individuals and organizations opt repeatedly for the familiar; the alternative is too terrifying to contemplate.

It doesn't need to be. The truth is, the majority of ailing enterprises have available to them at key strategic moments many more options than they are willing to acknowledge; they are simply too fearful or rigid in their thinking to entertain any departure from the past. This typically results from years, even decades, of the kind of exclusionary thought and action that, while it keeps an organization relatively homogeneous, proves in the long run to be a barrier to healthy growth. The closed, homogeneous organization invariably knows precisely what to do when the wolves are at the door. But at the same time it knows—even if it refuses to admit as much—that its reaction will bring at best a temporary respite from danger. Sooner or later, the wolves are bound to return, hungrier and more determined than ever.

No organization can expect to improve its performance if it continues to make reactive decisions when threats or temptations arise. Sustainable high performance is the product of an incremental series of sound decisions, and sound decision making requires honesty, a wealth of options, and workable means of evaluating risks. We dealt with the first of these three essentials in the previous chapter; we'll deal with the last in the chapter that follows. Our focus here will be on the second requirement for innovative decision making: the kind of collective open-mindedness that can jolt a hidebound organization out of its habits of reaction and replication.

As is true of the other techniques we recommend, open-mindedness is not of itself a cure-all or an infallible antidote to the malady of flagging or mediocre performance. And like its counterparts within the high-performance loop, a program of inclusiveness can be insincerely embraced or carried to ridiculous lengths. It's a relatively simple matter for an organization concerned primarily with appearances to indulge in ostentatious displays of how receptive it is to new people, ideas, and methods: all it need do is use its training function as a vehicle for advancing within the ranks every management trend or buzzword currently in vogue. This is a false and counterproductive approach; it is to true open-mindedness what glib moral relativism is to genuine tolerance. Both are charades meant to direct attention away from a stubborn commitment to the status quo.

THE PERILS OF HOMOGENEITY

Open-mindedness comes naturally to organizations that are in their formative stages of development. With neither a tradition to protect nor a substantial investment in a particular way of doing business, young organizations are ever on the lookout for individuals, concepts, and strategies that will bring them success. What's more, they lack the accumulated resources that might allow them to shop indiscriminately for solutions; financial strictures compel them to evaluate personnel, product ideas, and potential opportunities with prudent care. They try this, they try that, until finally they succeed or fail. And once they've achieved a performance breakthrough, they throw all their energies and resources behind the methods that have led to success. This is open-mindedness at its best: selective, nonjudgmental, and rigorously focused on the future.

The perils of inflexibility arise later on, when an organization has enjoyed an extended period of prosperity and has become committed to operational policies and procedures that exclude all others. What passes for innovation at this point amounts to little more than the grooming and refinement of entrenched policies in the areas of hiring, planning, decision making, training, and cost management. Which is all well and good, *so long as the competitive environment remains stable and the organization is more or less assured of an acceptable level of success*. This describes the milieu in which businesses and government operated during the thirty-year aftermath of World War II; largely unchallenged, they could do pretty much as they pleased. But then, abruptly, the world changed. Some observers date this fundamental shift to 1973 (the oil embargo by the OPEC nations); others to 1978 (the onset of the government's deregulation of business and industry); still others to 1980 (the election of Ronald Reagan, heralding the start of a decade of mergers, acquisitions, and intensified competition for investment dollars). The precise historical moment is unimportant here. What is significant is that vast organizational conglomerates suddenly found themselves saddled with the consequences of years of exclusionary and inbred policies.

That's what happened at the company where an executive we'll call Loren had worked for twenty-three years. During those years the firm, a manufacturer of telecommunications equipment and provider of related services, had held a commanding position in its market segment. Such was its dominance that the company was able to expand its operations widely and increase its earnings steadily; ongoing performance improvement seemed natural and effortless. With an abundance of resources and no real competitive challenge on the horizon, the firm focused primarily on refining its internal systems and practices. Included in the latter category were the company's hiring methods, which, by the early 1980s, had become nearly foolproof.

At this point in its development, the company knew exactly what kind of people it wanted to hire. Better yet, it knew just how to identify and select them. Over the years, it had employed an impressive array of performance analysts, psychologists, and statisticians to develop a sophisticated battery of tests designed to eliminate from consideration all individuals who failed to conform to the profile of the ideal candidate. This person would be pleasant, compliant, loyal, moderately intelligent, and devoid of strong or controversial opinions—the sort of individual perfectly suited to an image-conscious corporate bureaucracy concerned primarily with protecting its turf. The company successfully identified and hired thousands of these people during its glory years, and was lauded and rewarded for the uniform high quality of its corporate and field personnel.

But in the mid-1980s, the environment in which the firm had built and maintained its success abruptly changed. The deregulation of the telecommunications industry, in combination with the microcomputer revolution, altered the competitive picture dramatically: all at once, dominant players like Loren's company found themselves having to vie for the loyalty of customers whose business they had formerly owned. These industry giants had for the first time to contend with lean, aggressive upstarts who broke all the rules, or made up new ones while the contest was in progress. The new environment demanded innovation, risk taking, and flexibility—qualities that Loren, and many executives like him, saw as lacking within the ranks of their organization.

"Our people are good," Loren said vehemently. "They can present, explain, and deliver our solutions without missing a beat. But they don't think fast on their feet, and they're not what you'd call visionary in their outlook. This puts us at a disadvantage in today's crazy marketplace. We're always reacting, having to get back to the customer with a slightly less expensive or more streamlined version of one of our standard configurations."

In the early pages of this book, we talked about a typewriter manufacturer that had established and implemented hiring criteria that, in practice, sorted out the very kinds of employees it most needed. Loren's organization suffered from a similar malady. In employing state-of-the-art research and measurement technology to weed out those individuals who didn't fit its mold, the company had effectively closed its doors to the kinds of people and ideas it now needed to maintain its prosperity. When the firm issued an urgent call for innovation and risk taking, its members responded with a predictable array of tepid, maintenance-oriented marketing strategies and product enhancements. The company thus found itself in the untenable position of demanding creative and impulsive action from individuals it had selected *precisely because of their conventional thinking and relative lack of temperament*. This, in a nutshell, is how closed organizational systems become self-defeating. They rigorously exclude the kinds of people, ideas, and methods they most need to break free of stagnant patterns.

NEW PEOPLE, NEW IDEAS, AND NEW METHODS

To grow and prosper in an increasingly mutable world, the modern organization must open itself to individuals, ideas, and operating procedures that are *different*. We're not addressing the issue of staffing quotas based on race, gender, or age; these are superficial considerations that an organization can accommodate while continuing to remain closed off from meaningful change. We're talking instead about the need for an organization to embrace and encourage people and procedures that run counter to its ingrained dogmas and reactive tendencies. Without the constant (and, admittedly, often aggravating) challenge that arises from these sources, an organization is all too likely to lapse into replicative patterns that invariably justify themselves while contributing little to improved performance.

People
Open, thriving enterprises do not exclude people in ways that violate fair-hiring laws. Unfortunately, though, many organizations

have devised ingenious ways of complying with the letter of these laws, but not their spirit. The organization that makes a mere *pro forma* show of its openness to different kinds of people tends, in many instances, to remain closed to the contributions these people can make. What typically results is a tacit tokenism that undermines morale, lending weight to the notion that what an organization says and what it believes are two different things.

No outside force or agency can impose a spirit of true open-mindedness on a business, agency, or team. (Which explains why hiring quotas have yielded such indifferent results.) The organizations that have successfully opened themselves to new or different types of people have done so, we believe, primarily out of self-interest. They have come to recognize the perils of homogeneity; they believe in better performance through an altered internal chemistry. Some are wisely looking to break free of low-performance loops born of years of conventional, like-minded thinking. Others have found themselves repeatedly confronted with problems that demand skills or attributes in short supply among their internal ranks, while others have discovered that they need different types of people to take full advantage of unanticipated opportunities.

Consider the example of an agribusiness firm we once worked with. When the markets of Eastern Europe abruptly became accessible, the company's international marketers rushed in with offers of the kind of high-volume commodity deals it brokered with their traditional customers. But these new clients turned out not to be all that concerned with price-based supply contracts; they wanted instead to negotiate technology transfers and joint ventures. To compound matters, their representatives, having just emerged from an economic environment structured around five- and ten-year planning cycles, were uncomfortable with the pace at which the grain supplier wanted to move.

"We were at an impasse," recalled Leon, a vice president at the firm. "Our people had reached their wits' end. These new players struck them as antiquated in their assumptions and ridiculous in their demands. We thought more than once about scrapping the deal."

But instead of abandoning a potentially lucrative market, the leaders of the firm decided that maybe it didn't have the right kind of negotiators on its team. In an attempt to remedy the situation, the company hired several marketing executives and consultants who had lived for extended periods of time in Eastern Europe, as well as a few academic experts on the region. These individuals were assigned in groups of two or three to each of the current negotiating teams; their role was to provide a badly needed historical perspective to bear on what the company had come to view as an intractable business problem. They were also charged with the task of "reading the signs" the new clients sent out and translating them into requirements the company could address head on. As a result, the stalled negotiations began to move slowly ahead, with some of them leading to mutually profitable agreements.

The company's new, open-minded approach didn't end with this incident. The experience confirmed a suspicion that senior management had held for quite a while: they felt their enterprise had become too uniform in its makeup and too predictable in its thinking. They subsequently directed their personnel officials to cast a wider net when searching for potential employees. Over a period of two years, the population of the firm took on a markedly different cast, as more women, minorities, and people from unconventional backgrounds began to filter into the ranks. In short, the company opened itself to new people as a means of improving its performance. Along the way, it effectively preempted the problem of needing to take on token individuals to comply with government mandates.

Before moving on, we should mention that an organization's openness to different types of people extends well beyond its hiring practices. The great majority of ostensibly homogeneous organizations already have within their ranks numerous individuals who differ in terms more meaningful than their physical or cultural characteristics. We're talking here about the kind of strange individuals who somehow find their way into even the most monolithic organizations: mavericks, tinkerers, grumblers, and dreamers, as well as people given to odd dress, odd thought, and irregular working hours. The truly open organization not only makes a place for these people—it also listens to them. This doesn't mean that the organization has to act on outrageous protests or suggestions, or even be comfortable with them. But it does mean that weird opinions ought not to be rejected out of hand. Today's bizarre notion might well contain the germ of tomorrow's performance breakthrough.

It may be a mere coincidence, but the most successful enterprises we've observed number among their employees an assortment of former hippies, reformed ascetics, defrocked clergy, and people who seem to be walking contradictions: accountants with a loathing for numbers and bottom lines, human resource officers always looking for ways of automating high-level tasks and reducing professional staffs. Open-minded organizations do more than tolerate these nonconforming sorts; they also value them and treat them well.

Ideas

It's an ill-kept secret that much of modern organizational life is based on a mere handful of time-honored ideas and operating models. One is the notion of the classical capitalist, which casts each individual as a buccaneer bent on cutting a wide swath at the collective expense. Another is the model of mass production—of leveraging economies of scale and limiting individual responsibility to produce vast quantities of product at an ever-decreasing price. A third is the concept of bureaucracy, which implies an organizational structure built of accumulating hierarchical layers designed to exercise absolute control over a range of business activities. Most businesses and agencies are rooted in one or more of these notions, all of which more or less serve their purpose. Yet none is particularly new or flexible, and none seems to provide an answer to the kind of ambiguous dilemmas the world continues to serve up.

Open-minded organizations are well aware of this precarious situation; they know that some of their bedrock notions may no longer be working. That's why these enterprises persist in entertaining ideas that may have once seemed heretical, or hybrid notions that appear to contradict themselves. Take, for example, the problem of setting individual and group performance at odds with one another. Does the organization encourage the individual to excel regardless of the consequences, or does it constrain individual initiative in the interest of team, department, or company performance goals? The open organization is willing to test the notion that the two alternatives need not be mutually exclusive. Consider how Amanda at the data services firm, and Dave at the failing brokerage, struck a healthy and productive balance by combining the two. In both cases, senior management looked on the proposed solution as unworkable at best, and, at worst, subversive. Yet both organizations allowed the experiment to go forward, and in each case it reversed a deteriorating situation.

Another good example of how a new idea can reverse counterproductive organizational behavior is what ensued at a software development company when a manager named Ted challenged his organization's entire outlook on performance evaluation.

Ted was a smart guy; he hired people only on the basis of their software design and coding expertise, and only when he knew in his head *and* in his heart that they could do the work he planned to assign them. In the process, he sometimes skirted or bent the procedures set down by the company's personnel department. As a result, there was little love lost between Ted and the firm's senior personnel director. The conflict flared when, at the end of an appraisal cycle, Ted turned in a set of evaluations that rated every one of his employees as an above-average performer.

"This just can't be," the flustered personnel director protested when Ted submitted his appraisals. "Our performance appraisal policy is clear: employee ratings have to conform to a normal bell curve. That means 20 percent above average, 20 percent below, and 60 percent in the middle. You'll have to redo these appraisals if you want me to sign them."

Ted refused to revise his original evaluations. The personnel director then proceeded to call a summit meeting with the company president, who had approved the standard performance appraisal policy.

The session began amicably enough, with the CEO expressing a willingness to hear both sides of the dispute. The personnel director spoke first, reading the performance appraisal policy aloud and then citing the research on which it was based. He emphasized the firm's commitment to an appraisal policy based on performance relative to peers, adding that employees were not likely to improve unless management identified areas where they performed "below expectations." All in all, he made a sound case for his position—provided, of course, that certain assumptions were beyond questioning.

"I don't have a whole lot of research to quote," Ted said when it was time for him to speak. "But here is what I know. We say that we're committed to encouraging excellence, and that in the best of all worlds, *every one* of our employees would be a top performer. That's the goal, at least, and that's what I've always aimed at.

"But here we have a system," he continued, "that *establishes in advance that a certain number of our people—20 percent—will always be stigmatized as below average.* I mean, the contradiction seems obvious. I don't have any low performers in my group—I have two superstars and ten fine programmers. I'm not going to label any of them as below par."

"Well, what do you suggest, then?" the personnel director shot back, no longer so amicable. "It's easy to criticize . . . how would *you* identify and deal with the kind of performance problems inevitable in an organization of this size?"

Ted was ready for this. "What I'd do," he replied, "would be to get the 'problems' you're talking about out of the appraisal process. Those so-called problems are mostly our fault, anyway: they usually come up when we've made a bad hire or haven't found the right fit for a particular person. So I'd set up an appraisal form with only two categories: "Solid Performer" and "Star Performer." And if I had on staff someone I couldn't honestly put into one or the other, I'd refer that person to Personnel for remedial counseling, reassignment, whatever. But I wouldn't use that odd exception to justify a system that makes us seem like hypocrites."

The company president was persuaded: he agreed to accept Ted's evaluations as they had been submitted. He also directed Ted and the personnel director to work together in the coming months to develop an appraisal system along the lines that Ted had suggested. The firm subsequently adopted just such a system, and as a result the number of employees designated as below average dropped steadily, with no corresponding decline in overall organizational performance.

Methods

Methods are to ideas what actions are to thoughts. Although new methods often flow from a receptiveness to fresh ideas, they are not always based on a revolution in organizational thinking or a shift in fundamental principles. Being open-minded to new methods requires only that an organization look at alternative ways of doing the kinds of tasks or jobs it has always done. It's the simplest kind of innovation for an organization to achieve, and one that may evolve naturally from existing quality improvement, systems analysis, or strategic planning projects.

This is not to say that new methods do not sometimes involve some degree of adjustment in how an organization thinks about its operating procedures and goals. Until recently, for example, consumer goods manufacturers and retail stores had been engaged for decades in an ongoing war of mutual attrition. The manufacturers wanted to sell as much product as possible, to maintain brand recognition, and to smooth out production peaks and valleys; the stores, to buy goods at the lowest per-unit price and to have on hand enough product to meet customer demand. The weapons of choice for manufacturers in this fray were deals, coupons, and promotional programs, while the retailers wielded control over shelf space and local advertising. Back and forth the battle went for years, with neither side gaining a significant advantage. Then some bright soul discerned that the conflict, such as it was, was rooted in the problem of who would absorb the high cost of carrying excess inventory, and that each party had an interest in resolving this dilemma.

The concept of just-in-time inventory management had been around for years, but had repeatedly run up against two hard obstacles. The first was technological: the hardware and software required to capture real-time inventory data tended to be error prone and expensive. The second barrier was psychological: the management of inventory flow across company lines demanded a level of trust that was in short supply among long-time adversaries. But just as the microcomputer revolution removed the first obstacle, the success of Japanese manufacturing cartels struck hard at the second. As a result, manufacturers and retailers began to view themselves not as combatants, but instead as links in a chain of value that began with primary producers—farmers, miners, and refineries—and ended with the ultimate consumer. The once-abhorrent *idea* of an extended business enterprise, in combination with technological advances, yielded the new *method* we know as electronic data interchange, or EDI: former adversaries linked their computers via common networks and shared information they had once withheld from each other. This operating method has yielded stunning performance improvements for all the players involved. It has also changed the face of retail sales, bringing an increasingly wider assortment of products to customers at prices that often seem too good to believe.

But new methods like EDI, though cost-effective in the long run, are expensive to implement, and struggling organizations often lack the resources to avail themselves of the latest technological advances. As promised, none of our recommendations hinge on huge capital investments. We refrain from suggesting that a bogged-down business build new factories, for instance, or outfit its facilities with state-of-the-art computers, or buy up all its competitors. So let's turn now to an example of how a low-tech, low-cost new method can achieve startling results.

Remember Darlene and her staff of confused bank tellers? These tellers had been directed by headquarters staff to present an expanding array of financial products and services to the customers whose transactions they were processing. This hastily implemented program led to long lines at the branch, a decline in the number and frequency of customer visits, and a sharp increase in the number of errors the tellers made. These problems grew so severe that, as a stopgap measure, Darlene was forced to instruct her tellers to disregard their referral duties and to focus instead on fast and accurate customer service. She also had to acknowledge to her staff that senior management may not have taken into account the potential consequences of the teller referral program.

Yet a program along these lines remained a viable—perhaps even an essential—business strategy for the bank, which found itself competing with insurance companies, discount brokerages, and savings-and-loan institutions for customer dollars. Darlene was aware of this. Her problem was to figure out how to implement such a program without disrupting the traditional operations at the branch office. The solution she arrived at was so simple and straightforward that it came to be termed a "no-brainer" by the bank's marketing staff—none of whom, it should be added, had ever suggested it.

Darlene proposed to her manager that two signs be installed facing the entrance to the branch. One would direct customers who wanted fast, uncluttered service through a velvet rope cordon designated by an arrow; the other would point customers with special requirements or needs to a separate cordon. The two cordons fed into different clusters of service windows, where tellers stood prepared either to process transactions without ado or to present products designed to meet specialized banking and investment needs. Darlene's manager said the plan couldn't be adopted without approval from headquarters, and the home office marketing staff at first was less than enthusiastic.

"Some of them thought it was tacky," Darlene remembered. "They said it reminded them of the express lanes at supermarkets and discount stores. But that, I said, was just the point. They were the ones, after all, who had told us we needed to operate like a retail store."

Despite this initial reluctance, the plan was approved as a pilot project. The bank's marketing managers were willing to try anything that might resurrect their flagging teller referral program. And though it took some time to fine-tune the number of fast-service and full-service windows, a workable balance eventually emerged.

This new approach, which was eventually adopted in all of the bank's branch offices, yielded benefits that belied its simplicity. Tellers who felt locked into dead-end jobs came to view a position at the full-service window as a means of career advancement; what was once looked on as a burden came to be perceived as a reward. Better still, customers took well to the new arrangement. Once they became aware that express service was available within the bank, as well as at the drive-through window, more and more of them began to take advantage of this option. This, in turn, reduced the burden on the drive-through tellers, leaving them less prone to errors during hectic rush periods. It was that rare business scenario in which everybody seemed to win: tellers, customers, managers, and the marketers responsible for the program. Not to mention Darlene, who was subsequently promoted to the position of branch vice president.

THE TRAP OF FALSE OPEN-MINDEDNESS

You may be convinced by now of the need to open your organization to all sorts of outside influences. You may be willing to hire and listen to people with different backgrounds and unconventional attitudes, to evaluate each and every new idea currently floating around in the marketplace, and to scrutinize your methods and procedures in the hope of increasing their effectiveness. You may even be ready to embark on an organizational shopping spree, doling out piles of cash for innovative and flamboyant consultants, popular and provocative training programs, or company-wide re-engineering initiatives. You may have reached the point of frustration where you throw wide your arms and say, "That's it! We're finally going to bring in new blood and really shake things up around here."

We say: *Not so fast.*

Having extolled at length the benefits of opening up a closed organizational system, we have to point out that open-mindedness has its potential pitfalls. Foremost among these is the temptation to bombard a struggling company or work group with new training programs, management philosophies, and operating procedures. This temptation is especially strong among organizations that have struggled long and hard—but with little success—to boost themselves out of low-performance ruts. On discovering through painful experience that internal solutions don't work, such an organization often swings abruptly to the opposite pole, hastening to adopt every novel scheme or approach the world is currently serving up. It's relatively easy at this point for the organization to become infatuated with the notion and appearance of change, while remaining resistant to the tough-minded work required to bring about performance improvement.

This headlong rush toward the trendy and the new often lures an organization into a state of false open-mindedness, a malady now epidemic among our businesses, agencies, teams, and public service groups. We see symptoms of this malady in the corporation that proudly displays people of different genders and races on the cover of its annual report, but excludes these kinds of individuals from positions of leadership; in the football team that changes its offensive and defensive philosophies every other year, ignoring the root causes of its mediocre record; and in the government agency whose members are simultaneously undergoing so-called training in the areas of empowerment, customer focus, and quality improvement. In each of these cases, false open-mindedness serves not to encourage innovation, but instead to divert attention away from the fact that an organization is continuing to operate as usual, and to achieve its customary indifferent results. The chances are good that the corporate report with the happy faces on its cover will reveal yet another year of declining profits; that the football team will continue to lose more games than it wins; and that you'll still have to wait the better part of an hour to be served by the empowered, customer-focused, and quality-conscious clerk at the local licensing bureau.

In nearly every way, false open-mindedness conforms to the pattern of a self-defeating organizational behavior. Lacking the will or desire to bring about true change, the organization nonetheless feels compelled to show the world that it is moving in the right direction. To this end, it sets off in hot pursuit of an array of confusing management philosophies and programs without committing to any one of them. Believing in its heart of hearts that any given "solution of the month" will probably fail anyway, the organization refuses to allocate the resources or make the changes required to implement the new program successfully. Consequently, the program dies a lingering death, confirming the organization's initial misgivings about it. This cycle repeats itself over and over, until the patience of owners, members, and customers is finally exhausted, or until the organization runs out of money. In the mean time, organizational leaders have become even more firmly convinced that healthy change is impossible, and that their best hope for success lies in a return to the familiar. In the end, insincere open-mindedness is just another way of running in place.

How can a business or agency avoid this vicious, resource-depleting cycle? The burden falls on organizational leaders, who must do everything in their power to promote and sustain a climate of *true* open-mindedness among themselves and rank-and-file members. These leaders need to recognize the need to be highly selective about what to incorporate into their operations. Although an open-minded enterprise must be willing to entertain and evaluate virtually any potential solution to an endemic problem, it should adopt or incorporate only those ideas or methods that dovetail with its plans and goals. When it goes shopping for fresh solutions, the open organization ought to be looking for a good fit and durability. It ought to be wary of any approach that fails to meet these criteria, regardless of its stylishness or attractively low price.

This is where your organization's core beliefs come into play. If your company or work group has developed a clear and accurate picture of its core belief system, you can use this system as a means of evaluating proposed solutions to its performance problems. When considering a new philosophy, program, or procedure, you ought to ask the following questions:

- Does this alternative reinforce a healthy core belief we want to preserve or acquire?
- Does it counteract or expose as false an unhealthy belief we want to be rid of?
- Are we willing to take meaningful and highly visible action to support this alternative?

- Are we prepared to make a long-term commitment to this way of doing business, regardless of the setbacks we are likely to encounter?

If you cannot answer one of the first two and *both* of the last two questions affirmatively, then you probably need to look elsewhere for a solution to your problems. And should you decide to go ahead with a program that does not meet the above criteria, be sure to evaluate your motives honestly, making sure that you are not indulging for the sake of convenience or appearances in the no-win game of false open-mindedness.

TRAINING THE HIGH-PERFORMANCE ORGANIZATION

Training is a powerful tool for incorporating new people, ideas, and methods into an organization. Once organizational leaders have persuaded themselves of the viability of an innovative program or procedure, they should waste no time in deploying internal or external trainers to provide instruction in the new skills that rank-and-file members will need to make the innovation a success. The development and delivery of well-designed, company-wide training is one of the most meaningful and visible measures that organizational leaders can take to demonstrate their commitment to fresh thinking and the kind of performance improvement it can yield.

Like any other powerful tool, though, organizational training has the potential to do more harm than good. Organizations should always be aware of this, lest they fall into the habit of relying on retraining to solve problems that have little to do with skill deficiencies or knowledge gaps. In Chapter 5, we mentioned some of the more common abuses that can result from this approach: using a company's training resources to perform public relations tasks for senior management, exempting one or more key constituencies from instruction with company-wide implications, and implementing training programs that few organizational leaders truly believe in. We went on to point out that the consequences of these misguided efforts are often doubly disastrous. Not only do they fail to achieve their dubious ends, but they also cause the members of an organization to look askance at *all* training efforts—including those that are crucial for bringing about healthy change.

High-performing organizations train their people rigorously and continually. They have an obvious and legitimate reason for doing so: they are regularly introducing new people, new equipment, and new procedures into their operations, and training provides an ideal means of merging the old and the new. But these top performers are aware of the requirements for effective training as well as its limitations. So before they invest in the development or delivery of a particular training program, they ask and answer the following questions:

- *Does the training impart the information and/or skills that people need to perform effectively at a specific task or job?* Sound, well-designed training is geared toward communicating, and describing the application of, a particular body of knowledge or set of skills. A program that instructs electrical assembly workers in the operation of a new wave-soldering machine stands a good chance of achieving the objective of improving productivity or product quality. A workshop that purports to educate these same workers in the principles of "nonlinear thinking" ought to be subjected to considerable executive scrutiny.

- *Is the training timely?* Effective training is best delivered within a relatively narrow time frame. As a general rule, there's a six-month window of opportunity for training with regard to any major change in organizational operations. Training that is delivered more than three months in advance of the time when it's required is likely to be a faint memory by the time a change in equipment or procedures actually comes about. And training that occurs three or more months after a change has occurred is apt to prove redundant. The majority of those affected by a change will probably have already acquired on their

own the skills they need. Those who haven't are probably
not overly concerned with how well they do their jobs,
and thus pose a problem beyond the scope of
performance-oriented instruction.

- *Are the outcomes of the training measurable, and will the
  organization take the time to evaluate these results?* Too
  much of what passes for training in the modern
  organization is directed toward high-minded outcomes that
  can seldom be measured. Seminars and workshops that
  propose to improve employee attitudes, to transform
  followers into leaders, or to increase the self-esteem of
  individual members are, at best, difficult to evaluate in
  terms of their ultimate effectiveness. The leaders of self-
  defeating organizations are well aware of this
  phenomenon; they depend upon it to justify their
  haphazard training practices. Worse yet, they cite it as
  grounds for their failure to follow up on any of their
  training efforts, including programs whose results can
  easily be measured in terms of improved performance.

- *Is the organization willing to create or maintain a working
  environment that will support the training?* This, in our
  view, is the acid test that any training program must pass
  before it is loosed on the organizational masses. There's
  little or no point in teaching people new skills and
  approaches, then sending them back to an environment
  where it's impossible to apply this training. We once
  worked with a retail store that, in concert with a much-
  proclaimed commitment to customer service, dispatched
  all its point-of-sale personnel to a series of seminars on
  how to deal with problematic customers. Yet the store
  continued to measure the performance of its cashiers in
  terms of how many transactions they scanned into the
  registers and to thin their ranks to a point that made
  patient, cordial service next to impossible. To call such
  behavior self-defeating would be to give it more than the
  benefit of the doubt.

In summary, then, high-performance training is specific, timely, measurable, and, above all, supported by organizational policies and practices. A program that fails to meet any one of these criteria may be well intentioned, entertaining, provocative, or nicely suited to prevailing business and social trends; but training it is not, and the high-performance organization shuns the temptation to position it as such.

FIXING THE CLOSED ORGANIZATIONAL SYSTEM

Note that our criteria for high-performance training tend to exclude the kinds of warm, fuzzy personal enrichment programs that enjoy an enduring popularity among today's confused enterprises. Also excluded are the currently fashionable workshops and seminars on such provocative topics as diversity, group sensitivity, and gender politics. The reason we're suspicious of these training alternatives has little to do with the debatable issue of whether they actually work. Many of them are well intentioned and they are often embraced in the spirit of open-mindedness and healthy change. For all their apparent virtues, though, they serve ultimately to reinforce a pernicious assumption that self-defeating organizations invariably share: the notion that collective performance will improve once the behavioral and intellectual quirks of individual members have been effectively remedied. This is why self-defeating organizations so frequently find themselves in the business of fixing people, rather than fixing counterproductive patterns that yield consistently mediocre results.

Most organizations aren't very good at fixing people. Nor should they be; unless they are in the therapy business, their expertise lies elsewhere. When a nontherapeutic business or work group takes on the project of ministering to the maladies or psychological defects of its individual members, the results are predictably dismal. At best, this organization achieves a grudging, superficial conformity to officially sanctioned patterns of thought and action. It manages to program its people to be rigid, fearful, insincere, and dishonest. At worst, it undermines the credibility of its trainers, promotes cynicism, wastes money, and distracts itself from the critical chore of identifying and changing unhealthy patterns of collective behavior.

This cannot be emphasized enough: *a struggling organization's first order of business should be to repair or replace the self-defeating behavior patterns that thwart healthy activity and perpetuate low performance.* Until these patterns are changed or eliminated, any attempt at improving individual performance is likely to prove futile. Employees may return from a seminar or workshop feeling empowered, energetic, creative, and open to new alternatives. But if the system they return to remains fundamentally flawed or counterproductive, most of them will, like chameleons, once again take on the coloration of their surroundings. And rest assured that at least a few of them—often, sadly enough, the best and the brightest—will read the writing on the walls, and escape those walls at the first opportunity.

This is why the most crucial aspect of organizational openness is a willingness to take meaningful action that supports any new idea, method, or training program. Earlier we mentioned the disastrous predicament of the retail store that sent its cashiers off to be trained in customer service skills, but continued to pursue policies suggesting that its leaders didn't view customer satisfaction as a high priority. As a result, the cashiers soon forgot or disregarded most of what they had learned, and the store's patrons continued to complain vociferously about how they were treated. Because the company looked on retraining as a panacea to operational problems it was loath to address, it essentially squandered its precious training dollars and damaged in-store morale.

Consider, however, what happened at a regional telephone company that sent its customer service representatives to the same seminar attended by the store cashiers. Company managers correctly saw that improved customer relations could be achieved only if they supplemented this training with changes in their operating methods. Accordingly, they hired *more* telephone representatives to relieve the pressure on employees charged with handling customer complaints and inquiries. At the same time, they instructed their trainers to be on the lookout for any reps who seemed temperamentally ill equipped to the task of dealing with impatient customers, and to recommend that these employees be transferred to more suitable positions. And they insisted, moreover, that the training include a provision that would grant each phone representative the latitude to depart from the recommended customer-handling procedure whenever he or she deemed it necessary.

"We used to say around here that training works once in a blue moon," a customer service supervisor subsequently reported. "Well, this must have been our blue moon, because the new training and hiring programs seemed to work like a charm. The phone reps became more confident and productive, and our customers a whole lot happier. And best of all, it didn't cost that much in the long run."

People change only when their experiences indicate that change is in their best interest. The same can be said of organizations, which cannot possibly experience the benefits of improved performance until they depart from entrenched dogmas, then open themselves to fresh alternatives at strategic moments. Without this open-mindedness, the struggling organization will react time and again according to its tattered performance script. It will continue to make decisions whose predictable outcomes make the prospect for improvement seem increasingly remote. These kinds of decisions repeatedly afflict the weak and reward the strong, and skew the organizational performance picture for expedient or selfish reasons. Over time, such decisions rob an organization of its resiliency, causing its members to flinch at the mere mention of healthy, lasting change.

CHAPTER 11
Sharing Costs and Benefits

ORGANIZATIONAL leaders tell us time and again that their people are fundamentally hostile to innovation. They argue that even the most trivial modification of a traditional belief, policy, or procedure is apt to meet with stern resistance. They contend that their charges cling to outmoded practices the way infants cling to their blankets, emitting plaintive wails at the slightest hint of separation. To an extent, we agree. Within the confused and stricken environs of the modern organization, individuals are naturally disposed toward the familiar, which affords them both the promise of protection and the illusion of control. But we stop short of concurring with the conclusion that organizations cannot change simply because their members won't allow it. This belief has about it the quality of a self-fulfilling prophecy; it paralyzes an organization precisely at those moments when dramatic and unequivocal action is most needed. It provides the leaders of an organization with a convenient rationale for their hidebound maintenance-oriented policies. It also serves as a convenient escape clause in situations where even a moderately innovative course of action appears to have misfired.

"Well, what did you expect?" organizational leaders cry out in plaintive wails of their own. "The only way to improve is to make changes, and people just can't cope with change."

But is this really true? We find it curious that it's primarily in their on-the-job capacities that individuals are assumed to be antagonistic to fresh alternatives and improved options. In their personal lives, people have become, if anything, a bit *too* willing to embrace change; they switch brand loyalties, entertainment preferences, political allegiances, and even domestic partners with a frequency that befuddles market researchers and alarms social commentators. If last year's most fashionable bottled drink was pure, healthful mineral water, this year's might be a jazzy cola laced with food coloring, refined sugar, and caffeine. This season's top-rated television series may be a situation comedy based on the small foibles of suburban life, but in a matter of months it may find itself supplanted by a gritty, big-city cop drama. The political leaders in vogue at any given moment, whether young ideologues or gray eminences, live under the constant threat of being driven from power and replaced by their opposites. As options and the means of accessing them have multiplied, change has become a generally congenial rule of modern life.

On the basis of our discussions with workers, managers, and administrators, we've found that individuals and groups are not hostile to organizational change *per se* but rather to the array of cynical and ineffective policies that are often paraded before them under the banner of "change." Most rank-and-file members are more than ready to welcome clearly articulated initiatives that promise to advance their long-term interests. But they take a dim view of the heavy-handed solutions that reactive leaders are wont to impose on the organizational masses: the ostensible solutions we categorized earlier as replication techniques. When people have experienced change or innovation primarily as a negative phenomenon—a smoke screen for policies and practices that sorely afflict them while delivering little in the way of benefits—they are apt to regard new ideas and methods with an entirely justifiable suspicion.

This is why it's important for organizational leaders to make decisions with a steady eye on the full range of costs and benefits that may result. These costs and benefits ought to be evaluated not only in terms of their impact on an organization as a whole, but also on each of the enterprise's major constituencies. It's all too common for organizational strategists and decision makers to pursue alternatives that work solely to the benefit of ownership or senior management. Less common are policies that benefit rank-and-file members or customers at the expense of the company, but their long-term effect is the same. The favoring of one constituent group over its counterparts leads inexorably to patterns of replication that prove, in the end, to be mere short-term fixes or palliatives. They upset the delicate balance of interests on which high organizational performance is so often based.

THE FIVE ORGANIZATIONAL CONSTITUENCIES

Although it may present the world with a monolithic face and behave along uniform lines, the typical organization draws on the resources and skills of five discrete constituent groups: ownership, senior management, staff/line management, workers, and customers/clients. We call them "discrete" because they differ in terms of what they contribute to organizational performance and what they expect to receive in return. You might think of these groups and their interests the way we've shown them in the figure on page 232.

Each constituent group has its unique role and set of interests. Each must be regularly accommodated if an organization is to flourish and grow. Before you look at how an enterprise can bring off this delicate balancing act, consider how each constituent group serves as a partner in the long-term project of sustaining high performance.

As you read the descriptions that follow, keep in mind that it's possible for a single group or individual to function in multiple organizational capacities. This is especially true in small organizations, where one person may own the enterprise, serve as its senior manager, and even perform a variety of job-specific tasks. Even in large, complex corporate entities, the distinctions among internal constituencies often blur, with senior managers holding a large equity stake in the enterprise, or staff and line management doing a considerable amount of hands-on work. The phenomena of

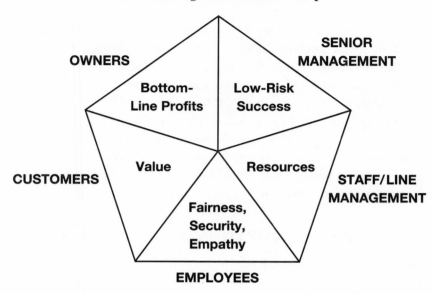

downsizing and flattening the organization have, in recent years, blurred many of the traditional distinctions among constituent groups and their individual interests.

The Interests and Expectations of Ownership

An organization's ownership is made up of those individuals or groups who hold an equity stake in its plant, equipment, cash reserves, and other essential resources. Directly or indirectly, ownership provides the dollars and authority an enterprise needs to conduct its business. An owner's official title and type of investment varies, depending on how and where organizational boundaries are set. If you're talking about a corporation, then ownership consists of company shareholders—particularly, those individuals or groups who hold a majority of the firm's stock. However, if the entity you're looking at is a division or department of a larger enterprise, its general manager or chief operating officer often functions as a *de facto* owner, securing funds, allocating resources, and charting a general course of action for what amounts to an independent enterprise. Government organizations and public agencies pose a more complicated scenario: although technically owned by the general public, they are under the operational control of elected or appointed proxies who, for all practical purposes, enjoy most of the prerogatives of legal proprietorship.

These prerogatives are what differentiate organizational owners from the members of other constituent groups. Regardless of the level at which you define an organization, its ownership is made up of the individual or group that holds the ultimate power of approval over any plan, decision, or operating strategy. Owners are granted this power in exchange for investing capital or assuming responsibility. So if you're looking to identify the functional owner of your organization, think of who stands to gain the most in terms of financial rewards or career advancement from its success—and, conversely, who will absorb the greatest loss if it fails or falls into a pattern of stagnant performance.

Because they risk their dollars and bear the ultimate responsibility for an organization's fate, owners have an overriding interest in bottom-line performance. This is both a blessing and a curse when it comes to cultivating long-term success. On the one hand, ownership's abiding concern about the bottom line tends to promote accountability among the other constituent groups: they know what is expected from them and, for the most part, they benefit from this knowledge. On the other hand, owners who are fickle, demanding, and obsessed with short-term gains are likely to encourage the kind of expedient decision making that leads, at best, to windfalls that can't be sustained, and, at worst, to the development of self-defeating organizational habits. Where ownership is not committed to long-term success, the prognosis for ongoing performance improvement is poor.

The Interests and Expectations
of Senior Management

Senior management provides an organization with vision and leadership. These are the people who decide what an organization will look like and what level of performance it ought to achieve, then offer general guidance on how these expectations are to be met. In large organizations, senior managers often carry such titles as president, chief executive officer, or chief operating officer. Their immediate staffs often serve in a senior management capacity, as do other corporate officers: the company controller, the chief financial officer, the head of legal affairs, the director of strategic planning. In an organization that is defined at a lower level of the corporate hierarchy, the role of senior management is often filled by a staff or line manager who has assumed responsibility for shaping the identity and steering the evolution of a division or department.

What motivates senior managers? In many instances, their interests are akin or identical to ownership's. A senior manager may, in fact, hold an equity stake in an enterprise, or may be compensated in the form of stock options or performance bonuses that augment an annual salary. Other top executives may be less interested in financial incentives than in burnishing their reputations or enhancing their credibility. The difference between these two approaches to organizational leadership has a major implication in terms of what senior managers are likely to expect of their people. Those with a financial stake in an organization will naturally be concerned with performance in terms of bottom-line profitability. Those keenly attuned to image-building may forsake high dividends and earnings per share in favor of a more modest success that conforms to an idiosyncratic personal vision or strategy. Both approaches have obvious strengths and weaknesses. Bottom-liners are prone to compromise an organization's future in the interest of achieving short-term success. Image-builders are apt to cling beyond the point of practicality to their own ideas, dreams, and pet projects, failing to maximize the benefits of any breakthrough that is not of their own design.

Regardless of the source of their motivation, senior managers share a common dilemma. Although they are burdened with many of the responsibilities of ownership, they often lack ownership's ultimate authority to say yes or no at key strategic moments. Senior managers can be overruled, second-guessed, dismissed, and replaced—and, with an ominous frequency, they are. This may explain why, in so many of the scenarios we've described, senior management is cast time and again in the villain's role; to the organizational masses, these leaders often appear to be self-aggrandizing, self-perpetuating, and always willing to hedge their bets.

Here, however, perception is often at odds with reality. Rarely have we met a senior manager who, for whatever reason, is not continually searching for a means of improving performance and achieving the grand breakthrough or organizational triumph. The problem is, in the real world these opportunities aren't all that readily available. Aware of this and aware, too, that ownership is sternly observing from the wings, senior management gravitates naturally toward low-risk approaches designed primarily to minimize potential losses. If not countermanded by personal courage or other organizational forces, this tendency becomes habitual and self-perpetuating. As senior management becomes more and more risk-aversive, it becomes less and less popular in the minds of the organizational masses.

The Interests and Expectations of Staff/Line Management

Once upon a time, the halls of business and government were populated by hundreds of well-groomed and well-spoken individuals who moved about with grace and confidence, but without apparent purpose. They held impressive but obscure titles, occupied spacious and comfortable offices, and indulged in frequent travel and long lunches. They were known as "middle managers," and, for better or worse, we'll probably not see their like in any number again. They were casualties of the recent spate of organizational downsizing, restructuring, and reengineering programs. Many were cut loose and left to fend for themselves in the job-poor wilderness. Of those who remained, a fortunate and opportunistic few were elevated into the realm of senior management. The rest were added to the hard-working ranks of our third organizational constituency: staff/line management.

These are the people who actually run today's enterprises. They are in charge of plants, divisions, departments, and projects; they are assigned measurable goals and rigorously held to them. They provide the organization with its operational expertise; they understand work flows, production processes, and the intricacies of intraorganizational hand-off points and boundaries. They know how to ship an order, manage budgets and schedules, acquire new equipment, or troubleshoot a stalled assembly line. Though they are often designated as managers, this need not always be the case. In small departments or organizations where the titular manager has assumed the role of planner and thinker, the line manager's role is often filled by a capable and experienced foreman, an expert equipment operator, or even a trusted clerical worker.

Where senior managers are often trapped between the contradictory imperatives of organizational maintenance and growth, staff and line managers are often faced with the dilemma of improving performance without disrupting orderly work flows and procedures. They are more caught up in the present moment than senior management tends to be; they decide in favor of efficiency or change largely on the basis of their most recent and pressing problems. This is both their strength and their weakness: they know how to react quickly and effectively, but may not consider how their decisions affect the larger organizational performance picture. They also are prone to become enamored of new tools, gadgets, and technologies. Because these devices often provide effective solutions to operating problems, staff and line managers may come to see them as the answer to every question.

What do staff and line managers expect from an organization? Well, like everyone else, they pine for promotions, pay raises, and job security. But these things aside, what operating managers need and want most are the *resources* required to sustain and improve performance. They expect adequate funding, functional (if not state-of-the-art) equipment, and, above all, qualified people. This often puts operating managers at odds with senior management and ownership, many of whom persist in believing that ill-trained, ill-equipped, and uncommitted workers can achieve performance breakthroughs if they are properly "managed."

The Interests and Expectations of Employees
Into this fourth constituent group we put any organizational member who neither holds an ownership stake nor fills a manage-

rial role. At first glance, this categorization might seem overly broad: what, after all, does a corporate attorney have in common with a secretarial worker at one of the firm's branch offices? As it turns out, quite a bit. Both provide the organization with two essential commodities: labor and technical skills. The company attorney with her knowledge of the law and the typist with his word-processing acumen are serving the organization in the same way. They are bringing their expertise and energy to the task of adding value to an organization's products or services. What's more, they are doing so with full awareness that much of the value they create will accrue to the benefit of other constituent groups.

Don't interpret this to mean that we view organizational employees as the poor, exploited masses. Most are adequately paid and relatively well treated, even in today's lean and increasingly mean organizational climate. And employees ought never forget that their organizations provide them with a context and an arena in which to perform. It's tough to make a living as a soldering machine operator, a quality inspector, or a policy analyst outside of organizational walls. With this in mind, rank-and-file employees should resist the temptation to frown on ownership and senior management's preoccupation with increased profits, or operating management's single-minded obsession with improved effectiveness and productivity.

For their part, the owners and managers of high-performing organizations need to acknowledge and respect a few fundamental expectations that rank-and-file members rightfully hold. The first of these is to be compensated at market value, at a level commensurate with their skills. Technological advances aside, it's absurd for management to assume that a worker earning seven dollars an hour will perform as well as a person earning twice that amount. (Unless, of course, the latter is grossly overpaid, which is another problem altogether.) Secondly, employees expect some measure of security; or, in situations where security cannot be guaranteed, fair and honest warning that their positions may be eliminated. And finally, what today's workers expect from their employers is a kind of *empathy*: a willingness on the part of organizational leaders to take their perspective into account when decisions are made. High-performing enterprises understand this, which explains why they shun the self-defeating practice of blaming rank-and-file employees whenever sales decline, profits slump, or quality problems arise.

The Interests and Expectations of Customers/Clients

Although they are not part of an organization, customers and clients play a vital role in its overall performance picture. They are the ultimate judges of how well an enterprise is doing; they vote with their dollars, ballots, and opinions. If they like an organization's products and services, they continue to buy, use, and endorse them. If not, they turn elsewhere, and organizational performance suffers. In this oblique way, they have as much control over what a business or agency does as do its owners, but with one crucial difference: customer approval or rejection of an organization's policies is delivered on a time-delayed basis. By the time it becomes clear that customers and clients have found an organization wanting, it is may be too late to turn the situation around. Consider the case of the American auto industry, whose customers seemed content for years to put up with inferior, over-priced cars. But in the 1980s, and apparently overnight, the public turned a cold shoulder toward these shoddy offerings, sparking an industry-wide crisis that has only recently shown signs of abating.

High-performing enterprises have taken to heart the lesson that automakers learned through traumatic experience: customers and clients matter, and when neglected or abused they strike back with a devastating vengeance. That's why so many organizational resources and so much energy has been devoted in recent years to identifying customer wants and needs, analyzing demographic trends and buying patterns, and surveying customer opinions. In general, this has been a healthy development. It has caused organizations to look beyond their sheltered walls for guidance and direction, and has inspired them to offer better products and higher levels of service at fair and competitive prices. Moreover, it has jolted many of our more imperious enterprises out of their traditional complacency, refreshing their awareness of marketplace dynamics. Customer service has become the gospel of many an organization, and with good reason.

But while it's important for a business or agency to listen to what its customers are saying, it's perhaps just as important for an enterprise to take such suggestions with a grain or two of salt. For one thing, customer opinion invariably lags behind the technological curve and ignores economic reality. Customers, clients, and political constituents are often lacking in expertise and information; they can offer general or amorphous guidance, but are seldom equipped to provide specific, workable solutions to an organization's problems. For another thing, customers and clients are notoriously fickle, which makes it precarious for any organization to revamp its policies, practices, and product line on the basis of this week's opinion polls.

An organization that is looking to improve its performance must always be willing to listen respectfully to the suggestions of its customers and constituents. But healthy, durable enterprises refuse to pander to the transitory whims of their clienteles. They know that they cannot possibly win every popularity contest, and they accept the occasional loss as one of the costs of long-term success.

COSTS, BENEFITS, AND ORGANIZATIONAL CONSTITUENCIES

Understanding the roles and interests of these five constituencies is one of the keys to making sound, healthy organizational decisions. And in the great majority of situations, lasting performance improvement can be achieved only if an organization clarifies and refines its decision-making processes. When an enterprise arrives at a strategic moment, it is essentially confronted with a choice between the low-performance loop and its high-performance counterpart. Once it has opted for one or the other, any measures that follow will reflect this initial choice. If the choice is shortsighted or skewed too severely in favor of a particular constituent group, it will yield consequences that cry out for expedient or biased remedies. But if it is insightful and well grounded, it will steer the organization in the direction of performance enhancement.

Organizational decision making goes habitually awry for any number of reasons. In a few rare instances, a business or agency finds itself in a situation where it truly has no viable options, and must of necessity opt for the least of several evils. This typically occurs when an enterprise has reached the end of its tether— when it has indulged in self-defeating patterns for so long that it has depleted its store of healthy options and adaptive resources. In most cases, though, low-performance decisions are the product of hastiness, short-term thinking, or a tendency to pander to the interests of a particular group. Each of these causes can be remedied, provided that each organizational constituency is honestly committed to the project of achieving long-term success.

The techniques that follow are designed to slow down the decision-making process, to clarify what we call the *cost/benefit narrative* an organization develops for a scenario, and to balance consequences among the five organizational constituencies. They do not constitute a formula for organizational infallibility: there's an element of risk involved in every major decision an organization makes. But if diligently applied, these techniques will more often than not result in decisions that an organization can justify without equivocation or denial. These decisions may not immediately put money in the bank, but they will allow an organization to emerge even from ostensible failure with its integrity and collective thinking intact.

Clarify Your Cost/Benefit Narrative

In moments of crisis or challenge, organizational leaders and strategists invariably look at the costs and benefits of each option available to them. Typically expressed in financial or other numerical terms, these projected consequences provide what seems to be an objective picture of what an organization can expect from each potential course of action it is considering. In theory, the organization looks at these numbers, then opts for an alternative that promises to deliver the greatest benefit at the lowest cost.

Now if the world really worked this way, no organization would ever make an ill-informed or disastrous decision, and accountants would reign as corporate kings. But in the mutable world of the modern organization, major decisions are seldom made solely on the basis of hard facts. They are based instead on subjective *interpretations* of seemingly objective data—or on the cost/benefit narrative that organizational leaders and planners construct from the raw numbers. No problem here; in healthy enterprises, honest decision makers formulate cost/benefit narratives that reveal significant truths about the prospects for long-term performance improvement. In confused or struggling organizations, however, executives and strategists tend to settle repeatedly on narratives that are improbable, skewed, or downright bizarre—and, even worse, to act upon these fanciful assumptions.

Self-defeating organizations develop distorted cost/benefit narratives for one of two reasons: they need to justify a course of action they have already decided to pursue or they want to rule out any alternative they deeply fear. Where executives and strategists are thus motivated, the process of analyzing costs and benefits becomes a hollow formality. The creativity these leaders ought to bring to bear on a problem is instead applied to the formulation of artful rationales meant to finesse problematic moments. How can they accomplish this feat? They can manipulate consequences and time frames, comparing this month's apples with next year's oranges. If, for example, the short-term benefits of a strategy are high, and if its projected long-term costs are low, the two can be juxtaposed in a way that supports whatever approach the decision makers wish to advance. Another clever tactic is to ignore or assign a minimal dollar figure to the qualitative costs that hasty, reactive decisions are certain to impose. Yet another is to develop cost/benefit narratives that perpetually favor the organizational powers-that-be, even though they might systematically undermine larger plans and goals. Skewing cost/benefit narratives via any of these means goes beyond mere rationalization. It is self-defeating organizational behavior in its most corrosive form.

There are ways of avoiding this self-perpetuating charade, and we advise any organization concerned with long-term performance to make consistent use of them. In the interest of clarifying cost/benefit narratives, organizational decision makers ought to make a regular practice of ignoring short-term benefits, assessing qualitative costs, and apportioning both costs and benefits among the five organizational constituencies.

Ignore Short-Term Benefits   The true cost/benefit picture surrounding a potential strategy or policy involves both immediate and deferred gains and losses. Come time for a decision, though, the former typically overshadow or obscure the latter. As we mentioned earlier, ownership and senior management are naturally drawn toward alternatives that promise a rapid return on investment and the appearance of organizational prosperity. This influential perspective frequently serves as a lens that magnifies short-term benefits beyond their actual significance, causing decision makers to opt all too often for alternatives that are merely expedient or temporarily lucrative.

To counteract this tendency, organizations that are in pursuit of long-term health and stability need to factor short-term benefits out of the cost/benefit picture when contemplating key decisions. There are at least two highly practical reasons for adopting this approach. The first is that it slows down the decision-making process, allowing organizational leaders and strategists to consider alternative—and, usually, more viable—cost/benefit scenarios. Ignoring potential short-term gains often has the effect of forcing decision makers to ask themselves if the course of action they are about to endorse is, in fact, in the best interests of the organization as a whole. Stripped of the allure of its immediate payoff, many a counterproductive policy or program shows its true colors, many of them less pleasing than they seemed during the course of a cursory or *pro forma* analysis.

The second reason for disregarding potential short-term benefits is that they are seldom fully realized. We pointed out in our discussion of organizational costs that the windfall gains of shortsighted decisions are frequently consumed in the process of minimizing consequences. The company that shuts down a facility and lays off its staff may seem to realize short-term gains in the form of reduced payroll costs, cuts in its operating overhead, and a one-time tax write-off. But the company ought to ask itself how many of these windfall dollars will actually end up in its coffers, and how

many will ultimately be expended in the form of severance packages, legal settlements, so-called performance bonuses bestowed
on bruised egos, and the subsequent procurement of the services
or capabilities the firm no longer has at its disposal. An honest
evaluation of these residual costs often robs reactive solutions of
much of their superficial luster, showing them to be at best break-
even propositions.

We worked with an auto executive who came to realize this
when his company was thinking seriously of shutting down its
glass manufacturing subsidiary. At first glance, the case looked
open and shut: the glass manufacturer seemed incapable of
improving its indifferent performance, and there were several
offshore suppliers waiting in the wings to provide auto glass at
favorable rates. But having recently experienced the ravages of a
similar cut-and-dried solution—one that involved liquidation of a
tire subsidiary—this particular executive was more than willing to
set aside the short-term benefits of the proposal at hand. He knew
that the closing of the tire plant had taken a dire toll, not only on
the laid-off workers and their families, but also on company morale as a whole.

He was also aware that once internal competitors were out of
the picture, the firm's offshore tire suppliers had begun to have
convenient second thoughts about the pricing policies they had
agreed to, and that quality problems had led to an unanticipated
increase in inspection and testing costs. These experiences left
him skeptical of the ostensible benefits of closing the glass subsidiary. By repeatedly raising danger flags when the matter came
up for discussion, he eventually persuaded the company to abandon this shortsighted option and to focus instead on helping the
subsidiary firm break free of its stubborn low-performance
patterns.

Assess Your Qualitative Costs Qualitative costs make organizations nervous. They are the trolls lurking beneath the jerry-
built bridges that businesses and agencies view as shortcuts to
high performance. Organizations know these nemeses by a variety
of common names: low morale, high turnover, territorialism,

reduced innovation. And while no one is sure of what they will look like or when they will appear, everyone is aware that they may spring up without warning and demand immediate redress. This is the essence of the problem that qualitative costs pose for struggling organizations: they are both undeniable and unmeasurable. Low-performing enterprises solve this dilemma by ignoring or denying potential qualitative costs. At decision-making time these consequences are simply left unmentioned, allowing organizational leaders to feign surprise when qualitative costs finally assert themselves.

A better approach to the problem of qualitative costs is to assign them the kind of *quantitative* value or impact that decision makers can comfortably deal with. This approach can admittedly take a lot of time, data gathering, and careful analysis; an organization needs to develop accurate and flexible models that are capable of comparing performance levels before and after a decision has been implemented. But several businesses and consulting groups have made significant progress in the area of assessing qualitative costs. As the long-term consequences of the recent rash of corporate retrenching and restructuring have come due, performance-oriented organizations have begun to assign dollar figures to the true costs of reactive policies. The figures at this point are crude, but nonetheless telling. We hear, for example, that it may cost a company as much as $10,000 to lay off a single low-level worker; or that a firm stands to lose a month's worth of net productivity per $10,000 of income for each employee that it dismisses or replaces. The implications of these figures are stunning. They suggest that a company that lays off 100 assembly or clerical workers incurs an immediate *$1,000,000* liability, and that replacing 100 employees with an average annual salary of $30,000 results in a net loss of *300 months* (3 months per worker) of net productivity. These are not insignificant numbers. They point to long-term costs that even a thriving enterprise would be hard pressed to minimize or absorb.

Another method of factoring in qualitative costs is simply to bring common sense to bear on the problem they pose. The executives and managers of high-performing enterprises lead with their hearts as well as their heads; they make strategic decisions as much by intuition as by raw numbers.

Zack, the owner of an injection molding plant, made staffing and competitive-bidding decisions with one eye clearly focused on qualitative considerations. He was aware that the success of his plant depended largely on its ability to fill large orders in limited time schedules, and that this often meant that workers had to put in long, stressful hours when delivery deadlines neared. But his knowledge of human nature also told him that he could count on these employees to rise to such challenges only if he, in turn, had demonstrated a willingness to accommodate their needs in fallow periods. He knew that at make-or-break moments, he couldn't legitimately count on the loyalty of workers who viewed themselves as mere pawns or chattel.

So while his competitors resorted to spasmodic mass layoffs and cutthroat bidding during economic downturns, Zack held his ground. He maintained a loyal and capable staff through thick and thin, then watched with detached interest as his rivals attempted to meet their unrealistic commitments through the efforts of surly, unreliable, and inexperienced workers. Year in and year out, Zack maintained a profitable, high-performing enterprise. His competitors, who rose and fell with the economic tides, often asked him how he did it.

"It's no great secret," he typically replied. "You treat people with respect. The company has its needs, they have theirs—we want to make money, they want good jobs. Balancing the two means you sometimes lose an order or live with higher than necessary labor costs. But in return, you get their best effort at crunch time, and that's when the game is won or lost."

Apportion Your Costs and Benefits Among Organizational Constituencies We now come to the key technique for making better and more innovative decisions. High-performing enterprises, we've discovered, are in the habit of evaluating alternatives according to their potential impact on ownership, senior management, line management, employees, and customers. Having developed a clear and unstinting picture of the costs and benefits of a particular course of action, these organizations take the further step of determining what it might mean for each of these constituencies. This doesn't mean that they unfailingly achieve a perfect balance among the five interest groups. Economic necessity or opportunity often forces them to make decisions that favor a particular constituency over its counterparts. But they do so knowingly; they don't delude themselves that they are pursuing a course of action "in the interests of the organization" when, in fact, it works primarily to the benefit of ownership and senior management. This awareness is crucial to an organization's long-term health. It prevents an enterprise from falling into the self-defeating trap of rewarding one constituent group repeatedly, and repeatedly penalizing others.

The inequitable apportionment of costs and benefits sets the table for long-term disaster. In recent years, we've witnessed countless scenarios where an organization has consistently implemented policies that benefit owners and top managers at the expense of all other constituent groups, almost invariably with cataclysmic results. The Wall Street scandals of the past decade come to mind, as do the savings and loan fiasco and the rash of leveraged buyouts that have left a few key leaders wealthy beyond their dreams, and their companies in utter shambles. You could argue that none of these organizations was overly concerned with long-term performance, and you'd probably be right. Still, their ultimate fate is revealing.

At the opposite pole lie those organizations that are obsessed with placating the rank-and-file masses, regardless of the larger consequences. Our national educational agencies, for example, have been so single-minded in advancing the interests of teachers and administrators that they have neglected the consequences for the taxpayers who fund and consume education services. As a result, we approach the year 2000 with an educational system ideally suited to the early 1960s: a vast bureaucracy constrained by rules, numerical quotas, and outmoded and discredited notions about what students need to learn and how they ought to learn it. And until recently, our auto industry tried to have it both ways, rewarding shareholders and senior managers with fat bonuses, and workers with similarly fat labor contracts. The cost of this cozy arrangement was passed on to customers in the form of declining product quality and escalating prices, and we all know how that panned out.

High organizational performance cannot be sustained if one or two constituent groups are perpetually rewarded or afflicted. Sooner or later, the organization will become top heavy, bottom heavy, or strapped for the resources it needs to continue to operate profitably. We recently worked with a software firm headed by an executive who seemed to have taken this notion to heart. He divides the net profits from each of the firm's contracts into two lump sums. Half the profits are deposited in a corporate account that can be drawn on only with stockholder consent. The other half are divided equally among all the company's employees, who can take their reward either as taxable income or as shares of stock in the enterprise. In the event that the firm loses money on a contract, the net loss is deducted either from the company account or the individual equity accounts, again on the basis of a majority vote. The genius of this approach is that it neatly merges the interests of both owners and workers; in many cases, they are one and the same. When performance drops, company owner/employees can opt either to tap into company resources or their own equity assets: they can choose, in larger terms, between long-term organizational viability and immediate personal gain. In a surprising number of cases, they opt for the former.

"It's worked out well so far," this executive told us. "At first we thought of giving performance bonuses outright, but that can be a problem: people come to expect them and get demoralized when we can't afford it. We wanted to give people a real stake in our success, but we needed to impress on them that ownership has its risks. Handing out bonuses only reinforces the idea that rewards are arbitrarily granted by management, rather than earned through cooperative effort."

BETTER DECISIONS YIELD LASTING BENEFITS

When you work from accurate cost/benefit scenarios and acknowledge the interests of their constituencies, you're drawn toward better decisions. For one thing, this process brings decision makers face to face with the full range of consequences that are likely to flow from an expedient action. This alone is often enough to dissuade them from their traditional remedies; the prospect of having to pay or minimize the costs of hasty reactions is seldom inviting. More importantly, the process of refining a cost/benefit narrative and evaluating the implications at all organizational levels has the effect of slowing the rate at which decisions might otherwise be made. And more than anything, struggling organizations typically need to *slow down*. Escalating or intensifying the pace of counterproductive activity does not make it any less self-defeating. It only defers until later the point at which an organization needs to take a contemplative and clearheaded inventory of where it is going and what it hopes to accomplish.

"When you don't know what to do, be sure to do it in a hurry." This seems to be the motto of all too many of today's self-defeating organizations. They mistake mere activity for meaningful action, and reaction for innovative response. They repeat the errors of the past, until finally their margin for error has been all but eroded. Then they throw up their hands, wondering why the benefits they have been pursuing never seem to accrue. On surveying the organizational ranks, they see only low morale, divisiveness, cynicism, and dulled thinking. They wonder what they should do. They pay others to tell them.

Our advice: *If you're unsure, do nothing—not, that is, until you've taken the time to assess potential costs and benefits thoroughly*. It's better for a self-defeating organization to take no action at all than to react under pressure in a habitual way. If your firm's last four reorganizations haven't improved performance, there's little reason to believe that a fifth will do the trick. If a half-dozen retrenchments have failed, it's unlikely that one more will turn the situation around. There's no surefire solution to the problem of improving performance over the long term. Organizational health results from action, and successful action results from decisions that appraise consequences accurately and balance them equitably. The benefits that flow from such decisions provide an organization with a lasting and invaluable advantage: an abiding faith in its ability to do the right thing.

CHAPTER 12

Maximizing Benefits and Owning Success

SELF-DEFEATING organizations are so preoccupied with what they do wrong that they often fail to capitalize on what they do right. Their stagnant performance and failure to replicate past successes leave them wondering if they have any viable strengths or special capabilities. They brood long and hard on the notion that the world may have passed them by. Meanwhile, they continue to pour resources and energy into the onerous task of minimizing recent miscues, patching leaks and polishing brass on an organizational vessel that remains firmly anchored. Believing they are ineffectual and immobile, they proceed to behave accordingly, disregarding any evidence that runs counter to their sense of collective futility.

Such evidence abounds, even in organizations with relatively undistinguished track records. The majority of self-defeating organizations are far too pessimistic about their prospects for success: in the absence of a recent triumph or breakthrough, they morosely conclude that they are saddled from top to bottom with patterns of low performance. This attitude is at least in part attributable to the winner-take-all mentality that has become pervasive in our increasingly competitive world.

When owners, customers, and organizational members themselves respond to modest or incremental achievement with an indifferent shrug, a company or agency is bound to start wondering what it is doing wrong. Once it has begun to wonder, an organization may fixate on those areas where it falls short of leaders in its field. Gradually (and, initially, without good reason) the organization's belief in itself is eroded. The enterprise then assumes a defensive posture that offers little true protection and scant opportunity for improvement and growth.

An alternative approach—one that successful enterprises incorporate with apparent effortlessness into their daily operations—is for an organization to maximize the impact of each and every positive result it achieves. High-performing businesses, agencies, and teams do not rise to their lofty status because they are infallible in their decision making and flawless in their execution of plans and procedures. They prevail instead by focusing on what they have done well and by doing more of it. They discern cells or pockets of high performance in the midst of ostensible debacles, celebrate innovation even when it does not immediately show up on the bottom line, and allow success—rather than failure—to chart the course for healthy organizational change. If they make a miscue, they acknowledge and pay the associated costs promptly, which allows them to proceed unencumbered toward a better day.

And when that long-awaited day finally arrives, thriving enterprises waste no time in taking full ownership of the success they have achieved. In a sense, owning the benefits your organization achieves is the opposite of blaming consequences on forces beyond your control. If your company or agency anticipates failure, you and your colleagues will always be looking for scapegoats. This momentarily relieves the pressure on your group, but at the same time robs you of the ability to control your fate.

If you're a member of a high-performing enterprise, however, you may seldom have reason to cast your fortune to the capricious winds. Instead of assigning blame, you and your colleagues probably focus on the benefits you've achieved. Without even thinking about it, you may well link these outcomes to positive aspects of your organization's character. You may do so consciously and deliberately, demonstrating how breakthrough ideas, effective performance patterns, and healthy thinking flow from sound beliefs and practices. In taking full ownership of its triumphs, your organization puts itself in the position to repeat them. It learns through experience how—and why—nothing succeeds like success.

MAXIMIZING BENEFITS

The executives and managers we've talked with sometimes have trouble telling the difference between minimizing and maximizing. Why, they wonder, does the one perpetuate low-performance patterns, while the other improves the chances for organizational success? Aren't they both legitimate ways of casting a favorable light on a less than attractive performance picture? Don't minimizing and maximizing amount, in the end, to more or less the same thing? No.

The key difference between minimizing and maximizing is a matter of focus and intent. Recall from Chapter 7 that minimizing is directed primarily at the lingering and unpalatable costs of reactive decisions and policies. Its goal is to deny that these costs exist, or, that failing, to alter how they are perceived in the collective organizational mind. The organization that compulsively seeks to minimize the costs of its actions is forever at odds with the reality of its performance. It depletes its resources and adaptive energy in a protracted conflict it cannot hope to win: a war against the truth.

In contrast, maximizing embraces the reality of the moment at hand. When costs are fully and promptly paid, the organization is free to focus on the benefits it has realized and to build on these healthy developments. Where the beleaguered, self-defeating organization sees only corrosive and ominous costs, the performance-oriented business or agency discerns signs of excellence, evidence of innovation, and grounds for legitimate hope. High-performing enterprises maximize as a means of achieving eventual success, then position this success as a rationale for system-wide change.

Identify Cells or Pockets of High Performance

Nearly every functional organization has within it cells or pockets of high-performance activity. (If it didn't, it would shortly reach the point of collapse or disintegration, as any number of the examples in this book suggest.) The manufacturer of generic pharmaceuticals that rates itself low on the innovation scale may, in fact, be regularly achieving significant breakthroughs in the areas of production scheduling and procurement. The midsized auto dealership that can't quite meet its competitors' prices may have much to offer in terms of sales expertise and follow-up customer service. The school district whose students seldom achieve stellar scores on their SATs may at the same time have a remarkably low dropout rate, or may be largely free of problems stemming from drug abuse and violence. Each of these organizations has, it seems to us, good reason for believing itself capable of growth and change. It simply needs to bring to bear on its relative weaknesses the attitudes and disciplines that characterize its performance in areas where it is strong.

When you identify clusters of high-performance activity, you help your organization in two ways. As we just suggested, you identify models for improving organizational effectiveness in areas where it may be lacking. Your firm's sluggish, depressed accounting department, for example, may stand to learn a lot from your energized and proactive sales force, just as your chaotic and ineffectual training group may benefit from adopting some of the operating principles of your results-oriented documentation team. This transfer of internal expertise constitutes organizational learning at its best and brightest. It provides a means of improving performance at a minimal cost. What's more, it casts doubt on the corrosive notion that your organization as a whole is floundering in the grip of some sort of collective performance malady. Once your department, team, or work group has acknowledged that its counterparts are excelling at their assigned tasks, it is less likely to seek solace in the belief that your organization as a whole is somehow irremediably flawed.

A few years ago we worked with a direct marketing firm that benefited dramatically from the process of identifying and building its internal strengths. The company sold personal computers, and no sooner had it finished celebrating a substantial sale to a key corporate client than a rash of angry customer complaints began pouring into its switchboard. Some of the machines, it turned out, came equipped with video boards that were incompatible with the monitors the firm had shipped. Others didn't have enough memory to run the required software properly, and still others had defective power supplies. Needless to say, the firm's slender profit margins were more than consumed by the costs of repairing, replacing, and reshipping the faulty or inadequate units.

Clearly this was a disaster, both in terms of the company's financial performance and its emerging reputation. But rather than looking for someone to blame for the problem—and, take our word for it, there was no shortage of both internal and external candidates—senior management chose instead to analyze the scenario in terms of what it said about the company's strengths and weaknesses. This proved to be much more than a search for the proverbial silver lining, in that it revealed the company to have serious production and internal communication problems. Despite these difficulties, the firm's shipping department had managed to perform flawlessly: the order had been shipped to the client exactly on time, there had been no in-transit damage to any of the components, and the shipping invoice had matched the customer's purchase order exactly. Why, the management task force wondered, had the workers at the firm's distribution center performed successfully under trying circumstances and amid the chaos of rushing to meet the delivery deadline?

The reasons behind this isolated instance of success soon became apparent. For one thing, the company had prided itself since its inception on its logistics expertise: it had hired only experienced and highly qualified people to perform what it correctly viewed as an absolutely crucial function. For another, the head of distribution had been planning to meet the shipment deadline, even while the deal was still in the works. At a time when even senior management viewed the sale as an iffy proposition, he had assumed that it would come about, and had scheduled workers and common carriers accordingly. He had also made it a point to have available in advance the required packing materials and hand trucks, and had made sure the distribution center wouldn't be training new personnel during the critical delivery window. His confidence in his own judgment, combined with a willingness to accept cost overruns if the sale didn't come off as scheduled, enabled him to succeed at a trying and complex task.

"More than anything he did, though, it was his whole *attitude* that impressed us," a sales executive recalled. "He saw meeting customer requirements punctually and precisely as his primary job. There was a lesson in that for all the rest of us."

This lesson had to do with how the members of the young enterprise viewed their respective roles, as well as where they stood on the issue of overall company performance. Most had regarded the pending sale from a constricted, short-term perspective. To management, it had seemed a fortuitous opportunity to reap windfall profits; to the corporate sales staff, a quick-and-dirty means of meeting quarterly quotas; and to manufacturing, a chance to get rid of costly excess inventory. Among these groups and individuals, only the distribution manager seemed to have factored customer satisfaction into his formula for first-rate performance. Company leaders were quick to discern this. As a result, they immediately incorporated detailed checklists of customer wants and needs into their proposals, contracts, sales literature, and advertising materials. In addition, they put all managers and workers through a series of seminars on customer-focused selling, and set up training programs that would provide sales representatives with the required expertise in both computer hardware and software. In subsequent years, the firm refined and scaled back its manufacturing operations, emerging eventually as a viable distributor of integrated computing systems for the corporate market.

Embrace Innovative Decisions and Actions

Top-performing organizations know the value of innovation for its own sake. They are aware that not every new idea, procedure, or proposed product will result in a dramatic reversal of company or departmental fortune. But they are aware, too, of their limitations when it comes to determining which particular innovation will lead to a breakthrough success. So like prudent gamblers, they improve their odds at what remains a game of chance by encouraging, embracing, and rewarding all manner of innovative thought and activity. Look inside any thriving enterprise and you're likely to see a constant shuffling of options, strategies, and suggestions. It may seem chaotic at times, but it's a madness with a method.

Stunning new products and levels of service do not appear overnight. Behind virtually every significant performance breakthrough lies a trail of trial and error, qualified triumph, and failed experimentation. None of these investigations or experiments may have in itself contributed very much to the bottom line; many, in fact, may have cost the organization considerable time and money. But each is likely to have added to the store of organizational expertise, laying a foundation for better and more informed decision making. Like individuals, organizations often learn more from failure than success. Aware of this, thriving enterprises systematically and continually promote within their ranks a spirit of investigation and inquiry. And perhaps more importantly, they tolerate—and, in some cases, even celebrate—the failure that results when people struggle to find new answers to old but vexing questions.

The alternative to embracing innovation in all its manifestations and outcomes is to do what so many self-defeating enterprises fruitlessly attempt to do: innovate only as needed or only on demand. In the course of their normal operations, these organizations systematically discourage new or unconventional ideas and methods. They are quick to disparage any fresh outlook on an ongoing problem; they dismiss at a glance any approach that diverges from their tried-and-true remedies. But then, when their lack of creativity gets them into trouble—when, for example, a competitor introduces a product or service that challenges one of their established offerings—they abruptly shift gears, demanding creativity and risk taking from the very masses they have flogged into a state of intellectual stupor. It's a scenario that never ceases to amaze people, and one that seldom yields more than a *pro forma* repackaging of shopworn products, procedures, and ideas.

A lot of the companies we've worked with—banks, insurance agencies, process-oriented manufacturers—see innovation as something outside their domain. They feel either that innovation is best left to hi-tech firms, the fashion industry, advertising agencies, and specialty retailers, or that it requires limitless research-and-development funding. But this need not be the case, as the experience of one savings-and-loan firm demonstrated to us. The situation was this: through one of its subsidiaries, the firm had developed a set of instructional materials for entrepreneurs who were preparing to start their own businesses. Everyone who looked at these materials—a set of videotapes, handbooks, and reference charts—agreed that they were among the finest available, containing information that any new business owner needed to have. The problem was that prospective business owners tended often to be short on cash and, hence, unable to afford the cost of the instructional kit. This left the company in the problematic predicament of having a wonderful product that was unfortunately targeted at customers who could not afford to purchase it.

The firm was on the verge of giving these materials away to its borrowers and writing off the development costs when a loan officer named Stan came up with an alternative. Many of his clients were current and potential small business owners, and all were looking to borrow money. Most also were in need of the kind of information and instruction included in the training kits. Why, he wondered, did the company not offer to add the price of the training materials to the amount borrowed by its small business clients, offering a slightly reduced interest rate if these borrowers agreed to buy the materials? This clever solution would, in the end, cost the company little or nothing, while allowing it to sell off the inventory of training kits at their fair market value.

This story would underscore the importance of innovative thinking even if it ended here—but it doesn't. As more and more borrowers began to purchase and make use of the training materials, word of their value began to spread throughout the small business community. The company started to receive phone calls from numerous small business owners, many of whom had no need to borrow money but wanted to order the instruction kit nonetheless. In a matter of months, the firm faced the problem of having to produce more copies of the same videotapes, booklets, and charts that had been collecting dust and taking up space at the subsidiary's offices.

"Talk about ironic," Stan later commented. "Here we were taking back orders for a product we had been ready to *give away*. And we were filling the orders at full retail price, which small businesses were suddenly finding the wherewithal to pay. It turned out we'd had a winner on our hands all along."

In this instance, a small measure of innovative thinking, in combination with a company's willing embrace of an unconventional solution, served to increase the perceived value of the lender's services and to create a new internal profit center. And innovation bred further innovation, as the firm's marketing staff suddenly began to come up with ideas for new collateral materials and creative ways of incorporating them into customer loan programs.

Make the Case for System-Wide Change

Organizations change only when their core beliefs are revamped, refined, or replaced. These beliefs, in turn, can be modified only through collective experience. When root assumptions lead repeatedly to failure, organizational members are eventually motivated to question the thinking that underlies an ongoing pattern of ineffectual action. This is why minimizing is so sinister in terms of its impact on long-term performance. It muffles or distorts the warning sirens a self-defeating organization ought to be hearing loud and clear.

The practice of maximizing benefits has the opposite effect on how a business, agency, or team thinks about itself. While it does not fail to take into account areas where performance improvement is needed, it amplifies the feedback an organization has received about what it does well. It provides organizational leaders and managers with the evidence they need to make a persuasive case for change and growth, leaving to habitual dissenters the chore of mounting an argument against demonstrated success.

Throughout this book, we've cited numerous situations in which an organization has built on a single instance of high performance or innovation to bring about system-wide change. In review, here are a few of them:

- The case of Dave, the new general manager at the stricken stock brokerage. Prior to Dave's effort, company headquarters had relied on a form of terrorism to wring improved performance out of struggling branch offices. But when Dave managed to turn a problem-plagued branch around through a program that combined honesty, openness, and an innovative compensation plan for individual brokers, senior officials eventually adopted this approach throughout the company. It displaced a self-defeating approach that relied in large part on restriction, retrenchment, and a good measure of managerial duplicity.

- The case of Darlene, the bank supervisor who found the courage to challenge an unworkable company policy—and, once the crisis at her bank had passed, the wisdom to find a way to make the policy work. Although her approach to directing customer traffic at the branch was at first dismissed as simplistic and obvious, it later achieved successful results that made it a cornerstone of the marketing department's teller referral program.

- Finally, the case of Ted, whose refusal to bend to a rigid and contradictory performance appraisal policy caused his employer—a software development firm—to revise the way it thought about evaluating individual employees. Ted, as you'll recall, saw little point in penalizing effective employees simply to accommodate an arbitrary rating scheme. The ongoing success of his department validated his approach to the thorny problem of appraising individual effectiveness. This success, in combination with Ted's willingness to make a persuasive case for change, brought about a company-wide initiative designed to maximize the contributions of its high-performing staff members.

Maximizing, in short, builds on the healthy actions and attitudes of the few to bring about change that works to the advantage of the many. It transforms dilemmas and crises into opportunities for productive change, and at the same time helps the organization break free of or avoid patterns that systematically undermine lasting success.

OWNING BENEFITS AND BREAKTHROUGHS

Owning organizational success is a much less mystical proposition that it might at first seem. It's often mistakenly viewed as a means of insincere self-congratulation, involving mass rallies, motivational speeches, and the singing of anthems and company songs. In reality, taking ownership of benefits and breakthroughs is pitched at a lower and less strident key. It's an ongoing process of identifying any beliefs, decisions, resources, and practices that have played a significant role in shaping an organization's success. It requires several of the attributes we've already seen in high-performing enterprises: an open-minded attitude toward alternative or unanticipated manifestations of success, a willingness to analyze and learn from behavior patterns that yield optimal results, and a forthright recognition of the causal relationship between collective behavior and its ultimate results. These habits of thought and action enable a business or work group to take full credit for the triumphs it achieves. They banish luck, fate, and blame to the wings of the organizational stage, and cast the spotlight where it truly belongs: on accountability and successful performance.

Embrace Renegade and Impromptu Initiatives

In *Adventures in the Screen Trade*, novelist and screenwriter William Goldman writes with acid wit about the movie industry's stubborn refusal to acknowledge any successful film it deems a "nonrecurring phenomenon." The examples Goldman cites are

The Four Seasons (1981) and *On Golden Pond* (1982). Although ranking among the top ten films of its year in terms of gross earnings, each was largely disregarded by industry executives. Why? Because in the judgment of the industry, both were dismissed as aberrations: movies that had achieved commercial success while flouting the conventional wisdom that called for the production of more action-adventure films, teen-oriented comedies, and sequels to previous blockbusters. *The Four Seasons* and *On Golden Pond* dealt, respectively, with the travails of middle-aged and elderly characters; and Hollywood had long since "known" that members of these demographic groups tend to account for a scant share of the film-going audience. In the collective mind of the industry, the success of these films remained inexplicable, and no major studio made any subsequent attempt to court the market segment they had clearly captured.

What this example suggests is that the movie business, for all its glitter and notoriety, is a business as hidebound as any other. Nonrecurring phenomena—or, as we prefer to think of them, products of renegade or impromptu action—arise on a perplexingly regular basis within even the most plodding and retrograde enterprises. Acting on their own, energetic or clear-thinking individuals develop effective and economical systems for accomplishing required tasks; in their spare time or on the spur of the moment, tinkerers and dreamers come up with innovative devices and concepts. When these small breakthroughs occur, however, self-defeating organizations shrug them off as lucky breaks, rarely pausing to consider the circumstances under which they have come about. These organizations simply cannot accommodate any instance of high performance that does not derive from the company rule book, resource guide, or roster of job descriptions. They would rather do things their way than do things well.

Thriving organizations, in contrast, embrace success in whatever shape or form it appears. Aware that existing policies and protocols amount to little more than templates for replicating past activities, they take their lead from windfalls and innovations that occur outside these established norms. We once worked for a successful trucking company that built one of its most profitable operations around an unplanned incident. In the middle of a severe blizzard, one of the company's dispatchers received a distress call from a driver whose unit had broken down on a remote, two-lane route. In response, the dispatcher contacted several firms that provided mobile repairs, only to be told in each case that the weather emergency had created a backlog of requests. On overhearing one of these phone conversations, a company mechanic suggested that he and one of his colleagues load an arc-welding unit onto a pickup and drive to where the truck was stalled. With no alternative at hand, the shop service manager gave the two mechanics the go-ahead, and they ventured off into the storm.

Three hours later, they arrived at the site of the breakdown, and quickly got the truck up and running. While they were working, however, the driver heard over his CB radio that two other rigs were stalled in the immediate vicinity. He asked if the mechanics might stop on their way home and see if they could provide assistance. They said that they'd see what they could do and, in the course of a long afternoon and evening, managed to get three more stalled tractors up and running.

Over the next few weeks, the company's service manager received calls from the owners of each of these trucks. They wanted to know how much they owed for the repairs the mechanics had made. Because the company had never rendered such services, the manager was at a loss, so he quoted an arbitrary figure in the neighborhood of $700. After a bit of negotiation, each customer agreed to approximately this amount. The firm subsequently realized more than $2,000 in unanticipated profits, all as a result of the initiative of two ambitious, hard-working mechanics.

When the firm's senior managers heard about this incident, they saw that it pointed to a new and potentially lucrative source of revenue. They began to explore what it would take to equip and staff a permanent mobile-service fleet, and to offer emergency repair service to other truckers. These discussions led eventually to the establishment of a new operating unit with its own drivers, mechanics, and specially outfitted repair vans. The unit remains profitable to this day, providing the firm with badly needed revenues during slack seasons and periodic economic downturns.

"It's something we never planned or thought much about," the manager of the unit recently told us. "And looking back, it seems like such an obvious way of buffering ourselves against things we can't predict. Prices may go up and down, shipping contracts may come and go, but trucks will always break down. And when they do, shippers and owner/operators will pay whatever it costs to get their rigs back on the road in a hurry."

Track Successful Performance Patterns

Owning benefits is often a matter of taking stock of the resources, skills, and practices that have contributed to your organization's successful performance. This approach differs significantly from the self-defeating organization's tendency to assume that it is inept and, consequently, to attribute any success it achieves to luck or external circumstances. The habit of compulsive blaming creates a climate that makes it difficult to maximize and own instances of high performance; if the organization is never to blame for its failures, then it stands to reason that it cannot really take credit for any of its achievements. This may well explain why struggling enterprises are so often unduly harsh in their self-evaluations. They struggle to survive in the worst of all possible worlds: one where failure is the norm, success is a fluke, and both lie outside organizational control.

To improve its performance, your organization must stand each of these corrosive notions on its head. You need to create an environment where success, rather than failure, is the rule, and where the organization itself—not some capricious external force—stands accountable for both the costs and benefits of its actions. As suggested earlier, this process begins when you identify areas in which your company or work group is already performing at peak level. You can then work backward from the successful or beneficial results achieved within these pockets of high performance; you can analyze retroactively the beliefs, systems, and behavior patterns that characterize your internal pockets of productive activity. And once you've determined how a particular division or department is managing to succeed on a regular basis, you can compare that group's performance pattern to the attitudes and practices of your enterprise as a whole. This comparison often yields surprising insights as to why an intelligent, well-intentioned organization is consistently falling short of the goals it has set.

We talked earlier about the computer marketing firm that had badly botched one of its first major corporate sales. In the aftermath, a management task force was commissioned to step back from the situation and determine how and why the company had failed to perform according to its plans. The task force looked at both strengths and weaknesses, discovering in the process that the company's shipping department had prevailed where management, sales, and manufacturing had come up short. With the aid of external consultants, the members of the task force tracked the shipping department's performance pattern, then compared it with the approach of the other players in the scenario.

The contrast between the two patterns was revealing. It suggested that the shipping department had clearly identified its goals and provided the required training and guidance well in advance of the crucial deadline, assuming from the start that it would succeed. By comparison, the performance pattern of management, sales, and manufacturing amounted to a virtual road map for disaster. It was based not on existing capabilities and resources, but rather on the perceived need for quick financial profit. Worse yet, it seemed to anticipate both problems and the cost of resolving them. Reduced to the bare essentials, the divergent internal performance patterns looked like the figure on page 264. These contrasting models provided the task force with a wealth of information and guidance. They were able to see that in focusing narrowly on short-term profitability goals, the company had overlooked such critical performance factors as customer satisfaction, employee training, and proactive scheduling and procurement. The firm as a whole had fallen into the troublesome habit of moving too fast and grabbing for too much, without adequately considering how such rash actions might affect its overall performance picture. But the shipping department, headed by an experienced and service-oriented manager, seemed to march to a different and more methodical drummer. The department's

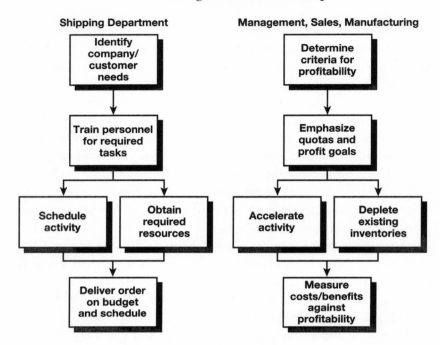

Tracking Performance Patterns

ongoing effectiveness not only demonstrated to the members of the task force that high performance was indeed possible—it also suggested any number of ways in which the firm might build on its current strengths.

Link Success with Core Organizational Beliefs

Tracking patterns of successful activity forces your organization to factor its strengths and assets into what might seem to be a dismal performance picture. This process demonstrates that your organization has successfully produced something of quality or value solely through its own expertise and resources. Your organization will soon come to see that it indeed can make a contribution to the world outside its walls, and that it can deliver quality, value, or service under even the most trying circumstances. Your business or agency may become inspired as a result of focusing on its success; you and your colleagues may discover new ways of replicating high-performance attitudes and actions that already exist within your walls. The process of owning and learning from success can't help but bolster your organization's confidence in itself, replenishing what may well be a diminished store of hope.

This process is not complete, however, until your organization establishes a clear link between what it is doing and what it collectively believes. And here, alas, is where a good many businesses and agencies stop short of closing what might otherwise stand as a viable high-performance loop. In some cases, they are simply so giddy with success that they lose sight of how it has been achieved; they are enjoying success too much to question it. More often, though, they are fearful of what a recent triumph or breakthrough might suggest about an organization's traditional identity and self-conception. In other words, they are afraid of fundamental change.

This fear is usually unwarranted. In most scenarios, pockets or incidents of high performance either confirm the validity of long-held core beliefs or suggest subtle ways in which these beliefs need to be modified. An organization may, for example, come into existence with a firm belief in technological excellence, only to be distracted down the line by price wars or distribution problems. In the process of ministering to a resultant performance decline, the firm may well reaffirm its faith in state-of-the-art technology, abandoning its ill-starred attempts to serve every market segment or potential customer. Similarly, a service provider that has expanded too rapidly or diversified beyond its capabilities may retreat from the ensuing chaos with a clearer and more refined sense of what it does best. There's much to be said for these back-to-basics strategies, which often yield a happy and sustainable balance between innovation on the one hand, and traditional strengths and beliefs on the other.

Sometimes, though, impromptu successes and healthy internal performance patterns underscore an organization's need to rid itself of beliefs that are no longer serving any productive purpose. These are situations where an organization's descriptive beliefs have become invalid over time, or where its self-evaluations have become so negatively skewed that virtually any measures the organization takes are tainted and compromised from the start. Tyler's chain of stores, which we discussed in Chapter 9, serves as an example of the former. The chain made up an organization that was clinging to an outmoded notion of its own uniqueness. Only when Tyler made it clear to his managers that the chain was "just another store," and backed this assertion up with hard facts, did store performance begin to improve.

The predicament of an organization whose core beliefs have become negatively distorted is perhaps best illustrated by Amanda's data services corporation, which we discussed in Chapter 6. You'll recall that the loss of key government contracts forced this firm into a hasty round of downsizing and restructuring. In the aftermath, the company was demoralized to the point where individual employees—among them, some of the members of Amanda's sales support teams—began to disparage their colleagues in discussions with customers. Though its descriptive beliefs (and, hence, its corporate identity) remained more or less intact, this particular firm was riddled with negative attitudes toward its leaders, managers, and prospects for success. Rank-and-file members like Chet had come to regard innovative action as prohibitively risky or difficult. With few exceptions—Amanda was one—they had withdrawn into cocoons of fear and loathing, looking primarily to protect themselves against what they viewed as a hostile and corrupt organizational environment.

Situations like these call for comprehensive, top-to-bottom change. Under such circumstances, organizational leaders need not so much to link beneficial results to existing core beliefs as to *take actions that exemplify and reinforce new beliefs and realities*. We emphasize this recommendation with good reason: it's much, much easier said than done. In our final chapter, we'll suggest a few initial steps a self-defeating organization can take to reshape the outmoded or unhealthy core beliefs that stand in the way of lasting performance improvement. We're convinced these measures can work—provided, of course, that a business, team, or work group is willing to cast old habits aside and assume full ownership of its ultimate fate.

CHAPTER 13

Shaping Core Beliefs Through Success

I F YOU'RE like us, you marvel now and then at how effortlessly high-performing organizations seem to achieve their ends and maintain their lofty status. You may wonder what these stellar companies, agencies, and teams know that the rest of us don't. How do they know precisely how and when to strike a blockbuster deal, build a state-of-the-art production plant, or introduce a breakthrough product? What magic enables them to avoid the flawed decisions and misguided strategies that send other enterprises reeling? Unless you're lucky enough to work for one of these powerhouses, you probably look on them the way the fifteen other major league baseball teams looked at the New York Yankees of the 1950s. You shake your head in wonder at their uncanny ability to make the right move at just the right time, to find a way to win regardless of the circumstances. You ask what they have that your organization doesn't.

One thing: *confidence.*

It's a special confidence born of repeated triumph and an abiding faith in positive outcomes. At times it may seem to border on arrogance, but once your organization has acquired it, you'll see it differently. Top performers in business, government, and sports know what success looks like, how it feels, and how it's achieved. This gives them at least two powerful advantages over their struggling counterparts. First, it provides them with the spiritual and material resources to take required risks; they don't allow imaginary fears to paralyze them at key moments. Second, they hold the other key advantage that comes with ongoing success: high-performing organizations believe that they are strong enough and smart enough to make any scenario work to their ultimate benefit, no matter how troubling it might first appear. Their ability to maximize any potential outcome disposes them toward innovative action. They know from experience that a new product or idea that doesn't pay off next month may well yield lucrative benefits a year or two down the line. They know that while nothing may succeed like success, sometimes nothing will succeed next year like today's apparent failure.

Your organization can develop this kind of confidence, this belief that it can prevail time after time. Obviously, it must succeed at what it sets out to do, even if its accomplishments are modest. It must then build on this small initial triumph, maximizing its benefits and reinforcing the attitudes and actions that brought about the successful outcome. First, though, your organization must feel that it *can* succeed, regardless of its past problems. In the words of the former Mets and Phillies pitcher Tug McGraw, your organization has "gotta believe"—in its strengths, in its resiliency, and above all in its capacity for healthy change.

IS LASTING ORGANIZATIONAL CHANGE POSSIBLE?

We stated at the outset that many of today's organizational leaders remain pessimistic about the prospects for lasting, system-wide change. They believe that their businesses or agencies are staffed by individuals who are intractably bound to traditional ideas, structures, and methods; and that these individuals, like most people, are apt to resist change until what often proves to be the bitter end. Although this point of view relieves executives and managers of the burdensome chore of transforming organizational character, it also steers them toward counterproductive courses of action. On the one hand, it points toward programs designed either to rid the organization of strong-willed members, or to "fix" people in the interest of rendering them amenable to any policy or procedure that management might choose to impose. But as we've noted on numerous occasions, most organizations aren't very good at this; they often end up purging themselves of valuable expertise, stifling innovation, and promoting duplicity among rank-and-file members. Alternatively, organizational leaders can focus on cosmetic change, resorting to the time-honored techniques of downsizing, restructuring, or automating their operations. And while this approach invariably whips an organization into fitter or shapelier form, it leaves unhealthy beliefs and performance patterns firmly in place. What typically results is a new, "improved" organization capable of doing the wrong thing faster and more effectively.

It's not that the people in charge of our major organizations are stupid or cynical. They often have good reasons for being skeptical when the topic of comprehensive change comes up; they have seen it attempted far too often, and with uniformly disastrous results. Like the rest of us, they have learned from experience, and their experience tells them that system-wide change is at best a long shot for success. No wonder that they tend to see it as a last resort, or as a project best left to the headstrong or the desperate.

These sentiments suggest why comprehensive organizational change so seldom succeeds. The problem is this: a business or agency typically embarks on such a program *in situations when its collective confidence and resources are at an all-time low.* So long as an organization remains marginally profitable or effective in achieving its ends—for as long as the ultimate costs of its counterproductive activity can be masked or deferred—its leaders will continue to pursue short-term or *pro forma* solutions to nagging performance problems. The fact is, organizational leaders and managers seldom contemplate the need for change until their existing systems are in danger of imminent collapse. This typically occurs when successive cycles of minimizing and blaming have all but eroded an organization's confidence in its ability to take command of a situation and reverse its outcome. It's precisely at this point that organizational leaders loudly trumpet the call to collective arms. The problem is, they are asking their charges to rise to the sternest challenge they will ever meet at a point when the organization as a whole is at its lowest ebb.

Yet healthy organizational change can be brought about, even under these trying circumstances. Ill fortune may breed despair, but it can just as easily yield a heightened resolve, causing an organization to marshal its resources and steel its nerves for the challenge that lies ahead.

The keys to transforming an organization's core beliefs are confidence and long-term thinking. If your business or agency is looking for a patchwork, short-term fix, you won't find it in the pages that follow. The process of changing a self-defeating character is often slow, incremental, and, at times, downright hard. But the benefits are well worth the effort. An organization with a sincere desire to break out of its self-defeating performance loop can realize these benefits in relatively short order and can build on them to restore its belief in itself.

CRISES OF CONFIDENCE

An organization suffers a crisis of confidence when its reactions to performance difficulties continually seem to create more problems than they resolve. As these problems multiply and deplete resources, the range of options available to the organization increasingly narrows. It finds itself bereft of the financial wherewithal or the collective will to break free of its traditional habits. The enterprise is left with only a few potential options at strategic moments, and with precious little faith that any of them will actually work. The organization is at this point a short step away from believing that *nothing it does*—no matter how atypical or innovative—will lead to performance improvement. The net result is a business or firm at once paralyzed and urgently disposed toward frantic, hasty action: an organization locked in the grip of self-defeat.

Take, for example, the electronics manufacturer discussed in Chapter 2. Having failed to recognize the impact that the personal computing revolution of the early 1980s would make on its revenues, the firm subsequently launched a series of retrenchment initiatives, reducing both its workforce and its investment in new plant and equipment. As a result, the productivity of plants like the one Ralph managed began a slow decline, which led to a further diminishing of the firm's annual revenues. To cut operating costs even further, the company then decided to lay off large numbers of its production workers and to restaff the plants with temporary personnel. Same reaction, same result: demand for the company's typewriters and adding machines continued to drop, causing senior management to instruct plant managers like Ralph either to improve productivity or face the prospect of shutting down. The problem was, meaningful productivity gains could be achieved only by outfitting the plants with modern equipment that members of the firm's flexible workforce lacked the skills to operate. With its traditional management solutions going nowhere fast, and with no viable alternatives in sight, the company seemed frozen in its tracks. It needed desperately to do something, but had no notion of where to turn. It had lost its collective will, and with it the faith in its ability to weather competitive challenges.

To understand how an organization can work its way through a crisis of confidence like this, first consider the factors leading up to it. Crises of confidence, we believe, result from three deficiencies in an organization's collective makeup: a lack of honesty, a lack of information, and a lack of evidence that the business or agency can achieve success. In the example we've been discussing, the electronics firm's senior management repeatedly refused to tell the truth—not only to plant managers and workers, but also among its own ranks. Top executives persisted in deluding themselves that the personal computer amounted to little more than the latest fad and, consequently, developing best-case strategic plans that in retrospect seemed ludicrous. This worked hand in hand with senior management's tendency to ignore or disregard new information about the marketplace and its requirements.

Company executives failed not only because they were

dishonest, but also because they remained largely uninformed about new technologies and innovative models for business management. This led them to replicate policies and strategies that were either outmoded or unworkable, and to achieve predictably unimpressive results. In the absence of any recent success or performance breakthrough, the organization as a whole saw little evidence that it could continue to operate profitably and effectively. In embracing this unhealthy belief in its own futility, the company closed its low-performance loop and transformed its apprehensions into self-fulfilling prophecies.

The high-performance techniques we've suggested here— truth-telling, open-mindedness, equitable cost/benefit sharing, maximizing, and ownership—can prevent this sort of crisis from arising. They can also help a floundering organization extricate itself from the depths of a self-inflicted malaise. To illustrate the way these techniques work, we need to add a few more elements to our picture of a typical high-performance loop. As shown in the figure on the opposite page, these new elements represent the results that each technique tends to yield. Individually and cumulatively, each of the high-performance techniques shown in this figure ministers to the lack of honesty, information, and recent success that characterizes the self-defeating business, team, or work group. Rigorous truth-telling provides such an organization with an accurate and timely picture of where it stands relative to the goal of high performance. Open-mindedness increases the number of alternatives available to the organization at strategic moments, allowing it to take advantage of the latest technological and managerial advances. This reduces the organization's reliance on expedient or familiar reactions. What's more, it increases the likelihood of making decisions aimed at long-term success—the kind of decisions that achieve a balance among the interests and expectations of internal constituencies. As a result, the organization has little subsequent need to justify or cover up the consequences of its actions. It can instead devote its time, money, and energy to maximizing the benefits it has realized. And maximizing benefits not only improves performance; it also shines the spotlight on what the organization does well and what it ought to be doing throughout its ranks. This process supplies the enterprise

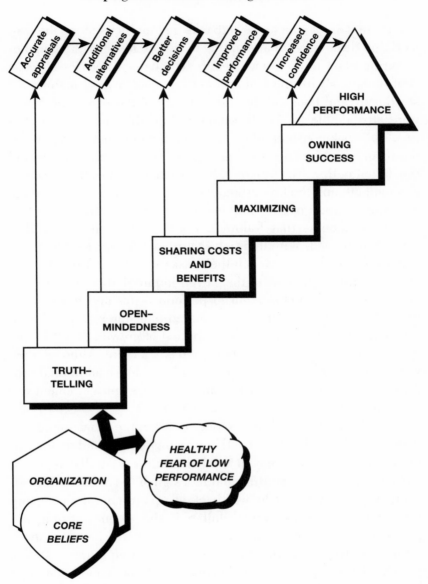

Escaping a Crisis of Organizational Confidence

with evidence of its capability to succeed, regardless of external events and circumstances. Its collective confidence is gradually restored, and from this confidence emerges a refined and revital-ized system of core organizational beliefs.

There will, of course, be setbacks and missteps along the way, as Ralph discovered in attempting to restore his struggling manufacturing plant to its former health. Throughout a series of tense confrontations with the managers of his company, he maintained steadfastly and honestly that the majority of the plant's problems were attributable to the ill-considered flexible workforce initiative. This took considerable courage on his part; many of those in the room with him had been among the most ardent advocates of this failed policy. Nevertheless, his insistent truth-telling eventually paid off, and the firm grudgingly agreed to allow him to create and train a group of core workers within the facility.

In the months that followed, plant productivity slowly but steadily improved. With their job security for the moment assured, employees began to approach their tasks with greater enthusiasm and concentration. Some of them even inquired about new equipment that would enable them to perform faster and more effectively. Ralph and his supervisors shared their interest, and began to pursue it actively when, after a period of growth, plant performance reached a plateau and remained stuck there. Although they were doing their best, the workers couldn't achieve additional productivity gains without new machinery, modern measurement devices, and improvements in plant design.

Ralph had expected that, sooner or later, the plant would run up against this wall. He knew that bringing output and quality up to the level that management wanted would eventually require a fairly comprehensive refitting and redesign of the aging facility. In many ways, he felt that he was back at square one: the company was reluctant to invest capital dollars in the absence of dramatic performance improvements that could only be brought about through a significant investment in plant and equipment. It was yet another classic business dilemma, and Ralph decided the time had come to present it as such to the company's top management.

The scenario that Ralph subsequently outlined before a committee of senior decision makers included the following elements:

- A summary of the productivity gains the plant had achieved through the establishment of a permanent, committed workforce. This chart also indicated the point at which plant performance had stagnated because of equipment and facility design limitations.

- A projection of the improvements in output and product quality that Ralph believed his workers could achieve if the plant were reequipped and refitted. Although these fell short of senior management's less than realistic goals, they suggested that the plant would soon be able to operate profitably.

- A set of proposals from equipment vendors and industrial designers that specified the costs of modernizing the facility. Included in these proposals were budgets and schedules for training workers to operate the new machinery and to implement new assembly procedures.

- A series of flowcharts illustrating how plant operations would be structured and managed subsequent to the needed changes. In explaining these charts, Ralph pointed out that line supervisors would assume a hands-on role in the new production and quality-measurement processes, and that the company would benefit from relieving them of certain redundant management responsibilities.

- A cost/benefit analysis that summarized how senior management, plant workers, and customers would profit from the projected improvements, and from the resulting capability to produce better and more diversified products.

In short, Ralph based his case for modernizing the plant on an honest assessment of the gains that had already been realized, on information from leading industry technologists, and on documented evidence of recent performance improvements. His unstated goal was to communicate to senior management the confidence that he and his workers had developed in their capability to learn, grow, and produce at optimal levels.

For all this, some company executives remained unconvinced.

They argued persuasively for closing the plant, limiting the company's product line to a few proven winners, and relocating their manufacturing operations to an offshore facility.

"It was crunch time," Ralph later admitted. "I was basically asking the company to decide whether or not it wanted to maintain a domestic production capability. Which, now that I think about it, was the decision they'd been flirting with for years."

The company executives sensed this too, which is why their answer to Ralph had ominous implications. "We're going to go ahead with your plan," said the senior vice president who delivered the news. "But I have to tell you, this is it. If things don't turn around fast, we're looking at a shutdown. We may have to cut our losses."

"I understand that," Ralph replied. "Thanks for giving us one last shot."

That last shot paid off well beyond senior management's expectations. In opting against the expedient and half-considered solution and putting its trust in a tenacious plant manager, the company broke out of its self-defeating loop. Management implemented a modified version of Ralph's proposal for modernization and selective worker training. As a result, the facility achieved a level of productivity once deemed inconceivable, and with a small staff of loyal, competent, and well-trained workers.

THE CIRCLE OF ACTION AND BELIEF

The focus of this book has been how your organization can help itself; how you can learn to stay away from dubious practices that undermine core beliefs and, ultimately, organizational confidence. In situation after situation, we've seen organizations manage to free themselves of old habits and achieve success under less than ideal conditions. What these groups and their individual members seem to share is a fearlessness in the face of mythical constraints, along with a fundamental belief in their ability to achieve realistic goals. This confidence serves as a foundation for the kind of thoughtful and innovative action that, over the long term, results in performance improvement.

But what, you might ask, about the kind of organization we've been discussing here—the business, agency, or work group whose character has become warped by ongoing patterns of self-defeat? Its leaders and members have little grounds for confidence, and its existing core beliefs may well be invalid or unhealthy. It lacks the rudimentary tools for fashioning healthy change. Believing that it cannot improve, it does not improve; and, consequently, seldom or never achieves the successful results that might bolster its confidence. Trapped in a low-performance loop, it finds itself precluded from taking effective action. It recognizes the need for comprehensive change, but hasn't the faintest idea of where to begin. So it holds long meetings and conferences, and sends individual members to workshops and motivational sessions. But still the problem remains, and the organization continues to struggle in place.

The problem remains, in our view, because it's a manifestation of the eternal riddle of the chicken and the egg: which comes first, action or belief? These two factors, along with the results they yield, form a basic behavioral loop that looks like the figure on page 278. The question facing the self-defeating organization, then, is where to initiate the process of transformation—where, in terms of our diagram, to attempt to broach the circle. And while circumstances may vary from organization to organization, our experience suggests that it's best for a stagnant business or agency to start at the top and *take decisive action*.

But not just any action will do. The self-defeating organization ought to be especially wary of any new policy or program that hints at the reactionary or replicative techniques it has used in the past. The struggling enterprise should also avoid hollow gestures and policies it may be incapable of seeing through to the end. Variations on old themes and theatrical pronouncements simply won't turn the trick; more often than not, they will only add to the cynicism that pervades the ranks. The members of a self-defeating organization need to be shown unequivocally that leaders and managers are serious in their commitment to healthy change. They need to see that their organization is at long last ready to walk the high-performance walk, as opposed to merely talking the talk.

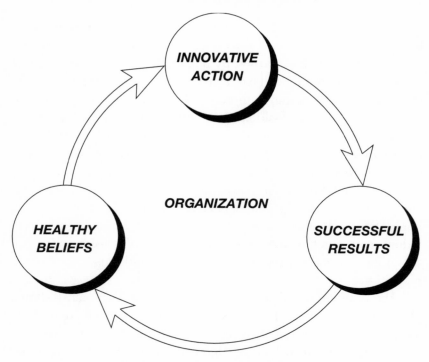

INNOVATIVE
ACTION

ORGANIZATION

HEALTHY
BELIEFS

SUCCESSFUL
RESULTS

The Circle of Action and Belief

The specific plan, decision, or program through which this commitment is demonstrated will, of course, vary from organization to organization. It will depend on the nature of the organization's business, and may well be constrained by scarce resources or other urgent circumstances. It may be as simple as a new departmental procedure for working with other internal units, or as complex as the retooling of an entire production facility. But regardless of its particulars, the self-defeating organization's first step toward comprehensive change should communicate three things: what the enterprise intends to do; how this course of action supports a healthy core belief; and the options available to individual members as the process of change unfolds.

Let's take a closer look here at each aspect of this, and at how an executive or manager might present it to an organization afflicted by low performance and a pattern of consistent self-defeat.

"Here is what we're going to do." This part of the message should communicate clearly any new procedure, policy, or method the organization plans to adopt. It should describe what will change, when the change will occur, and who will be accountable for its success or failure. And while we obviously can't specify the details of a particular organization's change initiative, we feel safe in saying that it should incorporate most—if not all—of the techniques that our high-performance loop comprises: truth-telling, open-mindedness, equitable sharing, maximizing, and eventual ownership of any and all results. These techniques are universal. They have helped dozens of self-defeating organizations see beyond their mythical fears and embark on a path that leads to performance improvement.

"This is what we believe." Recall that one of the root problems of the self-defeating business or agency is its lack of valid or healthy core beliefs. The second part of any call for system-wide change ought to speak to this deficiency. It ought to affirm without equivocation what the organization sees as the source of its strength. This may amount to nothing more than an accurate description of the organization's role and purpose; an identity statement that clarifies a primary activity and a broad criterion for successful performance. It may also confront and countermand any negative self-evaluations that have repeatedly compromised an organization's ability to achieve its potential. In any event, it should explicitly link a sound core belief with the measures the organization intends to adopt. This connection not only provides a rationale for the new course of action, it also posits a valid and healthy belief in situations where none exists.

"Each of us has a choice." The third component of a message heralding organizational change should pose an implicit challenge to the individual. It should emphasize that while the enterprise and its leaders are committed to performance improvement, they will probably not be able to achieve this goal without the help of rank-and-file members. "Each of us has a choice every day," the executive or manager might say. "We can choose between going about our tasks in a way that contributes to high

organizational performance, or we can muddle along as usual. The cumulative result of all our choices will determine if we prosper in the long run or continue to struggle, always fearful of the worst." Words to this effect can dispel the notion that management is in the way of imposing yet another unworkable or cosmetic program designed to conceal the consequences of poor decision making. In laying out the options and issuing a challenge, the leader of an organization admits that, in the end, collective success can be achieved only through the innovative actions of smart, dedicated, and hard-working individuals.

We don't guarantee that a change initiative communicated along these lines will ultimately prevail, or that it will be enthusiastically embraced by each and every organizational member. But we firmly believe that if you give them the opportunity, healthy individuals will opt in favor of effective policies and procedures, and will embark on an earnest pursuit of realistic organizational goals. The change message, along with the action or attitude it describes, can serve as the self-defeating organization's point of entry into the circle of high performance.

Once the circle is broached, the process has just begun. For the organization looking to wean itself of stagnant and reactionary habits, the problem of performance improvement is never ultimately solved. As challenges and crises continue to arise, this problem will continue to take on new dimensions and shadings. The healthy, evolving organization can never be sure that it has the right answer. It can be sure, though, that techniques like honesty, openness, fairness, and accountability will never fall out of fashion. Diligently applied, they ward off self-defeat and form an eternal loop of high organizational performance.

MAKING HIGH PERFORMANCE YOUR UNASSAILABLE CORE BELIEF

The world has come a long way since the time when organizational leaders with names like Vanderbilt and Ford could scorn the public, or command their employees never to complain about a problem and never to explain it. These industrial barons were sure of themselves and their world. They believed that resources were infinite, that markets were ever-expanding, and that their profits would continue to swell. Whatever you think of their well-documented failings, they held strong core beliefs—in progress, in growth, and in the notion of building business empires that would last forever. When they wanted to improve the performance of their companies, they simply demanded it. They got what they wanted by shouting louder, turning up the flame, tightening the screws, and stifling competition. The world was indeed their oyster, to be swallowed raw and whole.

The tides of history and technology have swept away the artificial borders and barriers that once afforded organizations the luxury of doing pretty much as they pleased. For most of our businesses and agencies, the era of hegemony and rule by executive fiat has long since passed. Today's organizational leaders are confronted simultaneously with a shrinking store of both internal and external resources; with a public whose demands for food, shelter, and transportation have become largely sated; and with competitive challenges from all sorts of unlikely sources. These circumstances are too numerous and complex to be subdued through brute force, or through the intensified application of techniques that have worked in the past. When brought to bear on a dramatically altered organizational landscape, these venerable techniques—replication, cost deferral, minimizing, and blaming—begin to work systematically against the prospect of long-term success. Gradually but inexorably, they deplete resources and undermine healthy collective beliefs, robbing once-vibrant enterprises of both confidence and flexibility.

There's a sad irony at work here. It's sad because a struggling enterprise, in moments of crisis or challenge, looks precisely where it ought not to look: to the techniques that have enabled it to prevail in the past. For the sake of novelty or public relations, these shopworn alternatives may be introduced under trendy or euphemistic aliases. Thus an ill-considered retrenchment may be presented as *downsizing*; an ineffectual shuffling of the organizational deck as *reengineering*; a wholesale restriction of individual freedom and initiative as *team building*; or a program of systematic indoctrination and fear-mongering as *retraining*. Much organizational effort goes into this chore of serving up tainted wine under deceptive new labels. Seldom, though, does the self-defeating organization confront the critical challenge of tracking the vintage to its source—of identifying the sour grapes from which its time-honored solutions are often distilled.

Were the organization to do so, it would soon discern a series of troubling truths. It would discover first that its traditional approaches were never all that effective. The organization would see that the layoffs, plant closings, and proliferating rules and regulations that enabled it to weather crises in the past were merely expedient reactions to scenarios that more appropriately called for introspection and considered decisions. It would see that these reactive "solutions" more often than not left in their wake toxic consequences, the cumulative effects of which seem only recently to have emerged. The problem-plagued business or agency would come to realize that it has in fact been working against itself for years, or even decades. It would discover, in short, that its self-defeating activities are rooted in the time of its greatest ostensible success.

This leads us to the paradox of self-defeating organizational behavior. It tends to be formulated not when your organization is young and struggling, or when hard times demand hard solutions; it arises instead in periods of relative health and prosperity. It takes root when you are flush with confidence. In heady times, you may fall prey to the assumption that continued growth and health are all but assured. You may delude yourself that your organization can do whatever it pleases, and that you'll always have world and time enough to repair any damage that results. It's at this point that your organization is most prone to depart from the sound core beliefs of its founders or charter members. A huge government contract resulting from war or natural disaster may tempt your organization into compromising its belief in providing quality products at a good price. The opportunity to reap windfall profits through a timely stock offering may distract organizational owners from their original commitment to self-direction and the collective good. The unanticipated success of a breakthrough product may lull company researchers and marketers into a somnolence that compromises a bedrock commitment to ongoing innovation. In each case, a level of success that might yield further success serves instead as fertile ground for the seeds of failure.

For this reason, you must be zealous in constantly promoting long-term high performance as a fundamental core belief. You should cite this belief as the explicit source of all of your organization's activity and link it whenever possible to the successes that result from innovative actions. Your belief in high performance should serve as a yardstick for measuring the potential outcomes of any policy or action, and as a tool for diagnosing your organization's health. Invoke it in support of anyone who tries to break your company or agency of its bad habits. Hold it sacrosanct and defend it at any cost against those who dismiss or challenge it.

Rest assured, this belief will be challenged. It will be challenged externally when uncontrollable circumstances seem to demand shortsighted actions or hasty changes of direction. What's more, it will be regularly challenged internally, as competing constituencies attempt to gain unhealthy sway over their counterparts. It will be challenged both actively and passively, whether in the course of plodding, aimless business meetings or in gossip whispered around the water cooler. In each of these instances, you need to rise to the occasion. Through your words and actions, you must demonstrate your commitment to high organizational performance, regardless of the resistance you're certain to encounter.

In this book, we've introduced you to several people who held and acted on their high-performance beliefs: Dave at the depressed brokerage; Darlene at the chaotic bank; Tyler at the troubled retail company; Ralph at the underperforming production plant. None would be mistaken as a charismatic or a visionary, but each had that special quality that we've come to view as a prerequisite for healthy organizational change. It's a simple virtue, and one that's unlikely ever to fall out of fashion. Your organization may know it as commitment, self-reliance, or stubborn persistence. We call it courage.

Summary

W E'VE GIVEN you a lot to think about in this book: lots of concepts, categories, techniques, and suggestions. To review the ground we've covered and to provide you with a convenient way of keeping all this information in mind, here is a summary of the major points surrounding each of the issues we've discussed. This is what you need to remember about core beliefs and organizational fears, the low-performance loop, and its high-performance counterpart.

CORE BELIEFS AND ORGANIZATIONAL FEARS

Your organization responds to crisis or challenge on the basis of its core beliefs and fears. If your core beliefs are valid and positive, and if your business or agency harbors a realistic fear of perpetuating low performance, it will follow the high-performance path:

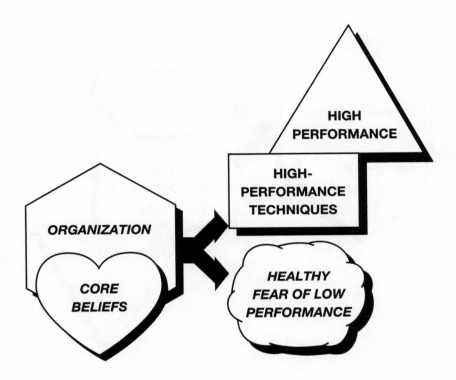

However, if your organization holds invalid or negative core beliefs, mythical fear will block the path to high performance and send you reeling along the road to low performance, as shown on the following page.

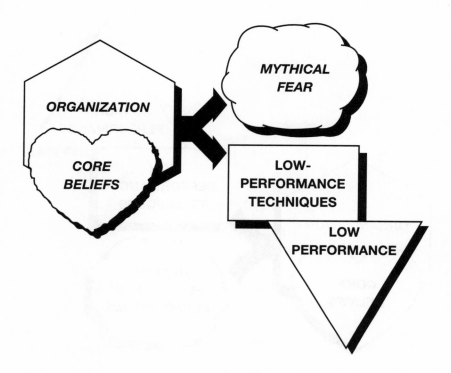

To escape or avoid a cycle of weak performance, you need to understand core beliefs and fears, and what they say about your company, work group, or team.

Your Core Belief System

Your organization's core belief system is the lens through which it views itself. As shown below, this system is a combination of *descriptive* and *evaluative* beliefs:

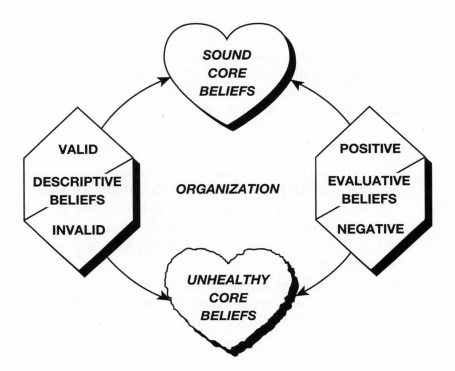

- Descriptive core beliefs define your organization's identity.
  When analyzed, they should specify your primary
  activity—for example, trucking, retail sales, or
  manufacturing—and a performance criterion that
  identifies the market segment you serve, or the level of
  quality or service you provide. Because you can measure
  them against reality, you can categorize your descriptive
  beliefs as *valid* or *invalid*. Only valid descriptive beliefs
  are healthy.

- Evaluative core beliefs are your organization's judgments
  about its performance, fairness, wisdom, and honesty.
  These evaluative beliefs are subjective; they're either
  positive or *negative*. Only positive evaluative beliefs are
  healthy.

- Certain combinations of descriptive and evaluative beliefs—for example, valid descriptions and positive evaluations—lay the foundation for high organizational performance. Others, such as an alliance of invalid descriptions and negative evaluations, clearly spell disaster. Your organization's core belief system probably falls somewhere between these extremes.

Organizational Fears

- There are two kinds of organizational fears: *mythical* and *realistic*. (See the figures on pages 285 and 286.) If your organization is caught in the grip of mythical fears, it probably shuns or avoids the very qualities that can restore its health: change, accountability, truth, and a focus on long-term success.

- Realistic fear is the legitimate fear of low performance. It can steer your organization away from hasty or trendy actions, and toward activities more in line with its healthy core beliefs.

THE LOW-PERFORMANCE LOOP

As you see here, the low-performance loop is a sequence of predictable activities that results when your organization reacts on the basis of unsound core beliefs and mythical fears:

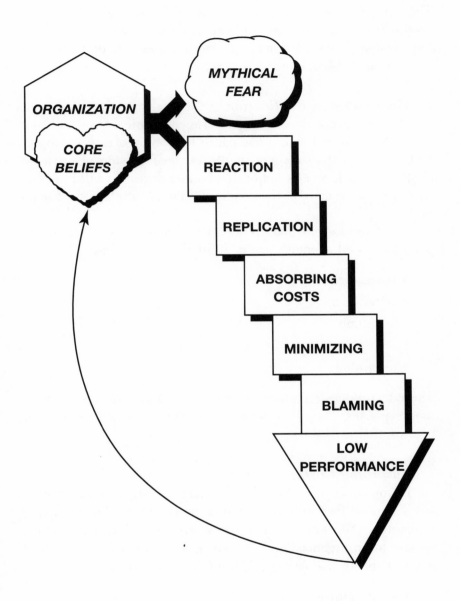

The low-performance loop is made up of five logical but counter-productive steps: reaction, replication, dealing inadequately with organizational costs, minimizing consequences, and blaming them on uncontrollable factors.

Reaction and Replication

If your organization is caught between mythical fears and core beliefs that are not sound enough to hold sway over your appre-hensions, it will react expediently at the first sign of crisis or challenge. Lacking new options and under duress, it will probably *replicate* one or more of the counterproductive strategies it knows best.

The five most common replication techniques that struggling businesses and agencies use at strategic moments are:

- reorganizing
- retrenching
- restaffing
- restricting
- retraining

These techniques are all reactive, backward-looking, and ineffec-tive responses. They yield toxic costs that will be difficult for your organization to absorb.

Absorbing Costs

If you've ever worked for a struggling organization, you're more than a little familiar with the customary fruits of reaction and replication. You know that in the wake of an ill-considered re-sponse to an organizational dilemma, a business or agency will need to absorb one or more of the following toxic costs:

- territorialism
- low morale
- high turnover
- low innovation

- negative reinforcement
- lost opportunities

Although unpleasant, these costs can be instructive—but only if your organization acknowledges them and pays them in full. They provide instruction about what you've done wrong, give you an accurate picture of your organization's performance, and provide a chance to escape the low-performance loop. But self-defeating organizations seldom take advantage of this opportunity. They choose instead to minimize and blame.

Minimizing

Minimizing is how your organization may try to hide or ignore the toxic costs it can't absorb. Financial cost justification is perhaps the most popular means of minimizing, even though it seldom works the way it's supposed to. The other common techniques for minimizing the costs of replication are:

- denying the consequences of counterproductive activity
- dividing the spoils (short-term benefits) of unhealthy actions
- romanticizing the past
- fantasizing about the future
- devaluing organizational losses

Minimizing may be a clever strategy, but you'll soon discover that it almost never works. The lingering consequences of unwise decisions and policies will impair your organization's performance, and you'll soon go looking for someone or something to blame for your failure to improve.

Blaming

As you can see in the figure on page 289, blaming is the technique that closes the self-defeating loop. When it blames an uncontrollable factor for its shortcomings, your organization temporarily relieves the pressure that may be bearing down on it.

Chronic organizational underachievers typically resort to one of the following:

- blaming customers, suppliers, and competitors
- fragmenting the organization
- embracing low performance as an organizational style

But when an organization indulges in this systematic finger pointing, it abandons control over its own fate. It admits it can do nothing to change or improve, and casts its fortune to chance. Even worse, it bolsters negative beliefs about itself, closing the loop of systematic self-defeat.

THE HIGH-PERFORMANCE LOOP

The high-performance loop is a model for improvement and change. You can tell by looking at it that this loop is designed to reverse the effects of its self-defeating counterpart. In one form or another, your organization's program for performance improvement needs to include the elements shown on the opposite page.

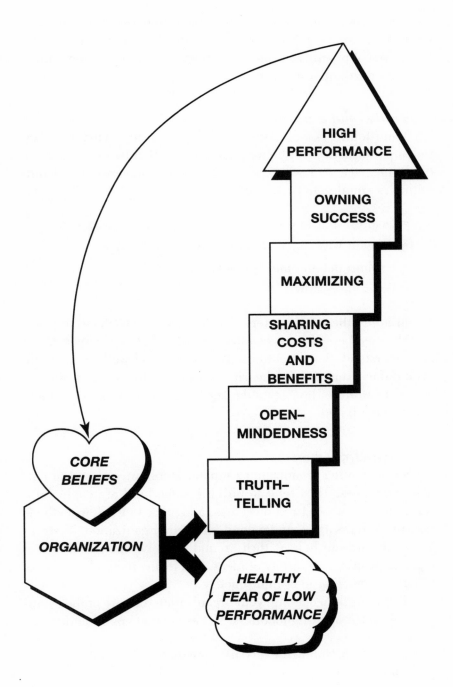

Through a program of truth-telling, open-mindedness, cost/benefit sharing, maximizing, and owning, you can help your organization break free of repetitive cycles of self-defeat or keep it from falling into this destructive pattern.

Truth-Telling Basics

Truth-telling is the bedrock technique for improving organizational performance. Without it, none of the other techniques in the figure on page 293 will work very well or for very long. Truth-telling is simple. You need only:

- Decide what to do.
- Explain why a decision or policy is necessary.
- Explain detours and setbacks.
- Describe results.

If you apply these basic steps regularly, you don't have to worry that the members of your organization will rebel at what you say or misunderstand your intentions. People respond well to the truth, even if they aren't used to hearing it. In struggling organizations, a moment's worth of honesty often succeeds where years of equivocation have failed.

Open-Mindedness

Self-defeating organizations remain stubbornly closed to outside influences. They tend to hire the same kind of people, subscribe to one or two tired old ideas, and stick to the few methods and procedures they understand. If your organization is struggling, one way to help it turn around is to be open to different types of people, to a variety of ideas, and to any method that seeks to put a promising idea into practice.

As you work to open up your organization, beware of the symptoms of "false open-mindedness." These symptoms include:

- a rush to embrace every new business trend and management philosophy

- *pro forma* gestures toward diversity, gender equity, or other political agendas
- frequent shifts in organizational policy, with minimal commitment on the part of leaders
- training that provides no measurable, timely, or meaningful instruction

To avoid the trap of false open-mindedness, use your organization's core beliefs to filter out ill-fitting programs and ideas. Before adopting a new program, ask yourself if it enhances a healthy belief you want to strengthen or if it counteracts an unsound belief you want to eliminate.

Sharing Costs and Benefits
To achieve lasting performance improvement, your organization *must* share the costs and benefits equitably among its constituent groups. In a typical organization, there are five of these groups:

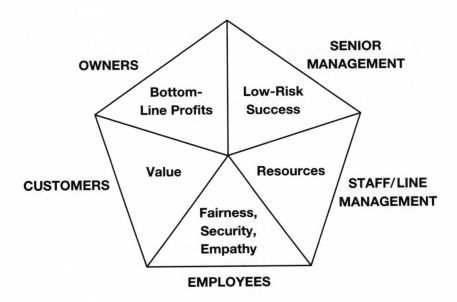

Your company or agency's ownership, senior management, staff/line management, employees, and customers have different interests and expectations, which often come into conflict. Serving one constituent group at the expense of the others weakens your organization as a whole, putting it in danger of collapse when it comes under pressure.

If your organization is sincere about sharing costs and benefits equitably, it must *clarify the cost/benefit narrative* for each major decision it makes. Here are a few simple steps for developing narratives that are fact instead of fiction:

- Ignore short-term benefits.
- Assess your qualitative costs.
- Apportion costs and benefits among constituent groups.

These steps make for sounder, broader-based decisions. These decisions will have wider support and a greater chance of success than strategies favoring a single constituent group.

Maximizing Benefits and Owning Success

These last two high-performance techniques help your organization realize its potential and learn from its expertise. Maximizing is a means of looking at what you've done well, even in the wake of a disappointing outcome. To maximize the benefits of your actions, try to:

- Identify cells or pockets of high performance.
- Embrace innovative decisions and actions.
- Use pockets of success to make a case for system-wide change.

When you practice these techniques, you create an atmosphere that allows your company or work group to take ownership of the benefits and breakthroughs it achieves. Owning these accomplishments builds confidence and bolsters valid, healthy core beliefs. Taking ownership is a process that involves:

- embracing renegade and impromptu initiatives

- tracking successful performance patterns from their ends to their beginnings
- linking success with high-performance core beliefs

These techniques complete the high-performance loop, giving your organization the faith and confidence that make success a habit.

There's much to think about here, so we encourage you to make copies of any of these diagrams and lists for your personal use. Try to keep these materials close at hand. Put them on your office wall or keep them in a three-ring binder. You'll find them invaluable when a supervisor or colleague confronts you with a troubling dilemma, then asks the eternal question: "OK, so what do we do now?"

APPENDIX 2

Counseling the Self-Defeating Organization

O RGANIZATIONS change best when they change from within. As several of the scenarios we've presented here suggest, lasting performance improvement is most often achieved when determined leaders, guided by internal expertise and pockets of effectiveness, break with the past and chart their own course for comprehensive change. That's why we've written this book as a self-help guide for struggling organizations. Your business, agency, or work group is most likely to change when you figure out on your own that something is amiss. After reading this book, you'll be in a good position to identify what's wrong and to figure out how to use your resources to fix it.

However, in two particular scenarios, your organization may need outside assistance to sort through and solve its ongoing problems. The first of these is a situation where organizational leaders are so mired in the details of a nagging problem or so beset by ownership's demands that they lack the time and breathing room to develop effective solutions. In a particularly troubling variation on this scenario, top executives and managers are fully aware of the need for improved performance. But they fail to act on this knowledge for fear of rendering themselves obsolete or redundant. If this describes your organization, ownership needs to bring senior managers back in line with long-term goals. Company owners must advise these executives and managers that they're being paid to solve, not perpetuate, ongoing performance problems.

The other scenario where outside consultants can help is the one we discussed in Chapter 3: the dilemma of an organization whose entire identity is based on its failings. When a company, agency, or work group views self-defeating activity as essential to its identity—when, in the terms we used earlier, an organization has become a Maintenance Crew, a Funhouse Gang, a Pep Squad, an Alumni Club, or a Cargo Cult—an adviser or analyst can track its unhealthy performance patterns and propose new alternatives.

But if you decide to take this route, you need to exercise great care in selecting your consultant or performance improvement team. The right kind of advice can patch cracks in your organization's foundation, or even rebuild it from scratch without disrupting your daily operations. The operative words here are *the right kind*. If you choose the wrong consultant, you may trigger another round of minimizing and blaming, and add another link to your chain of failure.

COUNSELING THE MAINTENANCE CREW

Like its self-defeating counterparts, the Maintenance Crew has a unique set of requirements and immediate goals. This organization is collectively depressed. Its reverence for control and loathing for change have kept it marching to a dull drumbeat. To move ahead, it needs permission to break ranks and shut out the sound of its familiar, plodding cadences. Its members must rediscover their natural aptitudes and enthusiasms, and come to see these assets can be brought to bear on nagging organizational problems. More than anything, the Maintenance Crew needs encouragement, along with a program of structured experimentation with a high probability of success.

The best consultant for this organization is some sort of motivational specialist. And not, mind you, just any kind of motivator—stem-winding orators are a dime a dozen, and often worth even less. The motivational specialist best suited to the predicament of the Maintenance Crew is a person who brings more to the podium than calls to action and lofty bromides about change. Before launching into his or her pitch, this individual must first be willing to bring to the surface and discuss frankly the long-suppressed rage and fear at the heart of the Maintenance Crew's depressed character. He or she must then craft a message that counteracts, rather than minimizes, these widely held misgivings and apprehensions. The motivator's ultimate challenge is to persuade dispirited people that performance improvement is possible.

To accomplish this feat, the motivational consultant must offer more than exhortatory rhetoric. He or she must also be ready to recommend a pilot project designed specifically to demonstrate the viability of organizational change. The consultant needs to take great care in developing this pilot initiative; his or her success may well hinge on its outcome. Generic or superficial approaches seldom fit the bill here. The members of a Maintenance Crew may seem gloomy or stubborn, but that does not mean they're stupid or naive. As soon as they see that the deck has been stacked in favor of easy success, they are apt to fold their hands and glower at the abashed dealer.

The all-too-real problems of the Maintenance Crew demand practical and specific solutions. We saw one such solution implemented within a troubled inner-city school district, where both administrators and teachers had grown weary of trying to meet the needs of an increasingly fractious public. A team of consultants designed a pilot program under which teachers would be relieved of certain administrative burdens in return for teaching elective courses in their special areas of interest or expertise. In order to enroll in these electives, students needed to demonstrate satisfactory progress in the district's core curriculum and to have avoided disciplinary sanctions during the previous semester.

Freed of curriculum constraints and ill-behaved students for three precious hours each week, many teachers experienced a renewed commitment to their jobs and, over time, to the possibilities of public education. They began to come up with ideas for new electives and to suggest ways of incorporating elective topics into the standard course of instruction. These suggestions proved invaluable when the district finally got around to the larger problem of revising its traditional curriculum, and with it the stultifying practices and procedures that had transformed vibrant educators into depressed functionaries.

COUNSELING THE FUNHOUSE GANG

The Funhouse Gang needs efficiency experts. This chaotic organization will benefit most from consultants who are more inclined to describe than prescribe. It needs consultants who are willing to undertake thorough analyses of how an organization is structured, how much it is spending to remedy internal chaos, and who is accountable for the repeated lapses that are draining the organization's resources. The efficiency expert needs to develop and present an accurate picture of how the organization is actually performing. He or she must strike a sharp contrast between current performance and the results a business or agency could achieve with a little accountability. The consultant must also persuade the Funhouse Gang that systemic chaos is seldom a sign of organizational health. To do so, he or she needs to emphasize that what appear to be random events are often the results of such low-performance habits as reaction, replication, minimizing, and blaming.

This is much easier said than done. Though they might claim otherwise, the leaders of chaotic Funhouse Gangs often have a substantial investment in rampant disorder. They may view potential remedies as striking precariously close to home. The senior managers of an underperforming discount retailer or fast-food chain, for example, may justify chaotic conditions at their outlets as the unavoidable consequence of the pressing need to cut payroll costs. Low-paid, transient, and ill-trained workers will inevitably make mistakes, these executives argue. And it's cheaper in the end to blame these regular lapses on system-wide chaos and absorb the costs than to hire and retain skilled, committed workers. The Funhouse Gang may find it more convenient to absorb the cost of chaos than to eliminate its root causes.

It's a tough argument to counter, especially when executives and managers remain focused on short-term performance. In this scenario, the consultant's major challenge is to force organizational leaders to look beyond immediate personal goals, and to bring these leaders face to face with the long-term implications of current organizational policies. The consultant needs to make senior managers realize that in tolerating or abetting chaos, they are themselves shirking their duty and shifting accountability for the ultimate fate of the enterprise to its future leaders. Current managers must be confronted, in other words, with the choice between acting now or leaving to their successors a legacy of endemic chaos.

In this way, a consultant with a knack for analyzing organizational efficiency can short-circuit the cycle of blaming and minimizing that chaotic enterprises use to defer or deny accountability. We saw this approach work effectively within the retail chain described in Chapter 3, where the installation of a network of malfunctioning cash registers underscored a pervasive bent for self-defeat through constant chaos. The business analysts the company subsequently hired to straighten out the mess prepared a series of decision matrices that diagrammed how the unwieldy registers had come to be installed in the stores. These consultants also developed a set of cost/benefit analyses that assigned a dollar amount to the ensuing chaos in each of the affected stores. These data persuaded senior management that it could not continue to make major decisions by default. Store executives saw that another three or four iterations of this pattern would not only perpetuate low performance, but might also make it hard for the company to survive.

COUNSELING THE PEP SQUAD

Pep Squads thrive on lies. To escape their low-performance loops, these booster organizations often require the services of consultants who specialize in telling the unvarnished truth. The latter are typically blunt-spoken individuals with a capacity to see through the jargon and glib assumptions from which self-defeating booster groups draw their lifeblood. Pep Squads seldom embrace these truth-tellers with open arms. Consultants who work with these organizations are constantly at risk of being ignored, or even dismissed. The fact is, many Pep Squads make a regular practice of hiring and firing truthful advisers. They hire them because they correctly but dimly sense that only the truth can provide viable answers to long-standing organizational problems. Then they fire them because the truths that they speak make leaders and managers uncomfortable.

How can a truth-telling consultant work with a booster group without getting fired before his or her job is done? Those who mean to counsel such an organization would do well to follow the lead of the famous detective Columbo. They ought to be prepared to present themselves at first as genial bumblers, too obtuse or disheveled to pose much of a threat. But all the while, they should persist in asking pointed questions: questions like, "What exactly does that mean?" and "Why are you in business?" Taken individually, these queries may seem simpleminded. But over time, and as the focus of discussion narrows, they can force a booster group to discover on its own the truth about its duplicity and counterproductive practices. Not until these truths are acknowledged can the organization embark on a course of healthy change. So long as the unpleasant truth remains implicit, the Pep Squad will continue to fear it and, as a result, to pursue policies and practices that perpetuate patterns of self-defeat.

As mentioned early in this book, we once worked with a weight-loss center that displayed all the symptoms of a classic Pep Squad. A few years later, with its profits slumping and government regulators not far from its doors, this organization was at last forced to face up to the unnerving truth about its business mission and its mode of operation. A gruff, brow-furrowing consultant led company management to the unavoidable conclusion that it was profiting from the dubious myth that its products and services could help clients achieve a permanent weight loss. The spirit of this myth had come to permeate the firm's character, creating a sunny, feel-good environment—one in which, paradoxically, few employees felt very good about what they were doing. Once this truth was out in the open, the consultant was able to recommend ways in which the company could use its expertise in the areas of nutrition and exercise to transform itself into something different and better.

Acting on this truth-teller's advice, the company soon modified its value proposition to the public. Instead of promising weight loss, it began to promote the concept of total wellness. Current and prospective customers heard the new message loud and clear. So, for that matter, did company employees. Relieved of the burden of living a collective lie, they no longer felt compelled to express their legitimate concerns in winking euphemisms and saccharine jargon. They began to speak openly and unequivocally about pervasive internal problems, thus providing management with an accurate and uncompromised picture of how well each center was performing.

COUNSELING THE ALUMNI CLUB
AND THE CARGO CULT

You'll recall that these organizations have become disoriented in time. Fearful of the present and the future, they focus their attention and energy either on past successes or on unrealistic dreams of the glories that await them far down the line. They are similar in terms of the guidance and advice they are apt to find most helpful. Like individuals who are impaired by compulsive remembering or fantasizing, they need to come to grips with the problems of the present. In therapeutic terms, they must learn to live in the here and now.

The last thing an Alumni Club or a Cargo Cult needs is a motivational specialist who either dwells on its past triumphs or exhorts it to rise to the challenges of the distant future. The task of ministering to these organizations is better left to a special breed of consultant: one who combines the skills of both the efficiency expert and the truth-teller. This individual faces a twofold challenge. He or she must first analyze and describe how the organization is expending resources in the course of its daily operations. How much money, this consultant must ask, is an Alumni Club spending, either directly or indirectly, for the purpose of burnishing or preserving its traditions? How much time and conversation does a Cargo Cult devote to planning for contingencies that seem remote at best, versus the time it spends on immediately improving its performance? Is remembering or "dream work" consistently consuming more energy than are the projects or problems at hand? In asking and answering these questions, the consultant should seek to demonstrate to the time-disoriented Alumni Club or Cargo Cult that it is not using its resources efficiently, and that it needs to start doing so at once.

This leads to the second, and more difficult, aspect of the consultant's challenge. Having shifted the organization's attention to the present moment, he or she must help the enterprise develop more productive methods and procedures for accomplishing its ongoing tasks. You probably know this activity as "process reengineering," a term that seems to cast it as the exclusive province of technologists and systems analysts. And while technical or industry-specific expertise is definitely an asset, it's not an absolute requirement for helping a time-disoriented organization break out of its low-performance loop.

We saw proof of this at an auto equipment supplier caught up in a spirit of nostalgia. In that particular instance, a simple analysis of how senior managers conducted their business meetings provided the firm with both insight and guidance. When presented with statistics and graphs that illustrated how much high-priced time executives spent discussing the exploits of legendary figures from the past, the firm's CEO directed the consultants to come up with a model for productive meeting management. Once this model was put into practice, executives found their regular meetings coming to an end much more quickly than they had in the past. They were able to make use of these windfall hours—a weekly average of three per senior executive—to deal with problems that had previously gone unattended or been ignored. A simple structural model had the net effect of increasing executive productivity and, more importantly, jolting senior management out of its habit of compulsive remembering.

Keep these considerations in mind if your firm finds it necessary to call on an outside specialist for guidance. And if you happen to be in the business of counseling problem-plagued organizations, you may find these guidelines useful when you are designing performance improvement programs for your clients or when you are marketing your services. Make sure that your talents and methods match the particular needs of the struggling organization you'll be proposing to transform.

Index

About the Authors

Robert E. Hardy is a state-licensed psychologist with a doctorate in counseling. As president of the consulting firm Hardy & Peters, he focuses on organizational change using assessments, high-performing and cross-functional teams, 360° directional feedback, and coaching. For several years he has taught a certified course at 3M aimed at maximizing individual performance, and he has worked with several national corporations and consulting firms. With Milton R. Cudney, Bob is the author of *Self-Defeating Behaviors*, a book on individual change. Hardy & Peters may be reached at (612) 897-5267.

Randy Schwartz is a writer and consultant who specializes in technical training and business communications. He has worked for more than twenty years with the process manufacturing, computer, and retail industries, accumulating a broad knowledge of both high-performing and low-performing organizations. He lives in Edina, Minnesota.